Inland Water Transport in India

About the Author

Born on 5th September, 1930, Professor Misra is an internationally known Geographer, Regional Planner, and Gandhian scholar. He has numerous books on his credit on Gandhian Thought, local and regional planning, rural development-urbanization, and ecology and environment. He did his Ph.D. at the University of Maryland, College Park, Maryland, USA in 1964 under the Fulbright Programme of US Government.

Professor Misra is known for his Growth Poles and Centre Theory now being widely used in urban and regional development planning all over the world. Micropolitan approach to rural transformation is his other major contribution to development theory. He has written/edited over 100 books and over 150 articles on various themes published both in India and abroad.

Among the positions Professor Misra has held from time to time, a few are listed below.

1. Professor, Department of Geography, Delhi School of Economics, Delhi University, Delhi (1987-1995);
2. Vice Chancellor, Allahabad University, Allahabad (1984-1987);
3. Vice Director and Chief Technical Adviser, United Nations Center for Regional Development (UNCRD), Nagoya, Japan (1979-1984);
4. Founder Director, Institute of Development Studies, University of Mysore, Mysore (1971-1979); and
5. Consultant UNDP, Teheran, Iran, 1975-76; and UN Research Institute for Social Development (UNRISD), Geneva, Switzerland (1972-73).

Professor Misra can be contacted at:
35/1, Stanley Road,
Allahabad -211001
Mobile: 91 9450869688
E-mail: sdf.misra@gmail.com

Inland Water Transport in India

R.P. Misra

CONCEPT PUBLISHING COMPANY PVT. LTD.
NEW DELHI-110059

ISBN-13: 978-93-5125-275-7

Revised and Enlarged Edition 2017

Published and Printed by

Concept Since 1974

Concept Publishing Company Pvt. Ltd.
Regd. Office:
A/15-16, Commercial Block, Mohan Garden,
New Delhi-110059 (INDIA)
Phones : 25351460, 25351794, *Fax* : 091-11-25357109
Email : publishing@conceptpub.com
Website: www.conceptpub.com

Cataloging in Publication Data—DK Courtesy: D.K. Agencies (P) Ltd. <docinfo@dkagencies.com>

Misra, R. P., 1930- **author.**
Inland water transport in India / R.P. Misra. — Revised and enlarged edition.
pages cm
Includes bibliographical references and index.
ISBN 9789351252757

1. Inland water transportation—India. 2. Inland navigation—India. I. Title.

HE691.M57 2017 DDC 386.0954 23

Preface to the Revised Edition

Inland Water Transport in India was published by the Institute of Development Studies, University of Karnataka in 1972. In the light of the keen interest taken by the Government of India in reviving and further developing the Inland waterways, it is being reprinted to provide the background information to the Government and other relevant agencies.

The concept of National Waterways was introduced in 1982 to promote the development of Inland water transport in the country. At present, out of six declared National Waterways, developmental works are being carried out on NW-1, 2, and 3 only by Inland Waterways Authority of India (IWAI). The first three National Waterways (NW-1, 2 and 3) are being developed for shipping and navigation by providing basic Inland transport infrastructural facilities, including navigational channel with required depth and width, aids for day and night navigation, and terminals at selected locations for berthing and loading/unloading of vessels.

Inland waterway refers to Inland water bodies like rivers, canals, backwaters, lakes, creeks etc. for transporting people and goods from place to place. India has a long history of Inland waterways, i.e. Ganga, Brahmaputra, Indus, Yamuna, Mahanadi, Godavari, Krishna, Kaveri, Narmada, Tapi and backwaters of Kerala were the main arteries of the country's Inland water transport system. They gave birth to a number of river ports and jetties. This system of transport declined when railways and highways emerged as the main bulk carriers of both passenger and goods in twentieth century. Diversion of water from rivers to irrigation canals made many of the rivers unsuitable for navigation. So much so, that today the share of Inland water transport in the

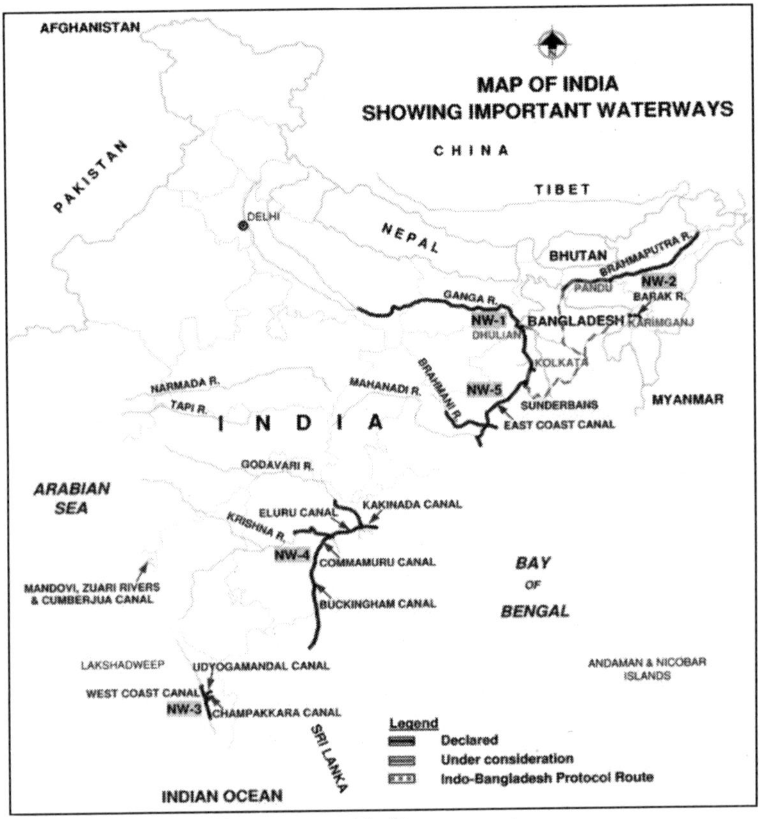

Fig 0.1: Important Waterways of India.

transport system of the country has come down to less than 1 per cent.

The total navigable length of Inland waterways as in 2015 is 14,500 km., out of which about 9,200 km. (5,200 km. of rivers and 4,000 km. of canals) can be used by mechanized crafts/steamers. Only 3,700 km. of major rivers are navigable by mechanized crafts, but the length actually utilized is only 2,000 km. As regards canals, out of 4,300 km. of navigation canals, only 900 km. are suitable for navigation by mechanized crafts.

Freight transportation by waterways is highly under-utilized in India compared to other large countries and regions like the United States, China and European Union. The total cargo moved in India (in ton-km.) by the Inland waterway is no more than 0.1 per cent of the total Inland traffic in India, compared to the 21 per cent in USA, 10 per cent in China and 7 per cent in EU. Cargo carriage in an organized manner is confined to a few waterways in Goa, West Bengal, Assam and Kerala. About 1.60 million tons of cargo is annually moved by Inland Water Transport.

Inland Water Transport in India is not a popular mode of transportation. This is mainly due to seasonal concentration of rainfall, fluctuating river regimes, devastating floods during rainy season, shifting river courses (in the Northern Plains) making it difficult to construct permanent jetty or wharf, diversion of large quantity of river water into irrigation canals that reduces the depth of water in the river and makes it unsuitable for steamers and mechanized boats, heavy silting and formation of sandbars, undulating topography in hilly and plateau regions leading to the formation of a number of rapids, and formation of delta and diversion channels making the mouth narrower for the entry of ships and large boats.

Realizing the potentials of Inland Waterways in moving goods and promoting tourism, the Government of India constituted a *Central Inland Water Transport Corporation Limited* (CIWTC Ltd.) in May 1967 as a Government of India Undertaking after taking over the business from a loss-making erstwhile River Steam Navigation & Co. (RSN & Co.) owned and operated by the Sterling Company. The Corporation is under the administrative control of Ministry of Shipping (MoS), Government of India. The head office of the Corporation is located at: 4, Fairlie Place, Kolkata-700001. The Corporation has three main functions: transportation of cargo through Inland Waterways; operational repair of IWT vessels; and operation and maintenance of four major and many minor terminals.

As the task of developing and managing the Inland Waterways of India grew and also became more complicated, the Government decided to set-up *Inland Waterways Authority of India* (IWAI) in 1986. IWAI is a statutory body in charge of the waterways of India. Its headquarters is at Noida, UP, east of Delhi and part of the NCR. It is responsible for building necessary infrastructure in and along the waterways, for surveying the economic feasibility of new projects, and also for administration and regulation of the waterways. The Authority also has its regional offices at Patna,

Kolkata, Guwahati and Kochi and sub-offices at Allahabad, Varanasi, Bhagalpur, Farakka and Kollam.

NAVIGABLE RIVERS AND CANALS

The most important waterways of the country are: the Ganga-Bhagirathi-Hugli, the Brahmaputra river, the Barak River, the delta and lower courses of the Mahanadi, Godavari and Krishna rivers, the lower courses of the Narmada and Tapi, the Zuari and Mandovi rivers in Goa, Kali, Shravati and Netravati in Karnataka, the back-waters and lagoons in Kerala and the Buckingham Canal in Andhra Pradesh and Tamil Nadu. Uttar Pradesh has the highest length of navigable Inland Waterways (2,441 km. or 17.01%) of the country followed by West Bengal, Andhra Pradesh, Assam, Kerala and Bihar.

River Ganga

The Ganga River provides an important Inland waterway for the country. It is a perennial river fed by Monsoon rains during rainy season and melting of the snow during dry summer days. On its 2,510 km. length from snow to the sea it passes through most densely populated parts of the country and nurturing a number of premier cities of north India like Hardwar, Kanpur, Allahabad, Mirzapur, Varanasi, Ghazipur, Patna, Munger, Murshidabad and Kolkata.

Despite heavy diversion of water to irrigation canals its main channel still maintains a depth of more than 10 metres from Patna downstream. Recently, the river has been made navigable up to Allahabad and regular steamer service has been started between Haldia and Allahabad. Some of the tributaries of the Ganga like Yamuna, Ghaghara, Gandak, and Gomati may also be utilized for navigation.

The Hugli River is an important distributory of the Ganga in its delta course and is intensively used for navigation between Kolkata and Diamond Harbour. Silting and consequent decrease in the depth of water is the main obstacle in this navigation. The Farakka Barrage Project supplies 15,000-21,000 cusecs of water through a 42 km. long canal to improve flow and clear silt deposits.

River Brahmaputra

Brahmaputra River is navigable by steamers throughout the year from its mouth to Tezpur and sometimes up to Dibrugarh (1,280 km.). It carries Assam oil, tea, timber and jute to Kolkata. Pandu, Jogighopa and Dibrugarh are important river ports. Navigation is difficult in the river due to barrier effects of Bangladesh, presence of river islands, sand banks and shoals and very strong current of the river during rainy season.

Peninsular Rivers

Peninsular rivers are seasonal and go dry during the dry season. Hence, these are not very suitable for navigation. Some transport is carried on in their lower reaches where ground is flat and quantity of water is satisfactory. Narmada, Tapi, Mahanadi, Godavari, Krishna and Kaveri are navigable in their lower courses.

Rivers Zuari and Mandovi of Goa transport iron ores, manganese and timber to Marmagao port. The creeks of the West Coast Rivers like Kali, Shravati and Netravati etc. also provide navigation facilities.

Navigable Canals

The Buckingham Canal (412.8 km.) is an important navigation canal in Andhra Pradesh and Tamil Nadu. It runs parallel to the eastern coast joining all the coastal districts from Guntur to South Arcot. It is 315 km. long north of Chennai and 100 km. south of it. Its northern part connects the Kommamur Canal of the Krishna delta, while the southern part terminates in Marakkanupi backwaters. The construction of the Vijayawada-Chennai rail line has adversely affected the canal traffic. It is now mainly used for the transport of salt and fire wood to Chennai city.

Similarly, Kurnool-Cuddapah Canal (116.8 km.), Son Canal (326.4 km.), Odisha Canal (272 km.), Medinipur Canal (459.2 km.), Damodar Canal (136 km.) and West Coast Canal (connecting major ports along the western coast) are also used for Inland navigation. Some of the irrigation canals of Uttar Pradesh and Punjab are also utilized for local transport.

NATIONAL WATERWAYS

India at present (2016) has six National Waterways (NWs). They have been developed by the Central Government of India through its own agency, i.e. Inland Waterways Authority of India (IWAI). The IWAI is a statutory autonomous regulatory body for the Inland Waterways Transport sector. It was set-up by the Inland Waterways Authority of India Act in 1985 and given responsibility of development, maintenance, and regulation of national waterways in the country. Along with IWAI, Central Inland Water Transport Corporation (CIWTC) also supports the IWT sector through transportation of cargo *via* Inland waterways and the operation and maintenance of the vessels and waterway terminals. The first national waterways established in India were the NW-1, 2 and 3 (in mid 1980s and 1993). They have a combined length of 2,716 km. With respect to freight rates, waterways are always cheaper than roadways and railways in base classes of goods and commodities.

The concept of National Waterways was introduced in 1982 to promote the development of Inland water transport in the country. At present, out of six declared National Waterways, developmental works are being carried out on NW-1, 2, and 3 only by Inland Waterways Authority of India (IWAI). The first three National Waterways (NW-1, 2 and 3) are being developed for shipping and navigation by providing basic Inland transport infrastructural facilities, including navigational channel with required depth and width, aids for day and night navigation, and terminals at selected locations for berthing and loading/unloading of vessels.

The NW 1 was declared as National Waterway on 27th October, 1986. It passes through Ganga, Bhagirathi and Hugli Rivers and runs from Haldia (Sagar) in West Bengal to Allahabad in U.P. Bihar and Jharkhand are the other States through it passes. The length of the Waterway is 1620 km. It is one of the most important waterways navigable by mechanical boats up to Patna. It has fixed terminals at Haldia, BISN (Kolkata), Pakur, Farakka and Patna including 2 fixed RCC jetties and 18 floating terminals at Haldia, Kolkata, Diamond Harbour, Katwa, Tribeni, Baharampur, Jangipur, Bhagalpur, Semaria, Doriganj, Ballia, Ghazipur, Varanasi, Chunar and Allahabad. Owned by the Inland Waterway Authority of India (IWAI), it is operated by the Central Inland Water Transport

Corporation (CIWTC). For more details of the facilities available at different terminals see Table 0.1.

Table 0.1: Land Area, Size of Berth and type of Terminals of NW 1

Sl. No.	*Name of Terminal*	*Land area*	*Size of berth*	*Type of terminal*
1.	Haldia	10319 sq m	200 m	Floating Terminal
2.	Botanical Garden Jetty	996 sq m	50 m	Floating Terminal
3.	BISN Jetty	11606.64 sq m	100 m	Floating Terminal
4.	Shantipur	8000 sq m	100 m	Floating Terminal
5.	Katwa	Pontoon placed on water front	30 m	Floating Terminal
6.	Hazardwari	Pontoon placed on water front	30 m	Floating Terminal
7.	Farakka	4800 sq m	80 m	Floating Terminal
8.	G.R.Jetty - 2	14606 sq m	216 m	Fixed RCC Jetty
9.	Rajmahal	Pontoon placed on water front	35 m	Floating Terminal
10.	Sahebganj	Pontoon placed on water front	35 m	Floating Terminal
11.	Bateshwarsthan	Pontoon placed on water front	35 m	Floating Terminal
12.	Bhagalpur	1000 sq. m	35 m	Floating Terminal
13.	Munger	3.4 Acre	35 m	Floating Terminal
14.	Semaria	Pontoon placed on water front	35 m	Floating Terminal
15.	Barh	—	27 m	Floating Terminal
16.	Buxar	Pontoon placed on water front	—	Floating Terminal
17.	Ghazipur	Pontoon placed on water front	35 m	Floating Terminal
18.	Rajgat	Pontoon placed on water front	35 m	Floating Terminal
19.	Allahabad	8.759 Hectare	35 m	Floating Terminal
20.	Patna	3.24 Acres	46.6 m	Fixed RCC Jetty

Nitin Gadkari, Minister of Shipping, Government of India, announced in July, 2014 that barrages will be constructed on River Ganga at every 100 kilometre and dredging of the river will be carried out to ensure a minimum width of 45 metres and depth of three metres to enable steamers to transport passengers and goods between Varanasi and Hugli in the first stage of its development. The proposal was based on a study by Danish Hydrological Institute of River Ganga between Allahabad and Varanasi, and

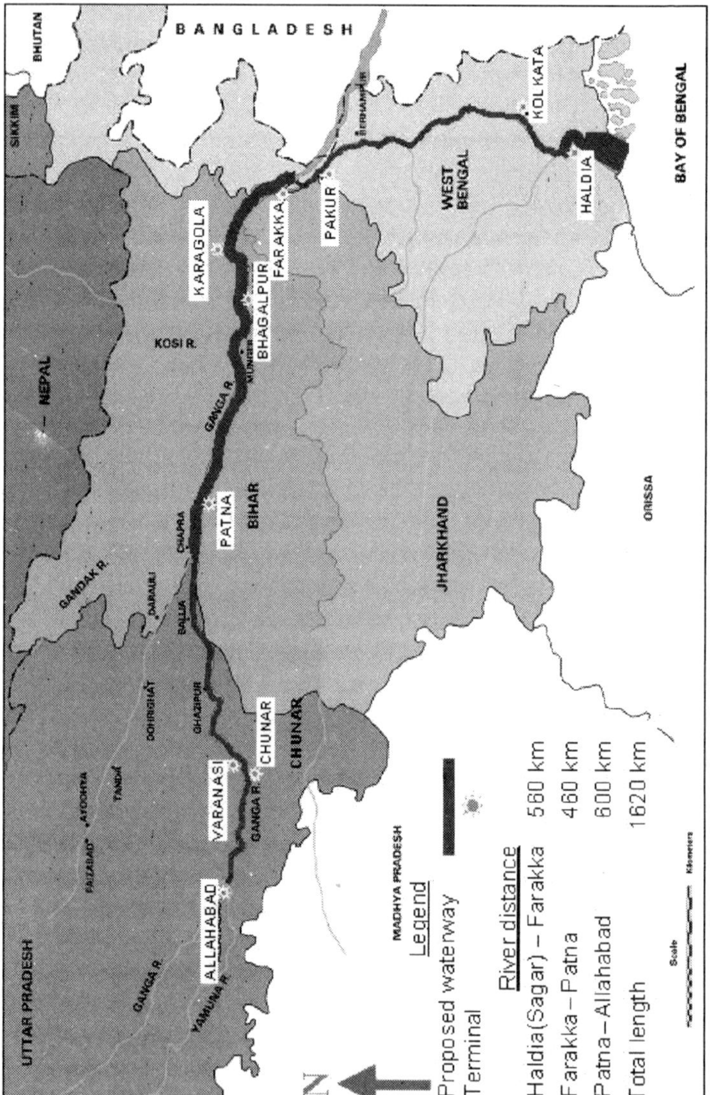

Fig. 0.2: National Water No. 1

between Varanasi and Buxur. The plan envisaged provision of a depth of three metres in the Ganga to make it fully navigable from Allahabad to Haldia by barges carrying 1,500-2,000 tonnes of cargo. The announcement was made after World Bank agreed to fund the initial 50 million dollars including technical support. The move was criticized by river activists and a number of professors of Banaras Hindu University.

In August 2014, a representation was sent to the Government of India and also to the World Bank by several experts on environmental and social impacts of training river Ganga to revive this waterway. The Government of Bihar also opposed the initiative to construct barrages on River Ganga stating that construction of barrages will convert Ganga into big ponds. The Inland Waterways Authority of India (IWAI) has responded by saying that there were no plans to construct any new barrage on the 1,620 km. stretch of NW-1 on River Ganga.

National Waterway 1

National Waterway (NW1) runs between Allahabad and Haldia and covers a distance of 1620 km. The rivers through which it runs are: Ganga, Bhagirathi and Hugli rivers and has fixed terminals at Haldia, Farakka and Patna and floating terminals at most of the riverside cities like Kolkata, Bhagalpur, Varanasi and Allahabad. It is the longest National Waterway in India.

National Waterway 2

This Waterway stretches on Brahmaputra River from Sadiya on Bangladesh border to Dhubri in Assam State. It is one of the major freight transportation waterway of North-East India and the third longest Waterway with a total length of 891 km. It was declared as National Waterway No. 2 on 1 September, 1988. It has eleven terminals, one fixed terminal at Pandu and 10 Floating terminals, one each at Dhubri, Jogighopa, Tezpur, Silghat, Dibrugarh, Jamgurhi, Bogibil, Saikhowa and Sadiya (Fig. 0.3). It belongs to IWAI and is operated by CIWTC.

National Waterway 3

National Waterway 3 constitutes Kottapuram-Kollam stretch of the West Coast Canal, Champakara Canal and Udyogmandal Canal. The waterway is located in Kerala and was established in February 1993.

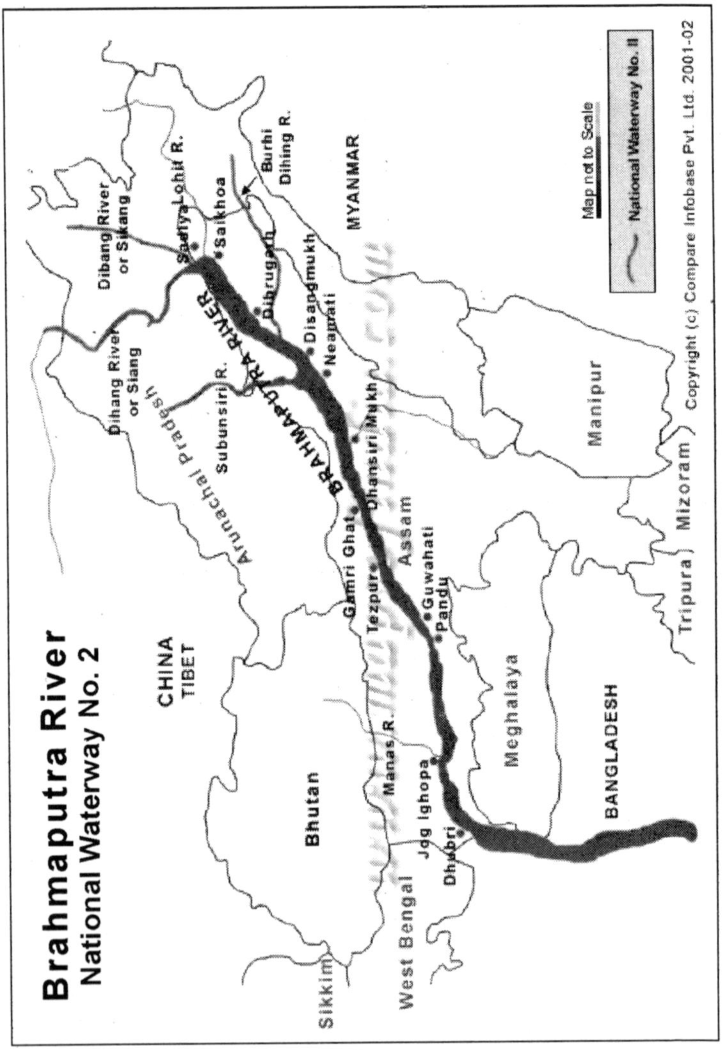

Fig. 0.3: Brahmaputra River National Waterway No. 2

Stretching for 205 km. between Kottapuram in the north and Kollam in the south, it has 9 fixed terminals at Aluva, Vaikom, Kayamkulam, Kottappuram, Maradu, Cherthala, Thrikkunnapuzha, Kollam and Alappuzha. It is owned by the Inland Waterways Authority of India and operated by Central Inland Water Transport Corporation.

The breakup of the 205 km. of the waterway is as follows:

West-coast Canal (Kottapuram-Kollam)	168 km.
Udyogmandal Canal (Kochi-Pathalam Bridge)	23 km.
Champakara Canal (Kochi-Ambalamugal)	14 km.
	205 km.

The waterways have always been an important mode of transport in Kerala. The total length of navigable ways in Kerala including rivers, canals and backwaters was 1,900 km. more than half (54%) of them being navigable rivers flowing from east to west. These 41 west-flowing rivers together with the backwaters form an integrated part of the Inland navigation system in Kerala. Kerala's Inland waterways pass through highly populated regions known for traditional industries such as coir, cashew, brick-making and fishing. On the main West Coast Canal between Kollam and Kottapuram, the Kochi-Edapallikota (120 km.) stretch was opened for cargo movement during November 1994, once the improvement works were completed by IWAI. The first phase of this development work included dredging to widen and deepen the canal between Kochi and Kollam. The work started during 1997-98. Capital dredging was started in Kochi-Kottapuram stretch (30 km.) in second phase during September 2002 except 4.83 km. Work in Kochi-Allapuzha sector was completed. Delays in dredging were caused by problems like disposal of dredged material, fishing nets, contractual problems etc.

Out of entire length of 205 km. of the waterway, the total shoal length has been estimated to be 87.16 km. out of which 59.75 km. has so far been dredged and 24.49 km. remains to be dredged. The total quantity which was to be dredged for deepening the entire shoal length was worked out as 40.33 lakh m^3 out of which 23.98 lakh m^3 has been dredged and 16.35 lakh m^3 remains to be dredged.

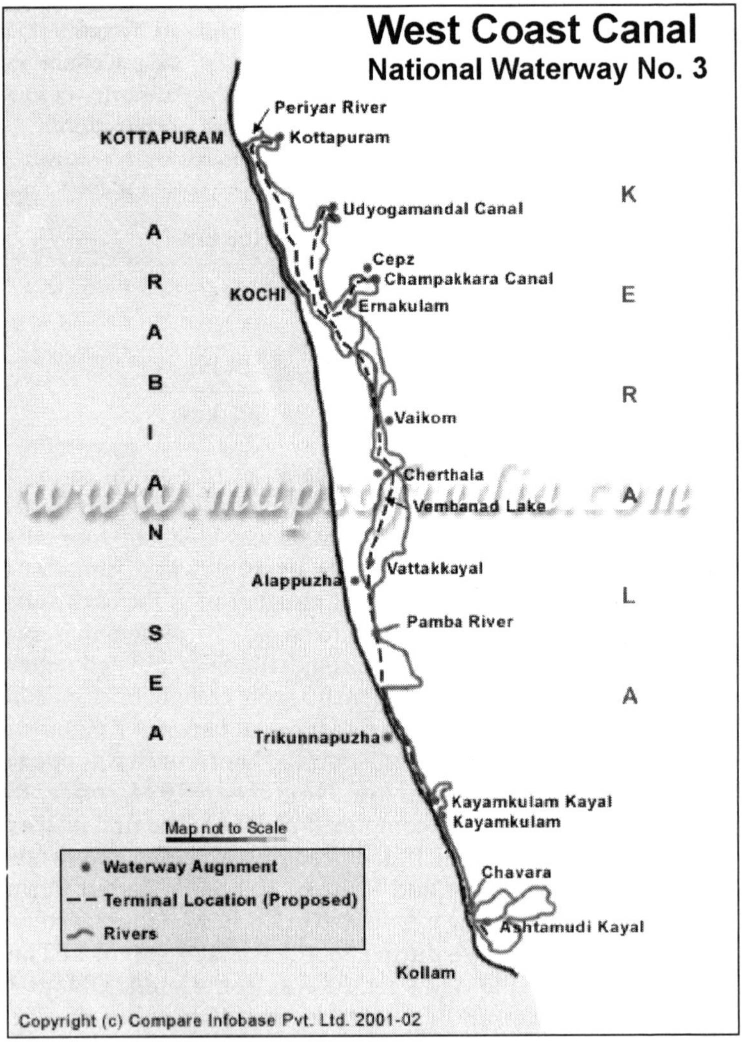

Fig. 0.4: West Coast Canal National Waterway No. 3

Project for providing and maintaining 24 hrs navigational aids by way of buoys and lights was completed during 2007-08 and now, the entire waterway has the facility for 24 hrs navigation since 2008-09.

Kerala's backwaters offer incomparable beauty and unique experience which have contributed to its inclusion in the list of 50 must see places in the world. These backwaters include the Kuttanad region, called the rice bowl of Kerala. Here paddy cultivation is done on fields which are below sea level. Lake Vembanad is the largest stretch of backwaters in Kerala; next in importance are Lake Ashtamudi and Lake Kayamkulam. The beauty of the tranquil backwaters of Kerala lies in the palm trees around them and hundreds of River Cruises between Kochi and Alleppey, also known as Venice of the East.

There are luxury cabins that take tourists from Kochi along the Lake Vembanad, to Alleppey. It is the largest backwater stretch of Kerala. And then, the tourists hire smaller country boats for rice excursion that includes visit to traditional Kerala family

Table 0.2: Terminal Accomodations

Sl. No.	*Terminal Location*	*Area (Hectares)*	*Acquired Length and Type of Jetty*	*Storage Facilities*
1.	Kottapuram	0.5823	30 m (RCC Jetty	200 sq m covered godown and 400 sq m open storage
2.	Aluva	1.331	30 m (RCC Jetty	200 sq m covered godown and 400 sq m open storage
3.	Maradu	2.0268	30 m (RCC Jetty	200 sq m covered godown and 400 sq m open storage
4.	Vaikkom	0.5184	30 m (RCC Jetty	200 sq m covered godown and 400 sq m open storage
5.	Thannermukkom	0.917	30 m (RCC Jetty	200 sq m covered godown and 400 sq m open storage
6.	Thrikunnappuzha	0.5057	30 m (RCC Jetty	200 sq m covered godown and 400 sq m open storage
7.	Layamkulam	1.6304	30 m (RCC Jetty	200 sq m covered godown and 400 sq m open storage
8.	Kollam (Quilon)	0.6208	30 m (RCC Jetty	200 sq m covered godown and 400 sq m open storage
9.	Alappuzha	2.2277*	—	—
10.	CEPZ	1.2234		—***
11.	Chavra	0.8061		—***
12.	Bolgatty	0.8000	Ro-Ro/ Lo-Lo service	Container terminal
13.	Willingdon Island	0.5000	Ro-Ro/ Lo-Lo service	Container terminal

residences. Water bodies in the cities of Kochi, Perandoor and Thevara were being used for navigation till some decades ago. Using the waterways, one can reach Kochi from Thripunithura in just 20 minutes; the road route takes close to 90 minutes during peak hours. Much of the raw materials of chemicals and fertilizers imported by the public sector FACT were transported through the Udyogamandal canal by barges.

This waterway has 7 terminals, one each at Kottapuram, Aluva, Maradu, Viakom, Thaneermukam (Chertala), Trikkunnapuzha and Kayamkula. Eighth terminal has also been completed by CPWD at Kollam. The terminals provide facilities for mechanical handling, with the help of 8 mobile cranes and 8 fork-lifts at each terminal.

Challenges and Potentials of Development

Many of Kerala's export-based industries that use Kochi port to route their shipments can grow considerably if the potentials of Inland waterways of the state are fully tapped. Kochi port is connected to Kerala's hinterland through Inland waterways which run virtually parallel to the Arabian Sea and link major trading centers. International Container Trans-shipment Terminal (ICTT) at Vallarpadam at Cochin Coast is one of such external factor which will create lot of future potential for IWAI in Kerala. The ICTT can attract more international cargo movement through India while at the same time reduce the freight cost of India's international trade. IWAI is taking steps to utilize such opportunities.

Two special terminals have been constructed near Kochi port to support the interchange of containers by LO-LO (Lift On, Lift Off) and RO-RO (Roll On, Roll Off) barges. Traffic may come to a halt in Kochi when hundreds of container-laden trucks take to the city roads and highways once the Vallarpadam container transshipment terminal also becomes functional. Presuming that a container will be loaded and another one unloaded every minute, almost 2,880 trucks will pass through Kochi's highways daily.

A number of industrial plants have come up on the banks of Udyogamandal Canal, including the public sector FACT and Travancore Cochin Chemicals (TCC). Though waterways are the cheapest, safest and most eco-friendly mode of transport, many of the navigable canals in Kochi are being contaminated by the wastes households, shops and markets dumped in it. The width of canals is getting reduced by encroachments from both sides. Some of the bridges such as the one at Kaloor are low level; they hamper the safe passage of boats. The Inland Waterways Authority of India and the KSINC have to take necessary action to correct the situation.

The NW-3 should be extended from Kottapuram to Hosdurg in Kasargodu and from Kollam to Kovalam. It's linkages to Velloor *via* Muvattupuzha River for 25 km. and from Muhamma to the eastern bank of Vembanadu Lake to Kumarakom and Nattakom also is necessary. Alapuzha should be linked to Nedumudy, Pulinkunnu, Chambakulam, Edathua and Parumala. The National Bank for Agriculture and Rural Development had approved a proposal for the development of the Mahe-Vadakara stretch of canal with a bottom width of 32 metres. The Valapattanam-Mahe stretch (58 km.) is the missing link and a major obstacle to the Inland navigation potential of the region. The survey of the project is over.

National Waterways 4

As early as 1993-95, IWAI commenced studies for developing a canal linking Kakinada and Chennai. In July 2006, the Minister for Transport and Shipping announced in Indian Parliament a proposal for development of NW-4 with a combined (river-*cum*-canal) length of 1095 km. The constituents of NW 4 are given in Table 0.3:

Table 0.3: Constituent of NW4

Stretch	*Length in km*
Kakinada canal	50
Eluru canal	139
Krishna river section	157
Godavari river section	171
Commammur canal	113
North Buckingham canal	316
South Buckingham canal	110
Marakkanam-Pondicherry section	22
Total	**1095**

The National Waterway 4 (NW-4) comprises nearly 690 km. of canal and 328 km. of river sections. The river section consists of two main rivers of Andhra Pradesh: Godavari and Krishna. The Godavari River section stretches from Bhadrachalam to Dowleiswaram, Rajahmundry. The Krishna River section stretches from Wazirabad, Nalgonda district to Prakasam Barrage, Vijayawada. The canal section covers Kakinada canal, the Eluru canal, Commamur canal, and the Buckingham canal. The Kakinada canal starts at Kakinada and ends at Rajahmundry covering a distance of 50 km. The canal gets its water from the Godavari through the Dowleswaram barrage and thereafter connects with Kakinada anchorage port.

The Eluru canal comprises two distinct irrigation-*cum*-navigation canals. These are: Krishna Eluru canal of the eastern Krishna delta and the Godavari Eluru canal of western Godavari delta. It runs for 139 km. between Vijayawada and Vijjeswaram lock at Sir Arthur Thomas Cotton Barrage. The Krishna Eluru canal takes off from the left bank of Krishna river on the upstream of Prakasam barrage through a head sluice at Vijayawada and meets Godavari Eluru canal at Eluru.The Godavari Eluru canal takes off from the River section of river Godavari at Vijjeswaram in Rajahmundry on the upstream of Dowleiswaram anicut through a head sluice and joins Krishna Eluru canal at East Tammileru lock. The Commamur canal runs between Vijayawada Seethanagaram lock and Peddaganjam lock for a total length of 113 km. It takes off from the Krishna River in Vijayawada on the right side upstream and joins the Buckingham canal at Peddaganjam Lock near Ongole.

The Buckingham canal is a tidal canal stretching from Peddaganjam lock to Chennai and further down south up to Marakkanam. It was constructed during nineteenth century along the Coromandal coast. The stretch of the canal from Peddaganjam lock to Chennai for a length of 316 km. is called North Buckingham canal and the canal from Chennai to Marakkanam for a total length of 110 km. is called South Buckingham canal. Marakkanam is connected to the Bay of Bengal at Puducherry by the Kalluvelly tank.

The length of the NW4 in the states of Andhra Pradesh, Tamil Nadu and Puducherry are as follows:

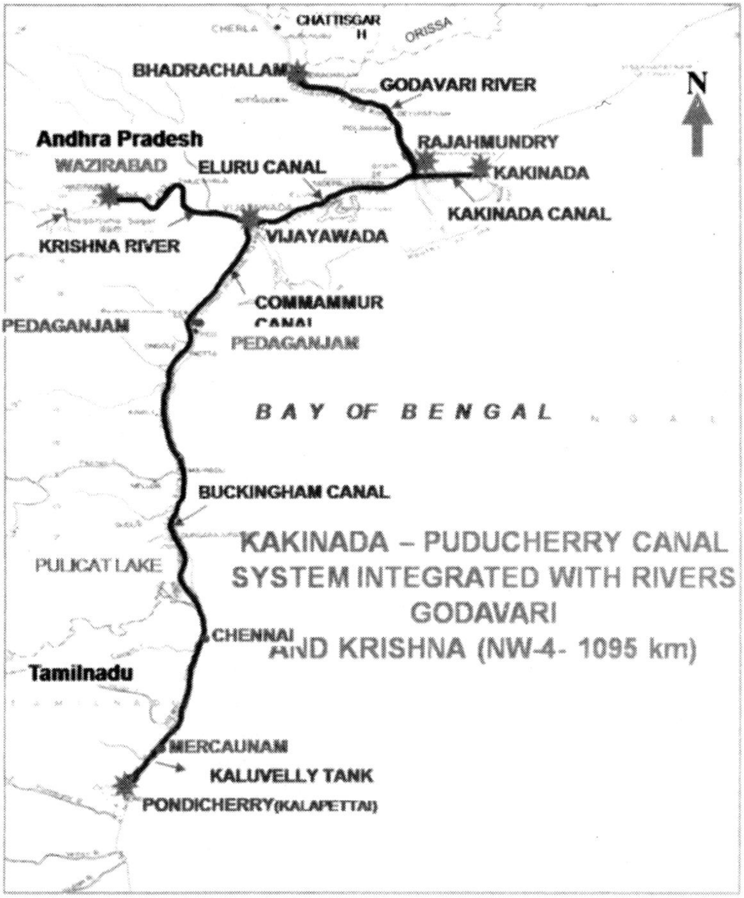

Fig. 0.5: Map showing stretches of NW 4.

Table 0.4: State-wise Description of Canals & Rivers

States	*Description of Canals and Rivers*	*Length in km*
Andhra Pradesh	Kakinada canal, Eluru canal, Commamur canal, Godavari river, Krishna river and North Buckingham canal (Peddaganjam to Andhra Pradesh – Tamil Nadu border at Tada)	895
Tamil Nadu	North Buckingham canal (AP-TN border at Tada to Basin), South Buckingham canal and Kalluvelly tank	210
Puducherry	Southern portion of Kalluvelly tank – Puducherry link	2

According to A.F. Fergusan who was appointed by Water and Power Consultancy Services (WAPCOS) for conducting traffic studies in NW 4 in 2005-06, there is no significant traffic in the waterway except for movement of country boats, which carry local produce. The main reason for lack of water transport is the absence of other infrastructure facilities and coordinated effort for improvements.

NW4 has been divided into four major cargo belts, namely Kakinada belt, Krishna belt, South Andhra Pradesh belt, and Chennai belt. Based on the survey conducted by Fergusan, the 11 million tonnes of cargo is expected to be transported through NW-4 every year. Types of cargo include coal, rice, food grains, cement, fertilisers, forest products, salt, and other bulk cargo. The Godavari river system flows through the Bhadrachalam forests and coal deposits. The Krishna River flows through limestone deposits and cement industries at Jaggayyapeta.

Krishna River (Wazirabad-Vijayawada)

Guntur has abundant resources of limestone which are of use in cement and steel industries. Main consumers of limestone are nearby situated cement and steel industries like ACC, Andhra Cement, Parthasarathy Cements and Industries Ltd and Gauthami Cements as well as Visakhapatnam Steel Plant.

Godavari River (Bhadrachalam-Rajahmundry)

The coal is a substantially available commodity in this stretch due to its nearness to Singareni Collieries (SCCL) mines. Coal fields are located in Kothagudem, Manuguru and Yellandu. Rice has a huge traffic potential in this downstream route up to Rajahmundry. In the upstream direction, traffic potential will be gained by transportation of forest products, wood pulp to Bhadrachalam where major paper mills like ITC Bhadrachalam and Andhra Pradesh Paper Mills (APPML) are located. Apart from this, many small paper mills are located in the East and West Godavari districts.

Kakinada Canal

Main cargo to be transported in downstream direction from Kakinada to Rajahmundry are coal, fertilizer, salt and rock phosphate. In the upstream direction, rice bran extractions, cement clinker and fertilizers will be the main cargos for transportation.

Eluru Canal

Rice and other foodgrains, rice bran extractions, coal, fertilizer and other general cargo are the substantive commodities which can boost the IWT in this stretch.

Commamur Canal

The stretch from Vijayawada to Peddaganjam (Ongole) is a vital trade link connecting Kakinada belt with south A.P. and Tamil Nadu. The major towns in the vicinity capable of promoting IWT are Vijayawada, Guntur and Ongole. Main traffic in the downward direction is rice and food grains. Forest products will form traffic in the upstream direction.

North Buckingham Canal

The canal can form significant traffic because of salt pans located all along the canal stretch. Rice, food grains, fertilizers, chili, peppers, tobacco, fish, granite and vegetables in the downstream direction from Peddaganjam to Chennai. In the upstream direction from Chennai to Peddaganjam, the main traffic consists of fertilizers from Chennai Fertilisers (MFL) plant located at Ennore and salt from Chennai.

South Buckingham Canal and Kaluvelly Tank

The canal stretch from Basin bridge up to Marakkanam can constitute significant traffic of salt and marine products because of salt pans and aquaculture shrimp farms all along the route. In the upstream direction from Pondicherry *via* Marakkanam to Chennai, the main traffic consists of salt, fertilizers and timber from Marakkanam, Thiruvallur, Kanchipuram, Villupuram and Puducherry.

NW-4 as Natural Barrier

The Buckingham Canal saved thousands of lives in the states of Andhra Pradesh and Tamil Nadu along the Coromandal coast from December 26 tsunami waves. Dr. B. Ramalingeswara Rao of National Geophysical Research Institute (NGRI), Hyderabad reports that the Buckingham Canal acted as a buffer zone and regulated the tsunami waves on the coastal region over 310 km. from Pedda Ganjam to Chennai. The tsunami waves drifted away towards the existing low-lying creeks at several places. The canal from Chennai (Marakkanam) to Durga Raya Patnam near Nellore and then to Pedda Ganjam, all along the east coast was filled with tsunami water, which overflowed at a few places and receded back to sea within 10-15 min. This saved the lives of several fishermen, especially in coastal Andhra Pradesh and parts of Chennai city.

Cost of Developing NW 4

The cost for developing waterways in India is approximately Rs. 0.5 crore per km., whereas developing a railway or roadway costs around Rs. 4-6 crore per km. As per estimates drawn by consultants M/s. RITES, the project will cost Rs. 542 crore (as per 2002 prices) and facilitate movement of 100 tonne vessels in the irrigation canal portion and 350 tonne in the rivers and Buckingham canal portion. The developmental works for NW-4 involve the widening of canal, dredging, excavation, bank protection, construction and repair of locks, modification of bridges and roads, navigational aids, and setting up of IWT terminals.

The cost of developing NW-4 is estimated by the WAPCOS to be Rs. 1515 crore. Phase one of the project envisages development of a stretch comprising Godavari and Krishna rivers, and Kakinada and Eluru canals, which has maximum cargo potential, at an estimated cost of Rs. 390 crore and land acquisition for remaining stretch at an estimated cost of Rs. 219 crore. Phase two of the project involves development of North and South Buckingham Canal, Commamur canal, and Kaluvelly Tank at an estimated cost of INR 906 crore.

During the Tenth Five Year Plan, Planning Commission has increased the budgetary provision for the development of Inland water transport infrastructure to Rs. 636.73 crore, against Rs. 150.00 crore in the Ninth Five Year Plan. For the year 2009-2010, the

Government released the following funds through Ministry of Shipping for development of IWT.

1. Rs. 62.68 crore as a grant to IWAI for development and maintenance of National Waterways (NW 1,2,3,4 and 5). And also for undertaking projects related to IWT promotion, training, IT activities etc.
2. Rs. 1 crore has been released for Technical Studies and R&D activities.
3. Rs. 1 crore has been released for Inland Vessel Building Subsidy Scheme.
4. Rs. 1 crore has been released for Central Sector Schemes for IWT Development in North-Eastern Region.

Delay in the Completion of the Project

Common factors attributable for delay in development of IWT are lack of infrastructure, absence of fixed scheduled services, poor navigational aids, lack of connectivity, longer river distances, multiple handling and limited flow of private investments. The Eleventh Five Year Plan envisaged development of six national Inland waterways. Although the Government demarcated five such National Waterways, the Shipping Ministry is unable to start the work on developing two of them (NW4 and NW5), as Planning Commission has not approved the development plans until now. Ministry of Shipping awaits the sum of INR 500 crores that it needs to carry out the development works. As a result of the delay in getting the Planning Commission's approval and the funds, the Ministry has suspended the plans for developing the Sixth National Inland Waterway. According to WASCO, the development work on NW 4 was to be completed in seven years. Earlier in 2002, it was to be completed in 5 years.

National Waterway 5

NW 5 is a proposed waterway covering the East Coast Canal along with Brahmani River and Mahanadi Delta [623 km. (387 mi)]. It thus connects Odisha to West Bengal using the stretch on Brahmani River, East Coast Canal, Matai River and Mahanadi River Delta. The 623 km. long canal system will handle the traffic of cargo such as coal, fertilizer, cement and iron.

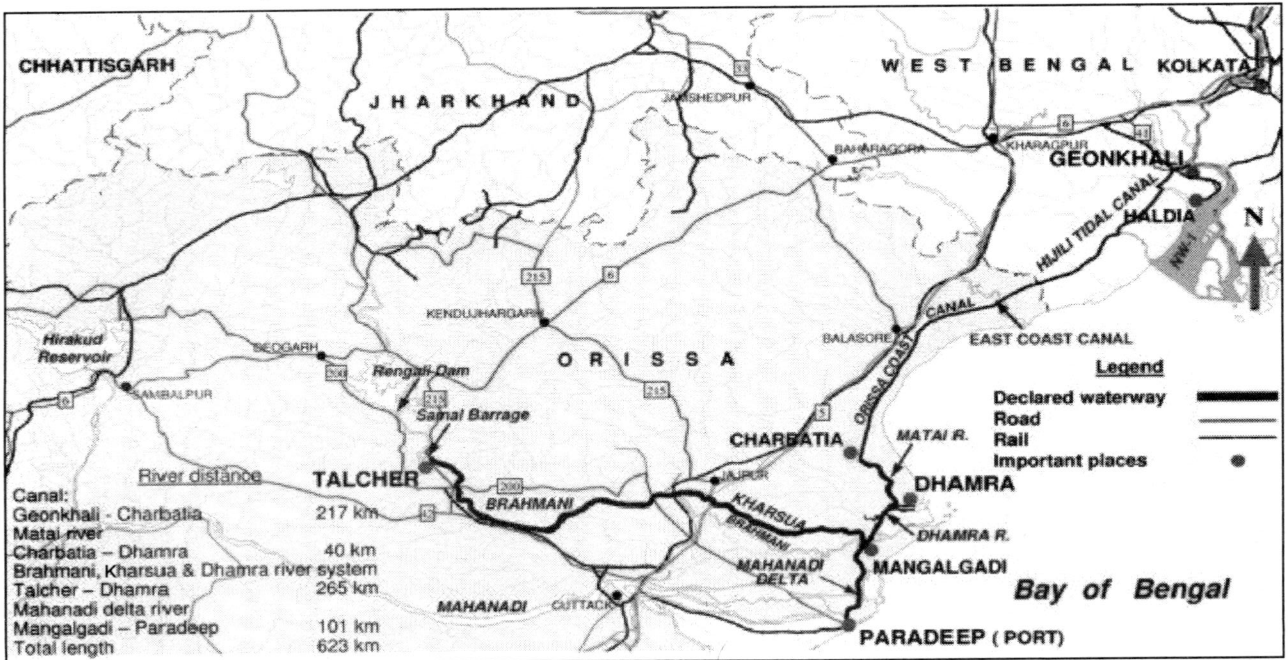

Fig. 0.6: National Waterway No. 5 (East Coast Canal integrated with Brahmani and Mahanadi delta river system).

National Waterway 6

Development of NW 6 was announced in the national budget of 2013-14. It is a proposed waterway in Assam State and will connect Lakhipur to Bhanga in river Barak (see Fig. 0.7). The 121 km. long waterway will help in trading between Silchar to Mizoram State. The project would be executed by the Inland Waterways Authority of India in two phases. The first will be completed by 2016-17 and the second by 2018-19, integrating the waterways in the north-east and helping cargo transport through Assam, Nagaland, Mizoram, Manipur, Tripura and Arunachal Pradesh. The waterway stretches between Lakhipur and Bhanga on the Barak River for 121 km. The waterway is owned by IWAI and is operated by Central Inland Water Transport Corporation.

Challenges and Opportunities for Inland Water Transport in India

Before examining the major challenges, we need to look at the impediments that have prevented this mode from being used more extensively despite its numerous advantages. Equally important are the advantages that the mode has relative to other modes. Mr. Gadkari, Minister for Transport and Shipping has introduced a Bill in Parliament listing 108 Inland Waterways which need to be developed in India. The Bill is ambitious, but without ambition nothing can be achieved.

Impediments in the Growth of IWT

1. Insufficient depths throughout the stretch of navigable waters.
2. Excessive siltation in major rivers from erosion of uplands and deforestation.
3. Navigation being relegated to the fourth position due to priorities to drinking water, irrigation and power (hydel) sectors that results in reduced draft.
4. Non-availability of low draft high technology vessels.
5. Non-availability of adequate navigational aids resulting in restricted sailing over long periods of time.

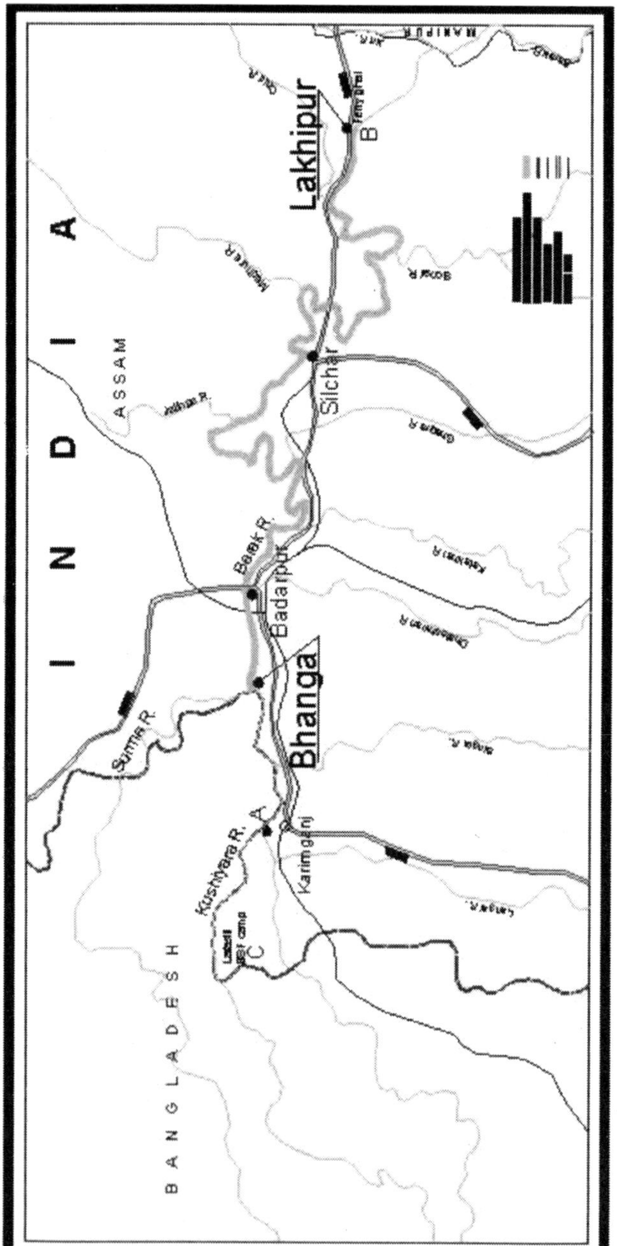

Fig. 0.7: Proposed National Waterway—River Barak (Lakhipur-Bhanga, 121 km.). Total Development Cost: Rs. 46 crore (at 2002 prices)

6. Non-availability of permanent terminals with adequate infrastructure for loading/unloading, storage etc.
7. Non-availability of bulk commodities along the water front.
8. Non-availability of return cargo on most of the routes.

Advantages of IWT

1. *Low capital cost.*
2. *Cost of development of Inland waterway*: It has been estimated to be a more 5-10 per cent of the cost of developing an equivalent 4-lane highway or railway.
3. *Low maintenance cost*: Cost of maintenance of Inland waterway is placed at 20 per cent of that of roads.
4. *Low fuel cost*: Inland Water Transport is a highly fuel-efficient mode of transport. This fact is borne out by the estimate that one litre of fuel can move 24 tonne km. of freight by road, 85 by rail and 105 by IWT.
5. *Cost-effective transport mode*: It has also been estimated that diversion of one billion tonne-km. of cargo to the IWT mode will reduce transport fuel costs by 5 million USD and the overall transport costs by 9 million USD.
6. *Need for Infrastructure building*: An analysis of the need for building essential infrastructure like mechanized handling at terminals and night navigation facilities reveals how these can translate into reduction of cost of transportation per tonne-km. over short haul as well as long haul carriage by IWT. It was observed that the TKM cost of movement would come down from the present Rs. 3.55 to Rs. 1.44 for a short haul of 100 km. and from Rs. 0.95 to 0.39 for a long haul of 2000 km. (TCS, 2004).

CONCLUDING REMARKS

When the reform process began in many countries, in the context of the transport sector, it was felt that a lot could be achieved by simply focusing on improving the efficiency and productivity of individual transport modes. However, given rapid increases in international trade movements, it was felt that only an integrated strategy involving all modes could be effective. In the absence of such an approach, there were major impediments including lack of competitive neutrality across transport modes, low quality and capacity of inter-modal connections etc. It has been further pointed out that current institutional arrangements do not appear to have provided the level of coordination and cooperation between modal jurisdictions needed to address certain issues. The traditional compartmentalized approach has, it is held, left a legacy of distortions that have created modal biases. The most commonly cited example is overuse of and excessive investment in road transport at the expense of rail and water transport. This point hardly needs to be emphasized here in a detailed way in the context of transport development in India. What needs to be emphasized is a required focus on development of a multi-modal freight transport system which can lead to improved productivity through elimination of the bottlenecks. In other words, we must move away from development and investment decision-making based on segmented modes, and many tiers of management, to an integrated nationally consistent multi-modal approach. The policy of encouraging Inland water transport has to go hand-in-hand with policies which encourage an efficient multi-modal transport system to emerge with each mode being used at least cost to the society as a whole.

References

1. Brahma, G.D.: "The Evolution of Perspective of Inland Water Transport in India", *RITES Journal*, April 2006.
2. GoI: *Report of the National Transport Policy Committee*, Planning Commission, Government of India, New Delhi, 1980.
3. GoI: *Report of the Steering Committee on Transport Planning*, Planning Commission, Government of India, New Delhi, 1988.
4. GoI: *Ninth Plan Document*, Planning Commission, Government of India. New Delhi, 1997.
5. NCAER: *Traffic and Economic Survey of Ulhas River—Thane Creek—Basin Creek*, National Council of Applied Economic Research, New Delhi, 1974.
6. Rangaraj, N., and Raghuram, G.: *Viability of Inland Water Transport in India*, INRM Policy Brief, Asian Development Bank, New Delhi, 2007.

7. Rao, P. and Kumar, M.: *Management of Inland Water Transport— A Case Study of the Godavari River Basin of Andhra Pradesh,* Paper submitted to the National Conference on Transport System Studies, Department of Economics, University of Mumbai, 1996.
8. Sriraman, S.: "Perspective on Inland Water Transport in India", *RITES Journal,* April 2002.
9. TCS: *Report of the Development on Coastal Shipping,* Tata Consultancy.

Preface to the First Edition

The purpose of this book is to discuss the role of Inland navigation in the transportation system of India and to assess the prospects of its future development in the country. Within the framework of the above purpose, the book is designed to meet the following objectives:

1. retrospective study of the part played by Inland navigation in the national economy and to identify the causes of its decline;
2. examination of the existing state of Inland navigation in different parts of India; and
3. study of the development of Inland water transport in India during the last two decades.

The book is based on the secondary data derived from various statistical publications and official reports. At places, these data are supplemented by field observations. The book is written for the general reader and aims at arousing public interest in one of the most neglected modes of transportation in India.

Inland Waterways have a chequered history in India. For a long time, they were the chief means of transportation in the country. With the advent of modern means of transportation such as railways and roads, their relative importance declined. By the late forties of this century, they were of national importance, only in the eastern states of the country. The partition of Bengal in 1947 bifurcating the otherwise one system of Ganga-Brahmaputra waterways into two, gave a stunning blow to the waterways of the region. Since Indo-Pakistan conflict in 1965, they have remained completely disrupted.

With the emergence of Bangladesh as a friendly neighbour in what was once East Pakistan, the situation has now undergone a complete change. The prospects of a coordinated development of Inland navigation on the Ganga-Brahmaputra system of rivers in India and Bangladesh have now very much improved. Steps have already been taken by India and Bangladesh to promote water transportation on the Ganga and Brahmaputra system of rivers.

To sustain the growth of the national economy, the Government of India has now decided to give serious consideration to the plan of creating a National Water Grid. This plan incorporates the proposal to link Ganga with Cauvery by a navigable canal. All this augers well for the development of Inland Waterways in the country.

The success of such a plan, however, depends to a great extent on the appreciation of it by the people. The time is now ripe for an intellegent public dialogue on this subject. Unfortunately, there is not enough published material in the market which can create necessary awareness among the people about this vital issue. This book is designed to partially fill this gap.

This book is divided into 10 chapters. Chapter one offers, a background for the book and compares the Inland waterways with other modes of transportation. Chapter two is devoted to the study of the history of Inland navigation in India and Chapter three compares Indian waterways with those of other countries of the world. Chapters four to eight discuss the present conditions and future prospects of Inland navigation in the Ganga plain, Assam, South-eastern states, South-western states and Western states of the country. Chapter nine discusses the problems and prospects of rehabilitating the Inland waterways of India. The last chapter deals with planning and development of Inland waterways. It reviews the plans chalked out in the past and suggests the stages in which an integrated plan for Inland navigation can be implemented.

There are three Annexures in the book. Annexure I consists of the three famous lectures of Sir Arthur Cotton on Irrigation Works in India. These lectures are referred to by many but very few have access to the originals because they were never published. Annexure II deals with coastal navigation in India and has been contributed by Mr. D. C. Jayasankar, Department of Post-Graduate Studies and Research in Geography, University of Karnataka. In

Annexure III, the National Waterways Bill, 2015 is given as introduced in Lok Sabha by Shri Nitin Gadkari, Minister of Road Transport & Highways and Shipping.

The book is designed to give a general and all-round picture of the status, problems, and prospects of Inland water transport in India. Perpectives of the study are generally geographic and non-technical. Those interested in the technical aspects may like to go through more advanced treatises.

The speed with which the book was published is praiseworthy. It, however, kept a few shortcommings unattended. For example, the scales used are not uniform and feet, metres, tons and tonnes often go together. I hope the reader will overlook these shortcomings. It is hoped the book will be of interest to all those who are involved in the development of water resources of the country, and will be of special interest to those who are interested in our Inland waterways.

As far as my knowledge goes, this is the first major publication on Inland Waterways of India. It should not be too much to hope that a more comprehensive book on this vital aspect of our economy will be attempted by more competent a person in not too distant a future.

Mysure **R.P. Misra**
November 1, 1972

Contents

List of Tables

List of Figures

1
Introduction

A. Background

Prosperity of a nation depends, to a large extent, upon the resources—material and human—it is endowed with. As these resources are not distributed evenly and equitably, the developmental processes the world over, have not operated with the same speed and intensity everywhere. The factor which minimizes the evil effects of these and which tends to distribute the bounties of nature and the fruits of social, economic and technological developments more evenly, is transportation—"the dominant economic fact of our age".

Transportation acts as a bridge between man the consumer and nature—the supplier. It also "enables a given flow of resources to produce greater results" by removing the obstacles in the way of their physical union. Regional specialization in the production processes will be impossible without modern transportation. The cotton goods of Mumbai or the jute goods of Kolkata are produced for markets which extend far beyond the immediate enviorns. Transportation is a decisive factor determining the size of market and hence also the price of commodities.

Transportation is a great unifying factor and has given rise to modern National States. Improved transportation was a major factor leading to the downfall of the Greek city states. "It rendered obsolete the small States founded upon the single city and its environs. At the same time, it created conditions favouring larger and more effective political units".[1] Had not the great empires grown in the fertile valleys of those mighty rivers which had acted as the highways of transportation? Even today river Ganga supports the greatest human congregation, a legacy of the time when it was navigable by large country boats from the point it descends to the plains down to the Bay of Bengal. Recent innovations in the transport industry have been the major contributory factors in the rapid growth of urban civilization.

Economic and social significance apart, transportation, is the foundation upon which the defence edifice of a nation rests. "Military and imperialistic considerations were doubtless uppermost in the construction of Roman roads, and similar motives have played a large role in the promotion of transportation in modern times".[2] Rapid expansion of railroads in India owes much to the military rather than economic and welfare considerations on the part of the British. It is, therefore, of little surprise that some of the modern developments in transportation are the by-products of the last two World Wars.

In view of the significant role played by transportation in the progress of man and his society, it is often taken as a barometre to measure the level of economic development and social change. A comparison of the network of transportation in the developed and under-developed countries of the world proves beyond doubt that it does reflect the overall social and economic progress achieved by a country. Most of the developed countries of the world have better transportation facilities than the developing countries have. The length of railways, roads, waterways and airways per unit area or per thousand population is invariably more in the developed countries than in the developing countries. The developing countries have to go a long way before they can come up to the level of the developed countries in matters of modern transportation. And unless the transport network which forms a vital element of the infrastructure necessary for social and economic development is expanded and improved, the progress of the developing countries has, at best, to be slow.

As a nation marches on the road to economic development, mobility of the people and the goods increases. Many products which did not enter the regional, national, and international markets before are transported from places of abundance to those of scarcity. Some of these have to be hauled to new destinations within a specified time and a given range of transportation cost. Still others require special arrangements for movement, lest they are damaged in carriage. All these different products and goods require different types of transport facilities. As each mode of transportation is different from others in matters of speed, bulk carriage, cost and transhipment facilities, a coordinated development of all these becomes necessary for a country.

The four main modes of Inland transportation which enter into transport planning are:

1. Waterways,
2. Roads,
3. Railways, and
4. Airways.

Waterways include all the navigable natural or man-made channels such as rivers, lakes, coastal backwaters, reservoirs and canals. Roads include all those land routes which are wide enough to be used by vehicular traffic. Railways consist of the land routes laid with iron rails on which vehicles move; and airways include the airplane and helicopter services. Pipelines and ropeways are the other modes of Inland transportation.

B. Inland Transportation in India

The history of transportation in India goes back to many millennia. We will look into it a little later. As at present, the country is poorly served by modern transport facilities. The inadequacy of the transport facilities in India was recognized by the planners from the very start of the five year plans in 1951.

The First Five Year Plan outlay on transportation and communication amounted to Rs. 517 crore which was 26 per cent of all public sector outlays. During the Second and Third Five Year Plans, investments in transportation and communication amounted to Rs. 1,261 and Rs. 1,486 crore forming 27 and 20 per cent of all public sector outlays respectively. Rs. 3,237 crore constituting over 20 per cent of all public sector outlays have been earmarked for transportation and communication for the Fourth Five Year Plan period (1969-1974) (Table 1.1).

Notwithstanding, the progress made during the last twenty years, India continues to be far behind the developed countries of the world in matters of transport facilities. As Tables 1.2 to 1.4 reveal, both in terms of area and population, India is poorly served by all modes of transportation. A great majority of people of India are still far away from all-weather roads, and railways; the airways have come only recently and serve only the larger towns. The waterways are confined to a few river valleys in the eastern States of the country.

Table 1.1: Public Sector Outlays on Transportation in India in Recent Years

	First Plan	*Second Plan*	*Third Plan*	*Three annual plans*	*Fourth Plan (Provisional)*
	(1951-56)	*(1956-61)*	*(1961-66)*	*(1966-69)*	*(1969-74)*
Railways	270	723	1,326	509	1050
	(55)	(65.6)	(66.6)	(47.0)	(39.7)
Roads and	143	242	–467	360	970
Road Transport	(30)	(22.0)	(23.5)	(33.2)	(36.5)
Inland water	Nil	0.72	3.07	6.23	13
Transport		(0.1)	(0.2)	(0.6)	(0.5)
Others	74	136	193	206	616
	(15)	(12.3)	(9.7)	(19.2)	(23.3)
Total	**487**	**1,101.8**	**1,989.07**	**1,089.23**	**2649**
	(100)	**(100)**	**(100)**	**(100)**	**(100)**

Note: Others include ports, shipping, civil air transport etc. Figures in brackets show percentages to total.

1. *Waterways*

Of the various modes of Inland transportation, the earliest to be developed in a country is apt to be the waterways.[3] In the early part of human history, riverways were the only possible highways for large-scale movement of men and materials.

Waterways are by far the cheapest means of transportation. The cost of haulage on the waterways is low as the base on which vessels ply is liquid and generates least friction. The cost of their maintenance is low as they use natural channels. Artificial channels like canals are often double or multi-purpose and hence can carry goods cheaply.

It is relatively slow; its route is fixed and requires transhipment at both ends. It is, therefore, suited to cheap and bulky commodities of non-perishable nature.

Many of the Indian rivers are quite suitable for Inland navigation; it is specially so with the northern rivers such as Ganga and Brahmaputra. They do not require costly ice-breaking and clearing equipment as they flow through warm lands and graded valleys. Transhipment of goods both at the originating and destination points is relatively easy.[4]

Out of a total of about 25,000 km. of potentially navigable waterways in India, not more than 8,000 km. are used for navigation by organized as well as unorganized steamer and boat services. A comparative picture of the development of waterways in various countries of the world as given in Table 1.2 shows that India has to do a lot before it can catch up with the developed countries of the world in matters of Inland water transportation.

Table 1.2(a): Inland Waterways in Selected Countries—1960-1965

Country	*Total*	*Length in km.*	
		Per 1,000 sq. km. of area	*Per 1,00,000 population*
USSR	96,000	11.0	40.0
USA	45,000	5.0	23.0
UK	4,000	18.0	8.0
China	40,000	4.2	5.7
Brazil	35,000	4.1	38.0
France	9,000	16.5	18.0
Netherlands	6,000	185.0	8.0
West Germany	5,000	20.0	8.0
India	8,000	3.5	1.6

Source: UN Statistical Year-book, *1968 and* Statesman Year-book, *1971.*
Includes channels suitable for steamer services only.

2. *Roads*

"Road is one of the great fundamental institutions of mankind. Its history dates back to the dawn of recorded history and beyond. Its beginnings are almost instructive with the man's first quest in search of food, water, plunder or sheer adventure. It develops with man's advance, it retrogrades with the breakdown of social order. A people without roads would be people without intercourse with the outside world...without the attributes of civilization. Man, the road builder thus cannot be separated from man, the builder of civilization".[5]

Roads can penetrate a far more rugged topography than any other Inland transport network. They are used not only by the vehicular traffic, but also by the people moving on foot or bicycles and are more easily accessible than any other mode of transportation. They supplement other modes by carrying the people and goods from wherever they are to the nodal points.

Road building was recognized as one of the primary duties of Indian rulers in the past. The well laid roads in Harappa and Mohen-jodaro indicate that road building was well advanced in India even as early as 3000 B.C. During the medieval times, a number of trunk roads such as the Grand Trunk Road were constructed. Nevertheless, the road network in the country before the British rule was not as well developed as one would expect in a country of vast distances and so ingenious a people. The reasons for this were: (1) animal driven vehicles did not require so nicely laid roads the like of which we find today; (2) trade and commerce was mostly localized; (3) political control over the whole of geographical India did not exist for a long enough time to encourage the tedious and expensive work of road construction on a systematic basis; and (4) techniques of road construction were still primitive and slow.

Because of the intense competition from the railways and also because of the fact that road development was the responsibility of the provincial Governments, road network in India during the British rule did not develop fast enough to integrate the country through a national grid. Further, most of the trunk routes were built along the railways and sufficient emphasis was not laid on rural transportation which alone could modernize the countryside.

After the Independence of the country, attempts were made to implement the Nagpur Plan chalked out by the Road Conference in 1943. According to this Plan, there were to be 3,31,000 miles of all types of roads in the country.

National Highways	16,600 miles
National Tracks	4,150 miles
State Highways	53,950 miles
District and Village Roads	2,56,300 miles
Total	**3,31,000 miles**

The added emphasis laid on infrastructural development during the successive five year plans has led to a progressive increase in road mileage in India. In 1969, the total length of roads in the country was 3,25,000 km. of surfaced and 6,47,000 km. of unsurfaced roads. But as apparent from Table 1.3, the existing network of roads cannot be adequate to the needs of the country. India is still far behind the developed countries in this regard.

Table 1.2(b): Road Transportation in Selected Countries—1968

Country	*Road length in km.*		*Number of vehicles in lakh units*
	Surfaced	*Total*	
USA	46,00,000	72,50,000	1,050
China	3,00,000	8,00,000	5
UK	3,35,000	3,35,000	150
Canada	5,45,000	760,000	80
Brazil	NA	10,89,000	26
France	NA	7,88,000	140
Sweden	26,000	98,000	23
Italy	—	2,85,000	120
India	3,18,000	9,14,000	12
Nigeria	—	45,000	0.28

Source: UN Statistical Year-book, *1969; and* Statesman Year-book, 1971.

3. *Railways*

The advantages of the railways are that they can carry at considerable speed, they can overcome moderate gradients, they can carry any amount of goods, and that they have a favourable natural and economic climate in India for efficient service. But railways cannot carry cheaply, require enormous outlay in initial stages and their track capacity is limited and of single purpose use.

The formation of the East Indian and Great Peninsular Railway companies during 1844-1945, set the stage for the development of railways in India. The first railway line (Mumbai-Thana) was opened in 1853. The main purpose for which the railways were brought to India is clear from the following paragraph taken from the despatch of Lord Dalhausie, the Court Director of the East India Company.

> The commercial and social advantages which India would derive from their (railways) establishment are beyond calculation. Great tracts are teeming with produce they cannot dispose of. Others are scantly bearing what they would carry in abundance, if only it could be conveyed whither it is needed. Every increase of facilities for trade has been attended, as we have seen, with an increased demand for articles of European produce in the most distant parts of India.[6]

With 25,000 miles of track, Indian Railways were the principal carriers of goods and people in the country at the start of this century. They were nationalized during 1930s, but the depression and the Second World War came in the way of their further development. The partition of the country in 1947 left 34,755 route miles in India.

In 1968, they had 60,014 route km. carried 6.1 millions of passengers, and 0.56 million tons of goods daily with a gross earning of Rs. 901 crore during the year. Indian Railways are the largest railway system in Asia and the fourth largest in the world. Yet, in relation to area or population of the country, they are not as developed as their counterparts in the developed countries of the world (Table 1.3).

Recognizing the significant role that Indian Railways have had to play in the national development efforts, considerable stress was laid on their rehabilitation and further expansion since Independence. By the end of the Third Five Year Plan, a sum of Rs. 3,152 crore was spent on them and the Fourth Plan has earmarked Rs. 1,050 crore for this purpose.

4. *Airways*

Civil Aviation is the latest addition to the transportation system of India. In 1969, Indian aircraft flews nearly 665 million kilometres carrying about 25 million passengers and 421 million kg. of cargo including mail. Since 1947, the passenger traffic handled by the aircrafts has increased ten fold and the cargo load has gone up by more than thirteen times.

Table 1.3: Railway Transportation in Selected Countries—1968

	Route km.			*Traffic (in millions)*			
	Total length (in 000)	*Length per 1,000 km. of area*	*Length per 1,00,000 of Population*	*Tons carried*	*Net ton km.*	*No. of Passengers carried*	*Passenger km.*
USA	352	39	160	1500	11,00,000	295	24,000
China	35	3.6	5	542	30,000	—	80,000
Canada	85	9	385	1,37,000	152	24	5,000
W. Germany	34	135	55	380	55,000	1,024	34,000
Argentina	43	15	195	20	11,000	481	14,000
France	37	67	74	243	63,000	610	38,000
Brazil	32	4	35	66	20,000	356	13,500
UK	30	133	580	200	22,000	425	29,000
Nigeria	4	4	7	—	1,613	—	390
India	60	20	11	205	60,000	2,230	40,000

Source: UN Statistical Year-book, *1969; and* Statesman Year-book, 1971.

C. Inland Water Transport in Indian Economy

The possible and potential role that Inland water transport can play in Indian economy depends largely on the nature and volume of Inland (inter-regional as well as intra-regional) and external trade of India. In the case of external trade, the waterways carry goods from interior to the ports. Geography of India offers such diverse natural, economic, and social conditions that inter-regional trade is indispensable. The bulk of the commodities entering the national market are also quite suitable for carriage by waterways (Table 1.4).

Table 1.4: Inland Trade of India in Selected Articles

(In 1000 quintals)

Commodities	*1956-57*	*1968-69*
1. Coal and coke	2,16,634	3,73,062
2. Raw-cotton	3,507	3,718
3. Cotton piece goods	3,260	1,689
4. Rice (not in husk)	16,407	17,256
5. Wheat	8,274	53,325
6. Raw jute	3,539	3,812
7. Iron & Steel products	19,165	76,807
8. Oil seeds	9,455	9,730
9. Salt	12,408	24,468
10. Sugar (Except Khandsari)	8,293	6,742

Note: India has been divided into 34 trade blocks. These figures relate to inter-block movement of goods and not to intra-block movement.
Source: India, 1960 and 1971.

For several commodities, the direction of movement is also parallel to the river channels of the country. As most of the mineral resources of the Eastern Plateau Region and many of the agricultural products like jute and cotton are not produced everywhere, opportunities for inter and intra-regional trade in these commodities is indeed great.

As years pass, India is steadily becoming an industrial nation. Industrialization and industrial development presuppose rapid and large scale movement of men and materials both intra-nationally and internationally. Waterways, by their very nature, have to play an important role in this context. The significant part played by the Lake Route in the development of the Iron & Steel Industry in the USA can be cited as an example.

Waterways are relatively cheaper operationally as the friction generated by water is far less than that generated by land. Improved water transport can encourage the movement of bulky, heavy and cheap commodities likes ores, grains, fuel etc. According to the Inland Waterways Common Carriers Association, USA, following are the comparative efficiency data of railway and water carriers.[7]

1. The relationship between the weight of a railcar and the quantity of cargo it can carry is 1:2, i.e. if the railcar weight 20 tons, the maximum quantity of cargo it can carry would be 50 tons. In case of barges plying in waterways, the ratio will be 1:5, i.e. a barge weighing 170 tons would carry 900 tons of cargo.
2. The equipment cost of a barge with one ton capacity would be Rs. 570, whereas the cost of rail equipment of the same carrying capacity would amount of Rs. 1,520.
3. In the case of diesel engine to be used both in the waterways and railways, the gallons consumed per 1000 net ton mile would amount to 315 in case of barges and 421 in case of railways.
4. In regard to labour productivity, the case of waterways is far superior. The ton mileage per operating employee amounts to 11 million in case of barges and only 3.5 million in case of the railways.
5. The average cost of maintenance and repairs per 1000 net ton miles amounts to Rs. 1.04 in case of towboats, and Rs. 2.94 in case of the locomotives and Rs. 0.67 for barges and Rs. 4.41 for railcars.

D. Limitations of the Waterways

Unlike the other modes of transportation, waterways can be developed only where water channel—natural or man-made—is available. The availability of a channel is, however, not a sufficient condition for the development of Inland navigation. Many other conditions must be met and a few of them are mentioned below.

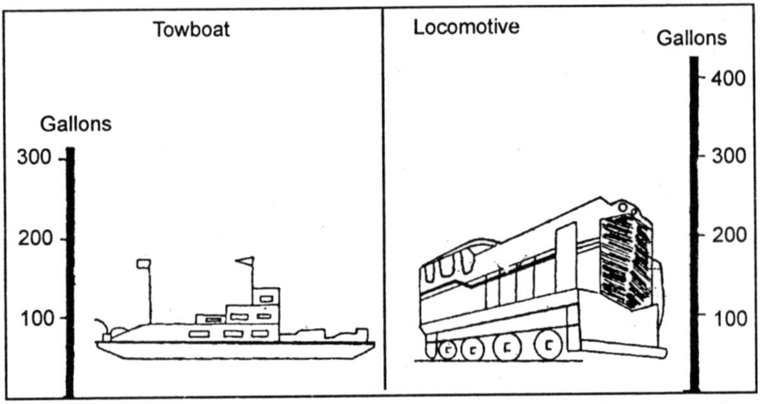

Fig. 1.1: Diagram Showing Ratio of Diesel Fuel Consumption (Per 1000 net Ton Miles)

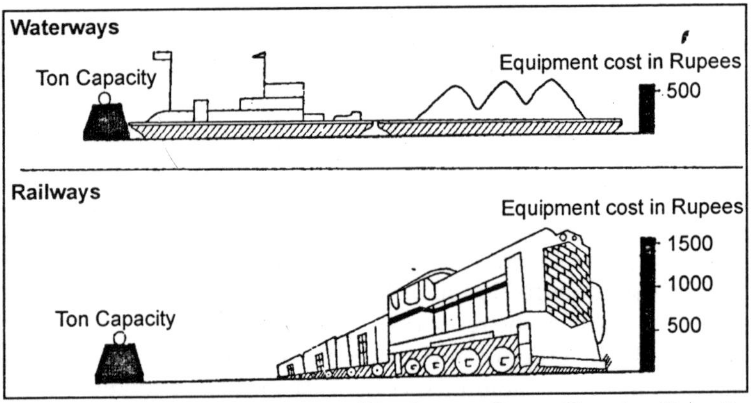

Fig. 1.2: Diagram Showing Ratio of Equipment Cost to Carrying Capacity

1. Depth of the Channel

Depth determines the types of vessels that can ply and also their capacity to handle traffic. A steamer that can carry itself at 2.5 feet draught carries 200 tons at 3.5 feet, and 400 tons at 4.5 feet draught a vessel can run only at a loss, with 3.5 feet, it can earn a profit and with 4.5 feet draught it will return much larger profits.[8] According to A. Pointon, at a draught of 6 feet, a flat can carry 26,000 maunds of cargo, whereas at a draught of 5 feet and 4 feet only 21,700 maunds and 15,350 maunds respectively.[9] In the USA, a standard minimum depth of 9 feet has now been accepted as essential for smooth navigation by modern vessels.

2. *Gradient of the Channel*

If a river is in the young stage of its valley development, its course will often be intercepted by falls and rapids. It will also have fast moving currents. These manifestations of the youthful stage of the river are not very conducive to Inland navigation. "It is estimated that the maximum fall permissible for a river to be used for easy navigation is one in 6336 or 10 inches per mile." As against this, roads can navigate a gradient of 750 feet a mile and the railways about 26 feet a mile.[10]

3. *Width of the Channel*

How far does the width of the channel come in the way of efficient navigation depends upon the size of the vessel used and the speed with which they navigate the channel. Modern vessels fitted with mechanical devices need a minimum width of 60 feet. Lesser width leads to bank erosion which in turn leads to the silting of the channel.

4. *Nature of the River Course*

The channel should be free from sudden bends, hidden bed-reefs, shoals and similar other permanent or temporary obstructions. Stability of the river course is also important. Expansion of canal irrigation in the valleys leads to large-scale diversion of water for irrigation. During dry seasons, only the lower reaches of many of these rivers remain perennial and navigational facilities have to be suspended in the upper stretches.

5. *Traffic Potential*

If the flow of goods is parallel to the channel, waterways tend to pay better. But, if it is against the channel, they have very limited scope for development and may have to limit their services to ferrying of goods and passengers from one bank to the other. Even when the flow of goods is parallel to the channel, the actual direction of flow would have its own impact on the development of navigation. If the goods are available only one way and are not available for the return journey, the services become uneconomic. The services going down-stream are cheaper than those going up-stream. Those waterways which have to carry bulky goods upstream and very light goods down-stream are less economic.

Some of the limitations of waterways mentioned above can be overcome through modern devices of river training and conservancy. The improved lock system which can be manned in minutes, the widening and straightening of the channels and the employment of high speed steam or diesel boats can overcome some of the drawbacks of the waterways. Opening of feeder canals and the application of hydrotechnical structures which straighten the courses of rivers, are other methods of improvement. But whether the country should invest in the improvement and development of the waterways or not, depends solely upon the cost-benefit ratio and role they can play in the national, regional and local transport systems of the country.

We propose to examine these issues in greater details in the following chapters.

References

1. M.L. Fair and E.W. Williams, *Economics of Transportation,* New York: McGraw-Hill, 1950.
2. T.C. Bigham and M.J. Roberts, *Transportation: Principles and Problems,* New York: McGraw-Hill, 1952.
3. Stuart Daggett, *Principles of Inland Transportation,* New York: Harper, 1955, pp. 25-26.
4. *Ibid.,* See also National Planning Committee (India), *Report on Transport,* 1943.
5. *New Popular Encyclopaedia.*
6. Cited by J. Johnston, *Inland Navigation on the Gangetic Valley,* Mumbai: Thaker-Spink, 1946.
7. Gokhale Committee Report on *Inland Water Transport in India,* 1959-60, Government of India.
8. Albert Robinson, *Navigation the Ganges by Iron Steam Vessel,* 1848, cited by J. Johnston, p. 116.
9. J. Johnston, *op. cit.*
10. *Ibid.*

2
Inland Navigation in Retrospect

Rivers have played a momentous role in shaping the history of mankind. All the great civilizations and empires had flourished in the valleys of rivers like Indus, Nile, Euphrates, Danube, Hwang Ho and Yangtse-kiang. The life blood of the civilizations of Sumer, Babylon and Assyria were the two great rivers of Mesopotamia—Tigris and Euphrates. Egyptian civilization was the product of the Nile and that of ancient China owed much to the waters of the Hwang Ho.

In India, it was in the vast riparian plains in the north and the extensive plateaux and valleys of the south, watered by the life-giving streams that take their rise in the icy-peaks of the mighty Himalaya and the gentle slopes of the Western Ghats, where the tendency towards union and coalescence, the *sine quart non* far the development of a great civilization, were widely marked. It was in the valleys of the Indus and Cauvery where the pre-Aryan culture of India reached its zenith. It was again in the flat plains of majestic Ganga where the Aryans wrote and chanted the Vedic hymns. In the later periods of Indian history, one notices with equal frequency the scenes of great conquests, grim struggles for power and the rise and fall of mighty kingdoms being enacted on the banks of these rivers of youthful vitality. The currents of history have moved in unison with the currents of rivers in India, so that, the history of these rivers, in the words of Pandit J.L. Nehru "would be far more important, far more living and real than all the trumping history books that you have. It would be a magnificent story, if it would be written properly".[1] So full of bounty these rivers are that after an incessant misuse and rape of several millennia, they still support one of the largest human congregations of the world.

The spiritualization of Indian rivers and the easy means of transportation they afforded, had greatly influenced the mobility of people, their ideas, goods and cultures. The varied topography, climate and cultural background of the populace of India tends to strengthen the forces of disintegration. The successive failures of emperors like Ashoka and Akbar to unite geographical India into one single political entity was due to these very forces. Rivers were the major forces of integration, but their development was localized and intermittent, so that, an efficient network of waterways capable of meeting the commercial, defence, and other needs of a nation of continental dimensions could not be evolved.

A. Period of Unmatched Supremacy (Up to 12th Century A.D.)

In the absence of modern modes of transportation such as air-ways, railways, roadways, and riverways were the only highways for the movement of goods and people in ancient India. The Ganga and Yamuna in the North, and Narmada, Tapi and Godavari in the South were extensively used for commercial navigation. Yet long-distance navigation in the rivers passing through different kingdoms was considered to be a hazardous task. The subsistence economy and the political problems apart, comparative insecurity kept navigation restricted to only short distances. The knowledge about the bed and the discharge of rivers was limited and hence, the boatmen and merchants were chary of navigating in channels where traffic may not be safe.

In spite of the fact that water transportation was largely confined to short stretches, riverways, in ancient India, had an unmatched supremacy. There was no other mode of transportation which could offer better services. Consequently, the boats and the rivers became a part and parcel of social and cultural life of the people. Their influence was not confined to boatmen and traders alone, they caught the attention of the artists, the poets, the writers, the philosophers and the religious teachers alike.

We read in the *Ramayana,* Lord Rama crossing river Ganga on a ferry boat at Shringverpur (near Allahabad) and paying the cess to the *Kewat* (the boatman), and elsewhere about Alexander crossing the river Jhelum by means of boats and attacking Porus. During the Golden Age of Indian history, the riverways attained special importance in the economy of the country. It happened because: (1) almost the whole of the Ganga valley came under the direct control of the Gupta dynasty and hence, through services from one end of the river channel to the other became possible; and (2) the unprecedented development of trade and commerce in that period necessitated large-scale movement of goods both internally and for export. This gave rise to a number of commercial and religious towns like Indraprastha, Mathura, Kaushambi, Prayag, Kashi, Pataliputra, Tamralipti, Kanchi, Kaveripuram, Uraiyur, Madurai, Kayal, Bhrigukachcha and Kapisa, either on the coasts busy with coastal traffic or the rivers navigated by country boats. The coastal towns were connected with the Inland river towns hundreds of miles away in the interior.

B. Period of Comparative Growth (12th to 15th Centuries A.D.)

With the fall of Hindu dynasties and the advent of Moslem rule in the tenth century A.D., riverways, declined in importance for the time being. During the Mughal period, we, however, notice a regeneration of the waterways. Feeder roads linking major riverways were constructed all over the country. But, during this period, the long distance traffic remained lamentably limited. This is evident from the fact that Mughal armies used riverways for transport of personnel very infrequently. The only occasion when Ganga was used for this purpose seems to be the invasion of Bengal by Akbar in 1574 A.D. The progress made in the development of river transport for commercial purposes can still be said to be remarkable. All along river Ganga, cargo and passenger handling facilities were provided and a large number of small towns hustling with life sprang up on both sides of the Ganga system of rivers.

Travelling along the Ganga one comes across several dilapidated and isolated remains of transhipment facilities built during the Mughal times. These structures, still standing boldly, though undermined at the base by the non-stop beat of the rippling currents of Ganga, had once been the Inland ports. The ruins of extinct cities (like Kara and Manikpur near Allahabad) which had once served as centres of commerce and trade and of the Mughal, structures like Mosques, Idgahs and travellers inns, still point to the glorious days of the riverways.

In the south, coastal services on the Coromandel and Malabar Coasts increased and trade between India and the countries of the

West and East Asia flourished. Indian culture, Indian religion, Indian thought and Indian merchandise had their venerable place all over the known world. Inland waterways were the arteries through which they could find their way to far off lands.

C. The Golden Period (1550 to 1850 A.D.)

We now approach a period which witnessed the ascendency of the riverways as the foremost transport arteries of the country. During this period long distance journeys were quite popular and safely undertaken. This period starts from the middle of the sixteenth century and continues till the first war of Independence fought in 1857 A.D.

It is pertinent to note that this period is also marked by closer trade and commercial contacts of India with Europe culminating in British domination. During the medieval and early Mughal periods the commercial relations of India with foreign countries were limited to South-West and South-East Asia. Indian exports to these regions consisted of fine and superfine manufactured goods of light weight used by the upper stratum of society. During the early part of the period under study, this aspect of Indian trade underwent a desirable change and common goods started moving long distances, so that, India became a bulk supplier of a variety of manufactured goods. During the British period, the pattern was, however, completely changed. Instead of India being the supplier of manufactured goods, it became its importer in bulk. In return for finished goods, India exported large quantities of raw materials. This gave a death blow to Indian industry, but helped the Inland navigation to grow at least temporarily.

The improvement in the law and order situation also encouraged river navigation. During the Mughal period, there was comparative peace. Although after the death of Aurangazeb, the insecurity of life and property became a rule rather than exception, the increasing power of the British East India Company in Bengal kept law and order under control in areas of its influence. As the hold of this Company over India increased, the general conditions of law and order also improved.

During this period, the population of the country, particularly that of the Gangetic Valley appears to have increased rather rapidly necessitating the movement of foodgrains from region to region.

This period is also remarkable for the emergence of a middle stratum in the society which demanded cheap and finished goods in bulk. These two factors gave considerable fillip to the already developing Inland navigation as there was no alternative medium through which bulky goods could be transported quickly and cheaply.

The introduction of mechanically driven vessels in the nineteenth century gave considerable impetus to the waterways. The riverways, being the free gifts of nature, did not require much initial outlay as roads and railways did and hence the discovery of steam power was apt to be used on waterways first.

Writing about the navigation in Ganga, Johnston states "the trade was not confined to the produce of the riverine tracts only, but extended in some cases to areas far removed from the rivers, when this entailed considerable carriage by road followed by transhipment. The main example is probably that of the cotton of Central India, which was brought to Kalpi on the Yamuna, and from there shipped to Kolkata. At the time there was no river of the world unless those of China be exception, on which there was so large a navigation as on the Ganga and its tributaries and no less than 30,000 boatmen found their livelihood from this source. Everyone who had a chance to live on the bank of the Great Ganga, says Major Rennel (1780), was struck by the constant succession of boats, moving up and down the river never appearing for a moment altogether clear; and as this was nearly the same at all the seasons and in all places, it leaves an impression of the extent to which this magnificent stream ministered to the wants of commerce and of the traveller, such as defied the attempts at computation. It was not only Ganga as a single stream that conferred these benefits; all the larger rivers that bring down the waters of northern mountains were navigable more or less throughout the year and almost to the foot of the first range."[2]

Commerce and trade being the primary objectives of East India Company, the unusal attention paid by them to the development of Inland waterways in the Gangetic system was, but natural. As new areas were acquired, the Company was forced to pay utmost attention to transportation as a measure of security. River navigation was the only means available readily and hence, it became the greatest beneficiary of Company's policies and programmes. Major Rennel, the Surveyor General of India, carried out the survey of the

Ganga down Allahabad at the instance of the Company in 1764. His successor, Mr. Colebrook resurveyed Ganga up to Allahabad in 1801 and up to Kanpur in 1807. As a result of a favourable report by Captain Thomas Prinsep on the suitability of River Ganga for steam navigation, Lord William Bentink took keen interest in the steam traffic, so that, a regular steamer service was started between Allahabad and Kolkata in 1834. The discovery of coal mines in Bengal made the steamer services cheaper by about 25 per cent.

With the introduction of steam power, river services became very popular. The steamers were sternwheelers of about 120′ × 22′ dimension with 40 to 90 nominal horsepower engines, giving a speed of 6 to 7 miles an hour. During rains when Ganga and its tributaries had sufficient water to allow direct service *via* Hooghly, it took 20 days to reach Allahabad from Kolkata. The return journey was, however, quicker and took only 8 days. During the dry seasons the steamers had to go *via* the Sundarban Creeks, as Bhagirathi (upper part of Hooghly) was not navigable by steamers, and hence, in this period up-journey took about 24 days and down journey about 15 days. In comparison to the present day, the freight rates were extremely high, but considering the time they were levied, they were not bad at all. Per cabin passenger charge amounted to Rs. 400 for journey from Kolkata to Allahabad and the cargo freight varied from Rs. 3 to 10 per maund depending upon the auction bid.

During 1844-47 Albert Robinson, started a new type of steamer that was run single handed rather than by towing boats or cargo flats between Kolkata and Mirzapur. But the service could not continue for long due mainly to the paucity of trained pilots although it took only eleven and half days to cover this long distance. However, steamer services continued to thrive and they went as far as Garhmukteswar in Meerut District, 393 miles up stream from Allahabad and the services up to Kanpur about 140, miles from Allahabad "plied with-much activity, the reach of the river at that military station having the appearance of a port on a small-scale[3]."

Apart from the traffic by mechanically propelled vessels, all the Gangetic rivers were studded with an array of innumerable country boats. In fact, the traffic, both passenger and cargo, handled by them was much more in volume than that handled by steamers. The number of boats plying on streams was in lakhs. The port of

Kolkata contained 10,000 tons of shipping built in India of a description calculated for the conveyance of cargo to England and the teak wood vessels of Mumbai were greatly superior to the oaken of old England. According to J. Johnston, "the volume of the upward and downward trade of the interior, with Kolkata alone by the Gangetic channels was, in 1881, valued at about Rs. 27 crore. At Bamanghata, east of Kolkata, 1,78,627 cargo boats were registered in 1876-77 at Hooghly 1,24,357 and at Patna 61,571. These figures, large as they are, represent only a fraction of the total number of boats on all the rivers of the Gangetic Plain."[4]

The last quarter of the nineteenth century marks a turning point in the history of navigation in river Ganga. This was the period of gradual decline which culminated in the final debacle in the first quarter of the twentieth century. The first challenge to the growing popularity of riverways was thrown by the Grand Trunk Road reconstructed between 1839 and 1842. But the usual inconvenience of animal driven vehicles destined for long journeys of hundreds of miles and the insecure law and order situation kept the road useful only for short distances. The construction of railways between 1855 and 1870 did not affect the riverways adversely. Instead, the traffic on rivers increased as large quantities of cargo destined to be carried by railways was transported by riverways to points nearer the railway lines. In this connection it may be noted that initially only trunk railway lines like the one connecting Allahabad with Kolkata were opened and rest of the areas were devoid of any other means of transportation except the riverways.

During this period of the ascendency of Inland navigation, South India was not lagging behind. The coastal traffic along the Malabar coast and the backwaters of Kerala had flourished incessantly. The Coromandel coast was equally bustling with country boats and the rivers like Mahanadi and Godavari were as much important in the south as Ganga and its tributaries were in the north. The economic history of Inland navigation in south India, however, does not devolve round these waterways. A navigation canal known as Buckingham Canal that follows the eastern coast of the Peninsula and was constructed as early as 1806 by an individual named Basil Cochrane was the focus of Peninsular waterway system.

This canal is still open for navigation by smaller crafts. Running parallel to the eastern coast, its major portion lies in the State of Andhra Pradesh and a portion of the Southern sector in Tamil Nadu. It is connected with Cannanur canal of Krishna delta, which in turn is connected with the Godavari delta canals. It make a continues stretch of navigable channel of about 451 miles along the eastern coast.

Initially, the canal was only 11 miles long and connected Chennai town with Ennore lake. It was then known as Cochrane Canal. A portion of it consisted of the natural channels formed by the backwaters of the Eastern coast and the remaining was cut through the strips of sand deposited along the coast by the waves of the Bay of Bengal. Subsequently, it was extended northward to Pulicat Lake, about 25 miles from Chennai. It suffered from frequent silting as its design and planning were not based on sound engineering principles of allignment etc.

The Canal became popular soon as a means of coastal transportation. The revenue derived from traffic in the canal was, however, not commensurate with the expenditure involved in keeping it fit for navigation all the year round. It suffered from one more handicap. The owner of the Canal had very little knowledge of the principles on which navigable channels are economically and efficiently run. His interest was limited to short-term returns and had hardly any perspective view of the Canal and hence had little, if any, interest in investing adequate capital on the remodelling of the Canal. His venture was, however, most praiseworthy as he could at least foresee the benefits that could accrue from the opening of such a Canal and could act single handed with a very crude knowledge of engineering devices and having no encouragement from the then administration.

Being one of the chief Inland waterways of Madras Presidency, the Government could not look passively at the deteriorating condition of the Canal. They took it over from Mr. Cochrane in 1837. Within two decades of this, plans were afoot to improve the working of the Canal. A lock was provided 9 miles north of Chennai, but was later abandoned and a new one was provided 8 miles north of Chennai in 1895. In 1878 the Canal which was than called East Coast Canal, was renamed as Buckingham Canal after the name of Duke of Buckingham and Chandos, then Governor of Madras Presidency.

By the year 1876, the northern section of the Canal had been extended to Krishnapatnam, 92 miles north of Chennai. Nellore which was a flourishing commercial centre of the time was only a few miles by road from this town. In the meantime a new project of constructing a 35 mile long canal south of Chennai was carried out, although it had no connection with the Buckingham Canal. During the Great Chennai Famine of 1876-77, these canals played an important role in the transportation of food grains to the famine affected areas. The administration was much impressed by the usefulness of the Canal and included its development as one of the items to be taken in hand as a part of general relief measure. As a result thereof, speedy extension to its present northern limit at Pedda Ganjam was undertaken and completed within a record period of two years. By 1882 the southern canal which was extended 60 miles south of Chennai was connected with the Buckingham Canal by means of a junction canal in the northern section.

In the years following, the condition of the Canal deteriorated once again. It was frequently silted up as there was no proper arrangement for cross drainage. During rains the muddy waters of the adjoining areas rushed across the Canal, breached the earth embankments and flooded the channel with salt laden water. An improved design of the canal was, therefore, adopted which had the provisions of:

1. Keeping the Canal at least 100 miles from the coastline;
2. Embankment on the eastern side of the Canal;
3. Flood gates on the western side of the Canal;
4. High Masionary sluices and long flush escapes for cross drainage; and
5. Locks to maintain a minimum depth of water.

This scheme was carried out in 1897, but the economic condition of the Canal could not improve much. The Canal from the very start was running at a loss, but the gap between income and expenditure was never so alarming as it was during the eighties for the last century and afterwards. The average loss amounted to about Rs. 25,000 per annum during the eighties and the subsequent years registered further losses. Table 2.1 gives an idea of the financial position of the canal between 1910-11 and 1921-22.

Table 2.1: Buckingham Canal: Receipts and Expenditure 1910–1922

Year	*Revenue in Rs.*	*Expenditure in Rs.*
1910-11	70,323	81,290
1911-12	75,883	1,34,028
1912-13	72,679	1,29,593
1913-14	74,663	1,44,554
1914-15	68,019	1,58,550
1915-16	69,019	1,34,462
1916-17	67,215	1,13,168
1917-18	79,239	1,30,325
1918-19	87,457	1,92,483
1919-20	81,784	2,21,332
1920-21	77,371	2,20,360
1921-22	79,200	2,38,670

Source: V.K. Sourirajan. "Buckingham Canal: A Survey—Historical, Geographical and Economic," *The Journal of Madras Geographical Association,* Vol. 3, (January, 1929).

The main goods carried by the Canal were rice, paddy, salt, building materials, timber, firewood and casuarina post. Of minor importance were cotton and wool—both raw and manufactured—dyes and tans, hides and skin, food grains other than rice and paddy, liquors, metals, oils, oilseeds, onions, provisions, spices, sugar and jaggery, tobacco, miscellaneous goods, bamboo, coal, and coke. The total volume of goods carried amounted to 1,98,566 tons in 1919-1920 and 1,42,284 and 1,56,005 tons in 1920-21 and 1921-22, respectively. The value of goods in terms of Rupees amounted to Rs. 15,376,699, Rs. 58,95,130 and Rs. 84,21,172 in 1919-1920, 1920-21 and 1921-22 respectively.

D. The Period of Decline (1850 to 1920 A.D.)

The decline of traffic on Ganga showed itself first in the upper reaches of the river and its tributaries where, due to diversion of large quantities of water to the Yamuna and Ganga canals constructed between 1825 and 1854, safe navigation became difficult. The decline at first was gradual, but between 1880 and 1890 it began to accelerate finally ending in a catastrophic and dramatic crash. In 1886-87 the traffic on Ghaghra-Ganga route to

Bengal amounted to 53,25,467 maunds composed of 46,88,515 maunds of export and 6,36,952 mounds of imports. After two years, it amounted to only 48,16,400 maunds of which 38,86,885 maunds represented exports and 9,29,515 maunds imports. The chief items of cargo for export were wheat and other food grains, oilseeds, and sugar, white salt, tobacco and iron were the items of imports (upstream service). The decline in the number of cargo boats may be taken as another evidence of setback suffered by Inland navigation. In 1905, the number of cargo boats on Gangetic rivers was 15,194 only, compared to 47,814 plying on Brahmaputra in Assam. By the year 1910, navigation on Ganga upstream from Allahabad was undertaken very rarely. The traffic down Allahabad was, however, still roaring and 1907 edition of the Gazetteer of Mirzapur District states that Ganga was navigated by country boats of 100 maunds berthen or even more during the rains. As many as 79 wharves were available on both sides of the bank for transhipment.

The above mentioned gazetteer further informs that "it is the custom of Mallahs, who form generally the class of boatmen and reside in the riverine villages, to leave the district after the Kali fair in August. If their boats are large, they take on cargoes of stone and grain; if they are small they carry passengers, the destinations being Sheorajganj, Dacca, Dulheri, Goalpara and even distant Assam. During the whole of the cold weather and uptil the month of April they work as boatmen or pilots in the timber carrying trade of the Bengal rivers; and then if the season is favourable and they have earned sufficient profit, they sail homewards on the east wind with cargos of rice, coconuts and similar things arriving in June or July. In good years as many as six hundred boats will return, but if trade is bad and earnings have been low, only half of this number may come home, the remainder staying on for another season of work."[5]

The situation on other rivers had also undergone considerable change. As far back as 1903, the Bahraich Gazetteer recorded that the "river traffic of the district is still of considerable importance, although it has been very greatly affected by the development of the railway system. The Ghaghra, Rapti and Sarju are all navigable. On the two, former, boats up to 1200 maunds and on the latter during the rains, large barges go up to Khairi Bazar and thence carry grain. The smaller boats used, will carry about 3 tons and draw 2 feet of water when loaded... The trade is almost wholly in grain and timber and very little now goes beyond Bahramghat, although at one time there was a considerable *traffic in sugar with Azamgarh*. Large quantities of sal logs are floated down the Rapti in similar fashion. Where, however, the forests are tapped by the railway, the river traffic has been almost entirely supplanted by the railway, which affords a means of transit that is not only more expeditious, but cheaper."[6]

By 1915, traffic in U.P. and Bengal-Assam riverways had shrunk considerably. The pattern of trade also was reversed and instead of exports forming the bulk of traffic, imports became dominant. In 1913-14, imports accounted for 2,07,669 maunds and export for 45,016 maunds only. As time passed this pattern of trade underwent further changes and in 1921-22, the total volume of traffic handled by waterways was a mere 1,10,089 maunds of which 83,196 maunds were imports and 26,823 maunds were exports.

1. *Causes of Decline*

As the foregoing pages indicate, the principal cause of the decline of Inland Navigation in India was the extension of railways at the cost of the waterways. We will now examine the factors that enabled the railways to out-compete the waterways.

It is argued that the railways afforded cheaper services over short hauls. To a certain extent the assumption does not seem to be baseless, but is open to doubts. It is not baseless, because haulage by waterways presupposes transhipment and considerable inconvenience and delay. The waterways are more profitably run in regions where the transhipment of goods, at least at one end of the journey is from steamers to ships and *viceversa.* And since on short distance haulage transhipment on both ends is from land to water or *viceversa,* the services naturally become expensive and slow. But, this in itself does not fully tell the whole story. In that case there was no reason why long distance haulage should have also declined.

Transport industry has two operational sides: (1) constructional side and (2) the organizational side. In neither of these two aspects the railways appear to have been cheaper in those days. These conclusions are fully supported by authorities like Sir Arthur Cotton, the great architect of the Cauvery and

Godavari canals. In his evidence before a Parliamentary Committee in 1872, he stated: "My great point is this that what India wants is water-carriage; that the railways have completely failed; they cannot carry at the price required; they cannot carry the quantities and they cost the country three millions a year and increasing to support them. That steam boat canals would have not cost more than one-eighth that of the railways; would carry any quantities at nominal prices and at any speed; would require no support from the treasury and would be combined with irrigation." Explaining further he said, "By 1878 the railways had cost 140 millions including debt for 5800 miles and carried 1,30,000 tons at 3½ pence and 7,00,000 passengers a day at 3¼ of a penny and required 4 million a year from Indian Treasury. The same sum would have made 60,000 miles of canals capable of conveying million of tons per annum at 1/10 or 1/12 of a penny and would have required no payment from the treasury even if they had all to be paid for solely as navigation, whereas most of them would have been paid by irrigation."[7]

J. Johnston writing on *Inland Navigation on the Ganga River* (1946) states that "though no authority can be claimed for the opinion unless and until there has been a complete survey of comparative cost, I am definitely inclined to the belief that river transport in India, on the purely engineering or technical side can be made a much cheaper proposition than the corresponding aspect of railway transport. I firmly believe that the main reason why railway transport killed river traffic was not because it was a cheaper technical proposition. It was cheaper only because the comparative security and the complete and detailed organisation of the railways made it so."[8]

The above opinions indicate that we cannot ascribe the downfall of Indian waterways to the comparative cheapness of railway transport. Railways had certain other advantages over waterways which made them a more profitable medium. Due to their speed and technical superiority they enjoyed safer runs than the waterways. The danger of pilferage, loot and accident due to grounding etc., were far more in waterways. The railways could also maintain control over the traffic of the area they served as there was no other means of transportation which could compete with them in matters of speed, organization, and regularity.

Moreover, as a result of the opening of several canals in the upper reaches of the Ganga and Yamuna, available draught for navigation was considerably reduced. Larger boats and steamers could not go further up as they used to do in the past. The cargo had to be brought to the river ports on smaller country boats or bullock carts and it had no organization which could handle traffic between river ports and the origin and destination points. The railways, on the other hand, were in a position to pick up and deliver goods at any station big or small. This facilitated the takeover of traffic by railways from the waterways running parallel to them. The poor organization and management of the river services was perhaps the weakest point that led to their downfall. Unlike the railways, they were owned by petty boatmen engaged in bitter competition among themselves. This kept the financial position of the owners weak and hence, during the time the railways started diverting cargo from waterways, they could not take counter measures to check the wreck that was clearly imminent.

The river services were subject to weather conditions more than the railway services. Sailing being the usual method used in upstream navigation by country boats, river services could not stick to the schedule due to frequent failure of wind. They had also no modernised equipment which could tackle these problems except by resorting to towing which was not an easy job at least in big streams whose tow-paths were traversed by numerous tributaries.

As the steamer services covered only a fraction of the total demand on waterways, country boats had to carry the bulk of the cargo. But such boats were hardly fit to meet the traffic requirements of the nineteenth century. There were several reasons for it. The most pertinent was the unsuitability of these boats to carry the bulk of the volume offered to them. Their design was old and fit only to small consignment destined for not very far off places. Apart from loading and unloading of cargo, a crew of 3 or 4 men was required for even a moderate sized boat carrying 500 to 1000 maunds down stream and 7 or more for a similar cargo proceeding upstream. By comparison a modern barge on European rivers taking 3000 tons (50,000 maunds) is manned by a crew of only 2 or 3 men. Apart from this, they were not very suitable for the carriage of grains and cotton during rains. And these were probably the only major agricultural commodities requiring large-scale transportation at the time.

Another factor that contributed considerably to the decline of waterways was the law and order situation along the river courses. The rapid decline of waterways and the consequent unemployment of hundreds and thousands of boatmen earning their livelihood from river traffic, turned them pirates and dacoits. In 1905, Mr. Bramley, District Superintendent of Police, Benaras reported that organized gangs of dacoits and pirates moved along the riverways (from Allahabad to Kolkata) in search of possible victims. It was clear, says the report, that crime of a very serious nature was rampant on all the waterways mentined, that life and property on the rivers was unsafe to a degree which could not be tolerated by the government of any civilized country, and that criminals made free use of trade boats in the guise of river traders as a cloak for the purpose of commission of crime. It further states that "the existence of a form of crime which looks much like a survival of real *Thaggi* of old is also strongly indicated by certain facts—from which it is clear that pious Mohammedans—are systematically decoyed by their caste fellows into making the '*Hajj*' pilgrimage to Mecca, and then either murdered or looted when in transit on the river."

The rapid increase in the crime on river Ganga and its tributaries had upset the merchants of the time, and it was, but natural for them to change over to railways even if they had to pay more. The actual position of merchants *vis-à-vis* the boatmen and the undesirability of utilising the boats when railway services were available is amply clear from the following extracts taken from a letter written by B. Sita Ram Roy, Honorary Secretary, Bengal National Chamber of Commerce to the Chief Secretary to the Government of Bengal on March 3, 1892:

> "At the outset my committee deem it necessary to state...that the *Mahajana* (merchants) have no cargo boats of their own, and that whenever they have to despatch goods, they look to the boatmen for such a purpose.
>
> "In fact, the boatmen and the *Mahajana* are two entirely different parties, very often being utter strangers to each other and having no relationship with each other, except

that the former lend their boats on hire to the latter at a certain rate per hundred maunds.

"Cargo boats are, as a rule, owned by the lower classes of Hindus and Mohamadans most of whom are unscrupulous and do not hesitate to abstract as much of *Mahajana's* goods entrusted to them as they safely can....

"The practice now followed in hiring cargo boats is that the head *Manjhi* (boatmen) has to be brought by the *ghat Manjhi*, a sort of broker and negotiator between the boatmen and the merchants, before the *Mahajana*, and he is at once engaged, contingent, of course, on the settlement of rates of hire per one hundred maunds. No question is then asked as to who and what he is, and no enquiry is made as to what sort of character he bears, but even if attempts were made to ascertain all these particulars nothing furher is known, except what might be had from the lips of the head *Manjhi* himself, for the majority of these boatmen never stick to their own villages, but go to such centres of trade and commerce whether far or near where they believe they will find ready engagement for their boats.

"The next step after a boat has been engaged and goods loaded into it after weighment in the presence of the *Manjhi*, is for the *Mahajana* to note down in *Khata* (account book) the names of the head *Manjhi* and his father and also the name of his native village and the police station to which it is subordinate.

"Where a *Manjhi* is honest and means no mischief or wholesale loot of the contents of the boat on the way to the place of destination, he gives a faithful description of himself, but where a *Manjhi* is dishonest and harbours wicked intentions, he is sure to give a fictitious description of names and places.

"Having successfully imposed upon the *Mahajana* in the manner indicated above and contemplating mischief from the outset, the head *Manjhi* with the crew weighs anchor and sets out on his journey, but very often, instead of going by the right route, he purposely deviates from it and looks out for the first favourable opportunity to dispose of the goods entrusted to his care and thus misappropriate the

> sale proceeds... The ill-gotten booty thus disposed of, the boatmen set out their way home. In the meantime, the consignee waits patiently week after week and even month after month hoping against hope for the safe arrival of the goods, but it is not long before that false hope vanishes and he sinks on blank despair. No goods are received and even no clue can be had of the missing boat or of its *Manjhi*. He starts on inquiry and sends information to the police, but to no avail for no *Manjhi* or the village of the name given to the consignor can anywhere be traced. The whole thing turns out to be mythical. Sometimes the dodge resorted to by the boatmen in order to allay all suspicion of foul play is that after disposing of the whole or a portion of the goods he purposely wrecks his own boat (which very often is an old worthless one). Then he circulates the story in the neighbourhood that his boat was caught in a storm or met with a serious accident and had gone down, the same information being also furnished to the *Mahajana* by a postcard....Apart from such cases of wholesale robbery, partial misappropriation of the goods by the *Manjhi* are events of daily occurance."[9]

All these factors mentioned above combined to make waterways ultimately costlier although their mile-to-mile running expenses were much lower than that of the railways. The circumstances in which the Indian waterways had to function during this period, would have impelled any National Government to take remedial measures. Unfortunately, the then Government adopted a very neglectful attitude towards the waterways and allowed the railways to out compete them to death. Had the law and order situation along the river-ways been as good as along the railways and had the boat and steamer services been treated on par with railways both would have prospered simultaneously.

One of the reasons for the preferential treatment given to the railways was perhaps the absence of a forceful public opinion which could impress upon the Government the desirability of having a simultaneous development of both railways and waterways. As such it became difficult for a Foreign Government having no roots in the soil to adopt a policy under which their own countrymen would cease to enjoy the benefits they had enjoyed in the railway construction projects. The British administrators could not realize that India wanted waterways as much as the railways. That the railways have to be given preference in places where the waterways cannot be developed and that the ever increasing population of India needed food as much as transportation. They failed to realize that they had become the rulers of a country which had no similarity with their fatherland and that India was essentially a land of agriculture and that her agriculture was a gamble in the monsoon. Had they understood the physical and human geography of India better, they would have introduced canals which could have solved the twin problems of food and transportation simultaneously. But Englishmen committed a geographical mistake. They needed few canals in their own country, and therefore, they neglected canals in India too.

The British Government not only discouraged the waterways by neglecting them altogether, but also allowed the railways to dislocate them wherever they could flourish on their own. The Ackworth Committee has pointed out specifically how ancient ports at Broach and the Buckingham Canal in Chennai had suffered due to the unfair competition put up by the railways. Firstly, railways were constructed parallel to the waterways and secondly, when they could not divert all the traffic from waterways, they used unfair means to outbid the waterways.

> "About hundred miles to the north of Bombay, Broach, a small, but ancient port is situated on the main line of Bombay-Baroda and Central India Railway. In the year 1908 an enterprising Bombay firm started a steamer service between Broach and Bombay. The Bombay-Baroda and Central India Company found that certain amount of traffic was being diverted. They, therefore, appealed to the Railway Board pointing out that the great bulk of the profits of the company went to the Government, the Goverment was interested in putting a stop to this diversion and they suggested that in order to enable them to impose on the through traffic for short distance to or from Broach rates sufficiently high to leave nothing for the steamer portion of the journey, the Railway Board should permit them to raise the classification of certain competitive articles to the highest class. The Board assented. In one case at least, that of sugar, the article was

raised from the first class to the fourth, in other words, the company's power to charge was increased four-fold. The steamer withdrew from the unequal struggle and the merchants of Broach not unnaturally protested. One sentence in the reply of the Railway Board deserves quotation:

"The contention... is altogether opposed to the universally accepted policy which recognised that the unfettered freedom enjoyed by sea transport agencies in the quotation of rates entitles railway administration to greater freedom when competing with water transport than is legitimate when competing amongst themselves." "The Broach case, though most surprising is not the only instance where railway companies have been accused, in dealing with water competition, of going or attempting to go to a length which seems to us indefensible. In Madras, our attention was called to three cases. Leading into Madras itself, there is a canal known as the Buckingham Canal, which was of considerable importance at one time, but whose traffic since the advent of a railway has greatly fallen off. It was admitted on behalf of the railways that they put in exceptional rates so low as to leave to them a very small margin of profit in order to divert traffic from the canal. Evidence was also given of an agreement between the South Indian Railway and the British India Steam Navigation Company, the effect of which was to induce the steamship company to cease to call at certain small ports and to leave to the railways a monopoly of the traffic. Again, a letter was submitted to us in which the Agent of the same Railway put forward a proposal that the Government should entirely close the small port of Tirumallarasal, and so force the local traffic on to the railway of which the Government was the owner. We think this is eminently a matter to which the Communication Department which, if our recommendation is adopted, will have charge not only of railways, but of canals and ports, should direct its attention."[10]

Before we close our discussion on the main causes of the decline of waterway, we must mention a few words about the causes that led to the downfall of steam navigation in particular although it could compete with railways in matters of speed and bulk carriage. As far as the neglectful attitude of the Government was concerned, the steam navigation was no exception. In 1911, six steamer companies with a fleet of 225 passenger steamers were plying on the Ganga system of rivers. In addition to this, they owned 19 cargo carriers. It was natural for these companies to expand their fleet as the country boats gradually went out of commission; but it did not happen. The reasons for this were that five of the six steamer companies were owned by the railways and hence their business was merely to supplement railways at ferry points etc. The question of their expansion, therefore, did not arise. Secondly, the withdrawal of water in the Ganga and Yamuna canals left very shallow draft in these rivers during the dry season; and thirdly, the steamer services also suffered from the pilferage of bamboo sticks demarcating the channel and related consequences of grounding and collision with country boats involving payment of damage etc.

The extremely shallow draft of Bhagirathi (upper portion of River Hooghly) did not allow the steamers to go straight to U.P. and Bihar from Kolkata for at least 8 months a year. The other two direct channels passing through Nadia District were Jalanghi and Matabhanga, but both were unfit for steamer services for one reason or the other. As a result, most often the steamers had to follow a detoured route involving 200 extra miles *via* Gorai distributary or they had to follow a more circuitous route *via* Khulna or Barisal and Goalundo, a diversion of over 400 miles. Such detoured routes naturally made the steamer services far more expensive and uneconomic. At the end of the nineteenth century the Gorai distributary was closed for steamer services due to the construction of a low level railway bridge across its head at Kushtia. Henceforward river services were routed through the Sundarbans and East Bengal channels.

The question of maintaining channel deep enough to permit efficient navigation in the Ganga was raised from time to time, but no effective step was taken to improve the situation. In the name of river conservancy, however, taxes were collected which further increased the burden on the water carriers. In 1867 an Act was passed providing for a levy of tolls on river Ganga between Dinajpur and Allahabad. The income which never exceeded more than Rs. 10,000 was distributed between the Districts of Ballia, Ghazipur, Benaras, and Mirzapur for river conservancy. Bramley characterised the working of this Act in following terms:

> "To begin with the tax falls entirely on the boats above the bar and thus the Allahabad and Mirzapur boats pay the whole of the sum realized, whereas it should be distributed over the entire shipping on the Ganga above Dinajpur and as at present arranged, all the boats below this bar, i.e. those in the Benaras, Jaunpur, Ghazipur, Shahabad, and Ballia districts, who use this channel, escape toll charges altogether. The rates of toll are high and in fact so exorbitant that from a correspondence in the toll office it appears that the India General Steam Navigation Co. Ltd., discontinued their services to Benaras on this account."[11]

Till 1900 A.D. no steps were taken by the Government to maintain a deep channel in Ganga between Kolkata and Patna. In 1901, a small dredger was bought for the purpose, but subsequent progress in this direction was not very encouraging. The canals constructed between 1776 and 1899, were not designed for navigation except here and there and the prospects of developing an integrated network of waterways in the future also became bleak.

E. The Period of Rethinking and Revival: 1920—to-date

The history of Inland navigation in India from 1920 onward is none too glittering, although since Independence greater attention has been paid to this mode of transportation. The experience of the transport bottlenecks of the two World Wars had a subtle and far-reaching effect on Government and public opinion. It was realized that even from a strategic point of view, it was necessary to develop Inland waterways. The spread of nationalism in the body politic of Indian society and the consequent liking for everything indigenous helped the waterways to get more attention both from public and administration. After the First World War, plans were chalked out for the development of navigational potential in the country. The depression of the twenties, however, discouraged the Government to take up any big scheme. The revenues from, railways too had considerably declined and hence, it was not considered to be an economic venture to take up schemes related to waterways. The Second World War and the threat to the eastern parts of British India comprising the provinces of Bengal and Assam and to Burma posed a great transport and supply problem to the Government. It was realized that much of these problems could have been considerably minimized, had there been in existence a commercially developed Inland navigational facility in the country.

Soon after India attained freedom, the National Government convened a conference of representatives of the interests concerned to consider the ways and means to promote navigation on river Ganga. The then Minister of Transport stated that "Government is interested in co-ordinating all forms of transport, river, road and railways, and that if the river services are found to be better suited to meet the needs of a particular area, Government would be prepared to consider its development even in preference to Railways or to make Railways co-ordinate their activities with the river services so as to enable the two to work in collaboration and that there will be no question of the Railways pulling all the freight away from the river services."

This conference can be said to be the starting point for a rethinking on Inland waterways. Subsequently, several conferences were held to discuss the problems connected with the waterways. In one of the conferences it was decided to take up for examination the possibilities of developing the navigational facilities on Ganga from Buxar to Allahabad. The question was remitted to a technical sub-committee consisting of the representatives of the Ministry of Transport, Central Water and Power Commission and the Joint Steamer Companies for a preliminary survey. In 1950-51 the committee concluded that as a result of the postponement of the post-war plans for industrial expansion in Uttar Pradesh and want of dependable statistics of traffic on the river, very little prospects of securing the minimum guaranteed return on the capital outlay involved in organizing the steamer services on this stretch of the river were in sight and hence commercially unjustifiable. This conclusion was probably inevitable as the Ganga Valley is the most well served region by roads and railways. The committee, however, felt that there might be scope for running the service either as far as Allahabad or Kanpur during the high and middle water season and had suggested the carrying out of a reliable census of country traffic at certain selected points.

The question of development of Ganga-Brahmaputra system of waterways was raised in a Conference held on 26th April, 1951 with the representatives of States concerned and the Central Government. The Conference recommended the setting up of the Ganga-Brahmaputra Water Transport Board with the Government of U.P., Bihar, West Bengal and Assam as members for the developments of navigation on inter-state rivers in North-East India.

With the start of the First Five Year Plan of India in 1951, the development of Inland waterways was taken up more seriously. An amount of Rs. 3.4 crore was earmarked in the First Five Year Plan for this purpose. Unfortunately, all this could not be spent, although grounds were definitely prepared for future progress. During the Second Five Year Plan a sum of Rs. 3 crore was allotted and several schemes were undertaken, important among them being the construction of an Inland port at Pandu (Assam). During the Third Five Year Plan a sum of Rs. 7.5 crore was earmarked for this purpose. The programme included a pilot towing project to be undertaken by the Ganga-Brahmaputra Board in Sundarbans, purchase of dredgers and launchers for Sundarbans and Brahmaputra and setting up of a central organization to advise on matters relating to Inland water transport. Provision was also made for the improvement and extension of the West Coast Canal in Kerala, improvement of Taldana and Kendrapara canals in Odisha and the development of navigational facilities in the Rajasthan canal. During the Fourth Five Year Plan, a sum of Rs. 13 crore has been earmarked for the development of Inland water transport.

The speedy development of Inland water transport in the eastern region where it has great scope for development depended much on the relation between India and Pakistan which were rarely good. The steamers and boats connecting Assam with Kolkata have to pass through what was formerly East Pakistan. After the 1965 Indo-Pakistan conflict, these services stopped operating. Further, during this conflict India lost a number of steamers and boats which were in Pakistani waters at the time the hostalities began. Thus, the development of Inland navigation in this region had become problematic. But now a new political situation has emerged. A friendly nation, Bangladesh, has emerged in the former

East Pakistan. It is now possible to have a fresh look at the whole problem of Inland transportation in the eastern region of the Indian sub-continent and to evolve a coordinated plan for the development of Inland waterways running through India and Bangladesh.

Notes

1. J.L. Nehru, Address to the Water & Power Commission cited in *Indian Rivers,* a booklet published by the Ministry of Information & Broadcasting, Government of India.
2. J. Johnston, *Inland Navigation on the Gangetic Rivers,* Thaker Spink, 1946.
3. Thornton's *Gazetteer,* 1854.
4. J. Johnston, *op. cit.*
5. *District Gazetteer,* Mirzapur, U.P., 1907.
6. *District Gazetteer,* Bahraich, U.P., 1903.
7. Arthur Cotton, *Lectures* at Chatham Military Engineering College, 1874.
8. J. Johnston, *op. cit.*
9. *Ibid.*
10. *Ackworth Committee Report on Indian Railways.*
11. Cited in J. Johnston, *op. cit.*

References

1. Sircar, B.K., *Inland Transport and Communication in Medieval India,* Kolkata: University Press, 1925, pp. 1-20.
2. Mukerjee, R.K., *History of Indian Shipping,* pp. 220-222.
3. *Travels of Peter Mundy,* Vol. II, pp. 87, 158, 224.
4. Rennel, *Memoirs of Hindusthan,* p. 255.
5. Stavorinus, *Voyages to the East Indies* (1768-78 A.D.), Vol. I, p. 468.
6. Carley, W.H., *The Good old Days of Hon'ble John Company,* Vol. I, p. 38.
7. *Administrative Report* of the U.P. for 1886-87 and 1888-89.
8. Gokhale, B.K., *Report on Inland Water Transport,* Ministry of Transport and Communication, New Delhi, 1959-60.
9. *North-Western Province Gazetteer,* 1883, pp. 87-88.
10. Robinson, Albert. *Navigating the Ganges by Iron Steam Vessel,* 1848.

3
Inland Navigation
Comparative Study

The decline of Inland navigation in India cannot be said to be peculiar to this country. In the United States of America and Europe it had met the same fate sometimes or the other. What is, however, peculier to India is that in other countries the mistakes committed were rectified soon giving the waterways their due importance. In India, they continued to be left uncared for and totally neglected for over a century. In the previous chapter we had discussed in detail the causes of their decline and concluded that they are far deeper than those merely based on economic considerations. This chapter offers further proof of this conclusion.

A. United States of America

In the United States of America, riverways played a momentous role in the past. In a virgin land covered with forests, rivers were the only channels through which the people and goods could move speedily. The development of the waterways was, therefore, started as early as 1782. The discovery of steam power and its use in the tow-boats during the first half of the nineteenth century made Inland Navigation more efficient. In the meanwhile, the opening of the lake route by linking the Great Lakes with each other opened few vistas for the development of Inland water transport in the United States.

River Mississippi, with its tributaries Ohio and Missouri, provided cross country transport lines at a time when no other means of transportation was at hand. Although till 1817, navigation on this river was conducted in a very old fashion using the flat boats, the ark, and the wood rafts for down stream journeys and the reel boats or barges for upstream coverages, it remained the chief means of transportation in Central U.S.A. The introduction of steam navigation gave further encouragement to it. But the construction of railways parallel to riverways created serious economic problems, and water transport except in the Great Lakes rapidly declined. The following data showing the quantity of cotton received at New Orleans (mouth of River Mississippi) is indicative of this trend (Table 3.1).

Table 3.1: Receipt of Cotton at New Orleans—1873 to 1904

Year	*Receipt by railway (bales)*	*Receipt by riverways (bales)*	*Percent of the total receipt by riverways*
1873	438,495	968,077	68.8
1875	406,076	750,080	64.8
1880	627,577	1,087,522	63.4
1885	1,018,261	680,376	40.1
1890	1,722,473	425,828	19.8
1899	1,835,177	343,450	15.1
1904	1,833,755	192,842	9.5

Source: F.H. Dixon, *A Traffic History of the Mississippi River System*, Washington D.C., Government Printing Office, 1909, p. 59.

The decline in the river receipt of cotton from 68.87 per cent in 1873 to 9.5 per cent in 1904—within a period of about 30 years—was mainly due to the diversion of traffic to the railways running parallel to the river channels, although the shift in the location of cotton producing areas was not of less consequence. Apart from the railway competition, the navigation channels were also unsuitable for improved crafts available then. Consequently, for about 25 years prior to 1920, there was hardly any common carriage on the Mississippi.

Around 1920 begins the period of rejuvenation of riverways. The story of the improvement of water transport in the U.S.A. is the story of concerted attempts on the part of several agencies, public and private, to offset the disadvantages of waterways by means of (1) canalisation to interconnect different waterways; (2) capital investment in modernised vessels to provide efficient services; and (3) legislative regulations and preferences to discourage cut-throat competition and to promote co-operation among different modes of transportation. Between 1910 and 1950, the United States opened and developed about 28,000 miles of waterways, 10,000 miles of which offer a draught of 9 ft. and above and have cost approximately Rs. 500,000 per mile. The result of this huge expenditure has proved most advantageous to the country. Leaving aside others, only Mississippi system of waterways carried as much as 138,144,871 tons of cargo in the year 1950. All the waterways except the lake route, together carried 297,694,832 tons the same year.

Tables 3.2 and 3.3 indicate clearly the growing popularity of waterways in the U.S.A.

Table 3.2: Cargo Carried by Mississippi System of Waterways in 1950

	Waterway	*Tonnage carried and type of cargo*
1.	River Ohio	48,589,227—coal, petroleum, steel, gravel and
2.	River Monongahela	28,509,901—Bituminous coal
3.	Missouri (not fully developed, schemes in progress)	1,609,304—gravel sand stone Petroleum, coal,
4.	Mississippi (Minniapolis to south)	66,922,594—aluminium ore, sugar, coffee, miscellaneous

Including the traffic handled by the Great Lake route which amounted to 1477 million tons in 1951, the total tonage moved by Inland waterways of the U.S.A. in 1951-52 amounted to nearly 1800 millions. In terms of ton-miles, the Inland waterways accounted for 170 billions as against 623.5 and, 184.1 billions for railways

Table 3.3: Cargo Carried by Inland Waterways of the U.S.A. (Except the Lake Route)

Year	*Net tons*	*Ton miles*
1931	179,735,000	9,233,362,320
1935	225,917,850	13,406,174,849
1940	366,235,582	22,411,961,000
1945	394,203,902	29,709,146,000
1947	262,282,074	34,548,917,000
1950	297,694,832	51,656,637,000
1955	362,555,910	97,662,567,000

Note: Figures since 1947 are based on better statistical methods to avoid duplication.

and intercity trucks in 1951-52. 119.9 billion ton-miles went to the Great Lakes, 36.7 billions to the Mississippi system, and the rest to other waterways.

The Mississippi system of waterways deserve special mention here because the physical conditions prevailing in this river are almost similar to those prevailing in Ganga which is the most important navigation channel of India. Like Ganga, it traverses very fertile lands and has parallel running roads and railways to compete with it. Both are the largest river systems in respective countries; both have Inland ports; Baton Rouge and Kolkata, both have fertile valleys and both connect the interior of the country with the sea. Even the shallow channel of Bhagirathi has its parallel in the Mississippi river.

Table 3.4: Statement Showing the Depth of Mississippi System of Waterways

River with segment	*Effective depth*	*Projected depth*
1. *River Mississippi:*		
Mouth of Mississippi to Minneapolis		
(i) New Orleans to mouth of passes	35′ and above	40′
(ii) Baton Rouge to New Orleans	35′	35′
(iii) Cairo to Baton Rouge	9′	12′
(iv) St. Louis to Cairo	9′	9′
(v) Minneapolis to St. Louis	9′	9′
2. *Illinois River:*		
St. Louis to Chicago:		
(i) Mouth of Illinois to Rock Points	9′	9′
(ii) Rock Point to Damen Av., Chicago	22′	9′
(iii) Damen Av., to Lake St. Chicago	21′	9′
(iv) Columet-sag canal to Blue Depond River and the Little Columet and Columet river to turning basin No. 5.	9′	9′
3. *River Ohio*		
Pittsburgh to Cairo:	9′	9′
4. *River Missouri:*		
(i) Kansas City to St. Louis	6 ½′	9′
(ii) Omaha to Kansas City	6′	9′
(iii) Blair to Omaha	4½′	9′
(iv) Mouth of Big Sioux River to Blair	3½′	9′

Water transport on this river has undergone a phenomenal change during the last few decades. Herbert Hooks once Secretary of Commerce thought out a plan for the development of a navigable channel, connecting New Orleans in the south to Chicago in the north, and then to further extend it northwards by interconnecting the Great Lakes by means of canals. It also included the trunk connection to Kansas City in the West and to Pittsburgh in the east through Missouri and Ohio rivers. In all, he planned to have a 9,000 miles of interconnected waterways, with a minimum depth of 9 ft. by training river Mississippi and its tributaries like Missouri, Ohio, Illinois and Big Sioux. The effective and projected depth in different sections of the rivers as in 1950 is given in Table 3.4.

River Ohio flows through a highly undulating topography and hence, the maintenance of sufficient draughts to permit all weather navigation at first seemed difficult. Its channel in its natural form was full of snags, rocks and sand bars and to make the situation still worse it was obstructed by a fall at Louisville. Conforming to

Fig. 3.1: Mississippi Waterway System

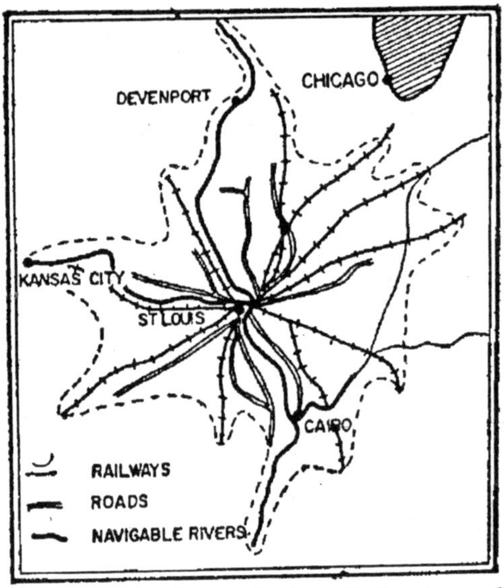

Note: The map shows how far goods from St. Louis can be carried for the same money.

Fig. 3.2: Isophodic Map of St. Louis and Environs

the topography of the valley, the depth of water in certain stretches was no more than 1 to 2 ft. To make such a river navigable by vessels requiring a minimum of 9 ft. draught was not an easy task. In 1830, a canal was constructed to bypass the fall at Louisville, but further programme could not be taken up until 1907. At present this river, with its 46 low dams, each provided with a lock 100 ft. × 600 ft. and sections capable of being lowered or raised in minutes stands as a proof of what human ingenuity can achieve in this respect.

Likewise plans to maintain a minimum depth of 9 ft. in the upper Mississippi and its tributary Missouri have also been completed. In this case, 26 dams with suitable locks within a stretch of 651 miles have been constructed for the purpose. The Great Lakes, *viz.* Lake Superior, Michigan, Huron, Erie and Ontario have been interconnected by St. Mary Falls canal, St. Clair and Detroit river route and the Welland canal. The St. Lawrence river, has been deepened further under a joint Canada-U.S.A. scheme to allow ocean going ships to enter the river ports like Quebec and Montreal. Its present effective depth is 27 ft.

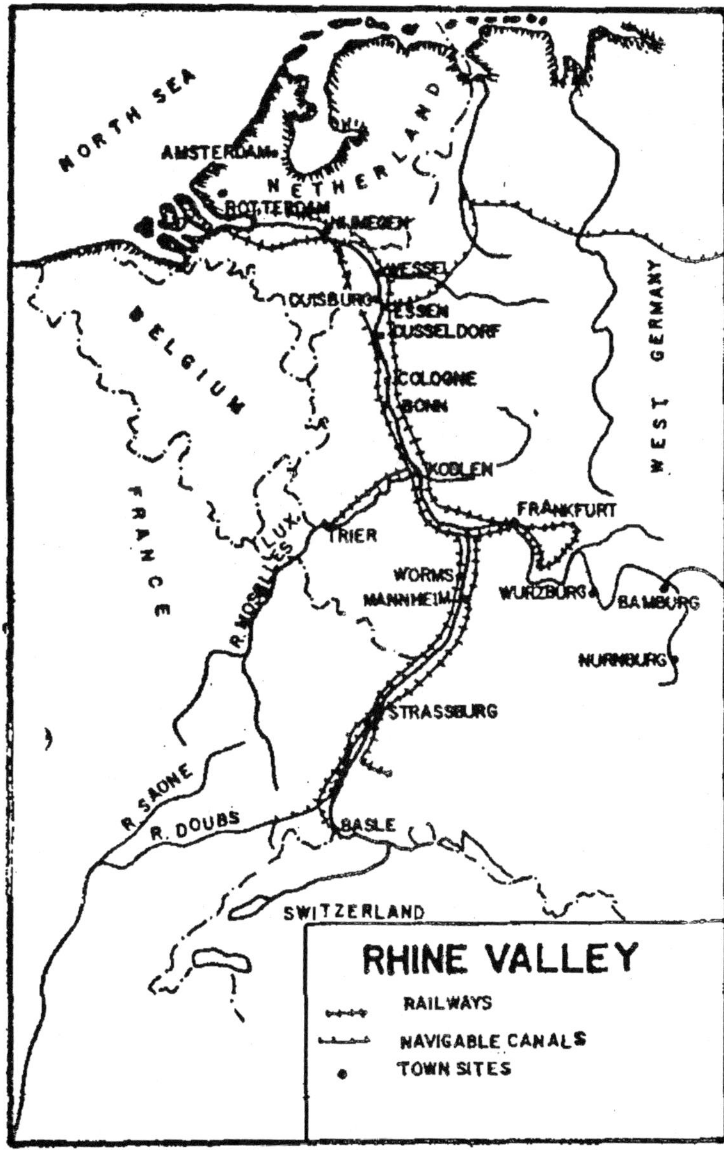

Fig. 3.3: Rhine Valley

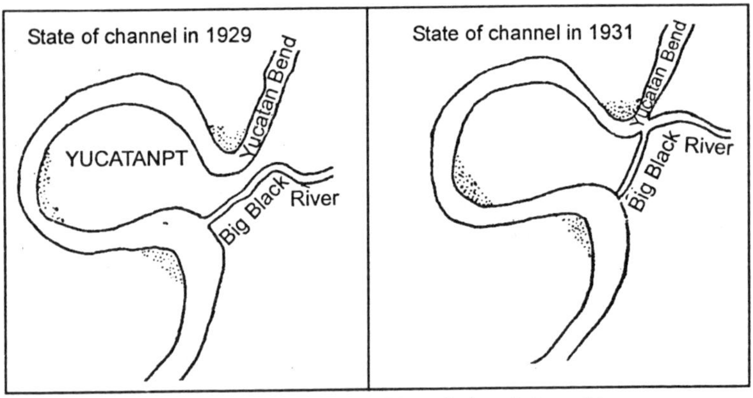

Fig. 3.4: Natural cut-off Mississippi River below Memphis

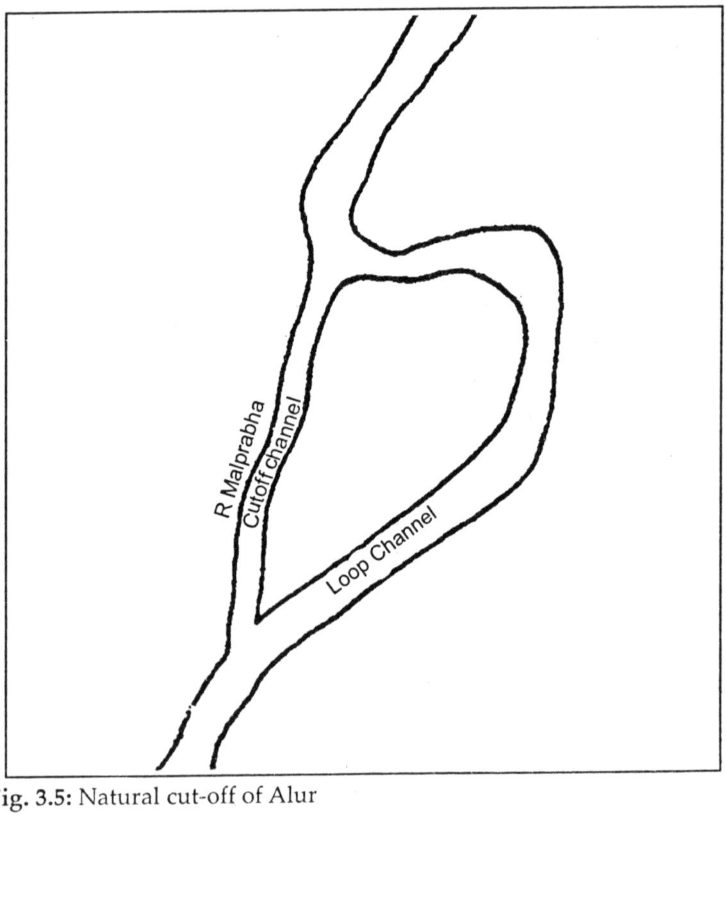

Fig. 3.5: Natural cut-off of Alur

B. Soviet Union

Nature endowed Soviet Union with a network of natural waterways both physically and economically suitable for Inland navigation. Rivers of the European Russia drain themselves in the Caspian, Black and Baltic seas. They provide an ice free navigation all the year round. Four major rivers of this region, *viz.* Volga, Don, Dneiper and Western Dwina, rank among the busiest Inland water channels of the world. One peculiar feature of the rivers of this region is that they all take their origin in the highland of Central Russia, so that, the distance between the sources of these rivers and their tributaries are very narrow. The gradient of the rivers being gentle, they have been used as navigable channels from ancient times. The inter-fluvial distances in the peneplaned central plateau necessitated portage. To overcome this, schemes to interconnect the rivers were prepared and executed. The possibility of connecting Volga with Don had been visualised as early as the seventeenth century. As the traffic potentialities of the region increased, new canals were constructed to avoid the portage. At present all these rivers are linked up with each other by navigable canals, the chief among which are the old Marunskaya system which connects Leningrad with the Volga at Shcherbakov, the Moscow canal, the White Sea-Baltic canal connecting Leningrad with White Sea at Belomorsk, the Dneiper-Bug Canal and the V.I. Lenin Volga-Don Canal.

Unlike the rivers of European Russia, the Siberian rivers emerge from Altai, Issayan and Yablanovy ranges just north of outer Mongolia. Almost every useful part of the watershed of rivers like Ob, Yenisei, Lena and Amur falls within the Soviet land and the main channels traverse the region at such convenient internals that it gives the impression as if nature itself desired to provide this vital region of Asia, a means of transport most suited to its topography, climate and settlement pattern. It is more so when one finds numerous branches of these rivers shaking hands with each other while flowing latitudinally defying the convention set by their consequent counterparts. All those rivers, with the exception of Amur which empties in the Pacific Ocean, flow to the north and discharge in the Arctic Ocean. They all suffer from the disadvantages of water freezing, but being open for more than six months, are able to meet the traffic demands of their hinterlands—backward as they still are economical.

As against the case in India and the U.S.A., Inland waterways in U.S.S.R. have never been neglected nor have they suffered from the unequal competition of the railways. The country is so vast, the economy so diversified and geography, so varied, that the introduction of railways to every centre of economic activity would neither be feasible nor justifiable. Consequently, one finds today Soviet rivers to be among the busiest water channels of the world. Recent plans as chalked out by the Government are designed to make most of the waterways deep enough to be navigable by moderate size ocean going vessels.

Volga is the most important river and accounts for about one-half of the water traffic handled in the country. The opening of the Volga-Don canal connecting the Caspean Sea with Black Sea has further enhanced the importance of this waterway. Its basin being densely populated and economically well developed the traffic potentials are fairly large. Timber, grain, fish and salt are the principal commodities that are offered for transportation. Its significance can easily be judged from the fact that it connects a great number of big towns of the Soviet Union such as Astrakhan, Leningrad, Moscow, Knibyshev, Kazan, Gorky, Yaroslav, and Kalinin.

C. China

Not much is known specifically about the progress made by China in the development of Inland navigation. Riverways had, however, played a vital role in the Chinese economy. Rivers like Sinkiang, Yangtse-Kiang, and Hwang-Ho are navigable for long distances and their valleys are densely populated and economically well off. Towns like Wuchow, Canton, Changsha, Chungking, Ichang, Shansi, Hankow, Nanking, Sining and Tainan are located on rivers. Yangtse-Kiang is, however, the most important navigable channel of China. In the words of R. Smith, "it is the greatest of the river thorough fares by which the commerce of Asia has been supported. Running from west to east through the heart of China, it has nearly a thousand miles of waterways for ocean steamers and much more for native boats. The Yangtse is the great commercial artery of China for two reasons, firstly, because it has navigable branches flowing into it from north and south, and a far reaching system of canals that open up great tracts of territory. Secondly, because there are large and dense populations depending upon these waterways."

Yangtse provides a 25 ft. deep channel from Shanghai at its mouth to Hankow, a distance of about 630 miles, navigable by vessels of 4,000 tonnage all the year round and 10,000 tonnage during the summer. Country boats ply as far up as Ichang, nearly 1,000 miles west of Shanghai. Its delta is intersected by a network of navigable canals.

D. United Kingdom

The canal boom of 1845 created hectic activites in Inland navigation, so that, by the start of this century approximately 300 miles of canals in addition to 20,000 miles of navigable river channels provided through services between different centres in U.K. According to W.L. Ires, Principal Traffic Officer, British Waterways, the industrial revolution could not have secured in Great Britain as it did, but for the canal era from 1760 to 1830. But the prosperity of canal itself could not continue for long and started dwindling after 1830. Unfair competition by the railways was largely responsible for it. The railway companies went as far as to acquire the ownership of canals so as to eliminate the waterways completely.

Several committees and commissions went into the problems of waterways and recommended certain measures for their restoration, but no effective steps were taken until 1947 when under the Transport Act, they were placed under the charge of the British Transport Commission. Another committee under the Chairmanship of Leslie Bowes was appointed to inquire into the economics of the entire system on a broader basis. The Committee suggested the creation of an Inland Water Transport Corporation to manage the entire system of Inland waterways on the ground that the British Transport Commission is busy in multifareous activities related to Transport in general and cannot be expected to give the attention this mode of transportation required.

The existing navigable Inland waterways of the United Kingdom are about 1400 km. long. Out of this about 1600 km. are navigable by small boats with a carrying capacity of 30 tons or less and 1,200 km. constituting the canalised rivers etc., are navigable by crafts of 50 to 400 tons capacity, depending upon the available draught. The other 800 km. are hardly used for commercial purposes. The British Transport Commission, that is responsible for the management and maintenance of 3200 miles of these waterways owns some crafts of its own, but the bulk of traffic is carried by independent operators.

E. West Germany

Today Rhine is perhaps the busiest Inland waterway of the world, but only a century back it could hardly accommodate small country crafts up to Strasburg, 300 miles Inland. During the last quarter of the nineteenth century, navigation on this river underwent a remarkable change. This development is particularly notable in view of the fact that by this time most of the industrial centres were interconnected with railways. This 800 mile long river drawing through several European countries such as Switzerland, France, Germany and Netherlands, carries more commerce than Mississippi does and 5 times of what Danube carries. Despite its shallowness and short run, this river is unique in connecting the heartland of Europe with the open sea.

The effective depth of the channel varies from 6.5 ft. in the upper reaches to 10 ft. in the lower reaches, so that, it is navigable by ocean going steamers and small ships up to Cologne, while the stretch of channel lying between Cologne and Strasburg is navigable by crafts of 600 tons or more weight. Its tributaries are equally developed for navigation purposes.

Considerable amount of money was spent by the German Government in the development of Rhine as a navigable waterway between 1920 and 1940. It is now navigable up to Basel farther up Strasburg from the North Sea. The main factors that have contributed to the development of Inland navigation on Rhine may be described as below:

1. It drains in North Sea which is the busiest water body of the world;
2. Its valley and the land around are rich in agriculture and minerals;
3. It has even flow throughout the years and is free from freezing during winters;

4. It passes through a densely populated and industrially advanced region;
5. It connects several commercial and industrial centres of Europe; and
6. The introduction of modern vessels and canalization programme carried out in the valley and its tributaries.

Apart from the Rhine system of waterways, Germany has developed many other channels navigable by modern mechanically propelled vassels. The total length of German waterways is about 5,000 km. of which 3,500 km. constitute riverways and the rest canals. The combined volume of traffic handled by them amounted to 133.7 million tons in 1956. Keeping in view the important role played by this transport system of the country, the Germans, have taken keen interest in its further development. In 1957, a sum of Rs. 30 crore was spent on it, although the total revenue receipt did not exceed Rs. 6 crore. It has now crossed its developmental stage and is now the premier waterway of Europe.

F. France

The Inland waterways of France have a chequered history. They have met several challenges in the form of competition from other modes of transportation. During the two world wars and the intervening depression they suffered severe damages. They have, however, been so much a part and parcel of the French economy that nothing could dislodge them from their original status.

The rivers Garonne, Loire, Seine and their tributaries flung out to the north-west after taking their rise in the central plateau. The Rhone flows to the south and empties in the Gulf of Leons after traversing the region lying between the central plateau and the Alps. So, well-distributed are the navigable rivers in this country that they offer a well-knit network of navigable channels.

Prior to 1879, navigation in these rivers was conducted in a very rudimentary fashion. Although there were several canals connecting the riverways with commercial centres, their design and dimension were so different from each other that even medium size vessels could not navigate them for any great distance. In 1879, a plan commonly known as standardization scheme was carried out, whereby the canals were constructed to a certain standard measurement which was thought to be enough to accommodate crafts of 280 tons carrying capacity. With this standardization, the French fleet of Inland waterways grew up rapidly and a peak figure of 15,000 vessels reached in 1913. The existing length of all the navigable channels totals over 1,000 km. out of which about 4,000 km. comprise canals and the remainder 5,000 km. of rivers. In 1956, the total volume of traffic handled by them was 61.6 million tons.

The budgeted expenditure on the development of French Inland Waterways amounted to Rs. 110 million against the total receipt, Rs. 10 million in 1954.

G. Benelux Countries

Belgium, one of the smallest countries of Europe, has 1,500 km. of Inland waterways out of which 800 km. are riverways and the remaining 800 km. canals. Land being low, other means of transportation are far less suited to Belgium and hence considerable amount of expenditure has been incurred by the Government during the last quarter of the nineteenth century for the development of waterways. River Schelde with its tributaries like Nete, Dyle, Demer, and Rys are connected by a multitude of canals. There is no major city of Belgium and the adjoining French territory which is not served by waterways. In 1956, total traffic handled by the water-ways amounted to 55 million tons. The Government spent nearly Rs. 17 million as against the receipt of about Rs. 6.6 million for the improvement of Inland waterways.

In Netherland, the condition of Inland waterways is still. The physical conditions being the same as in Belgium, the waterway have a natural advantage over other modes of transportation. But the most fortunate feature of the country is the presence of the lower reaches of the Rhine and an Inland sea-lake known as Zuider Zee. The ratio of the length of navigable waterways to the populated area of Netherlands is the highest in the world. The development of Inland waterways has been done as a part of several multipurpose projects involving flood protection, land drainage, reclamation and water transport. Total length of waterways amounts to over 6,000 km. out of which about 1000 km. are riverways and the remainder are canals. In 1957, a sizable sum of Rs. 270 million was spent for the waterway improvement although the total revenue receipt hardly reached the figure of Rs. 5 million.

H. India

Looking at the drainage map of India one is struck by the presence of a number of perennial rivers intersecting the country from all directions. Navigation on these rivers was apt to be the foremost transport system in early days. The navigable rivers like the Ganga, Yamuna, Ghaghra, Brahmaputra, Mahanadi in the north, Godavari, Krishna and Cauvery in the south and Narmada and Tapi in the west pass through agriculturally and commercially rich areas. The navigability of these rivers is, however, confined to their lower reaches alone except in the case of Ganga and Brahmaputra.

The combined route km. of navigable water channels in India with perennial flow of water amounts to approximately 40,000. This figure includes all navigable rivers and canals. Of this total, hardly one-fifth is used at present for navigational purposes. According to the estimates of J.J. Surie, a Netherlands expert on Inland waterways, deputed to India by the U.N., the existing length of Indian waterways is about 9,000 km. out of which 2,500 km. are navigable by mechanically propelled vessels. Out of the 2,500 km. the two states of West Bengal and Assam share 1,740 km. while Bihar shares 680 km. The remaining 80 km. is shared by the other 12 states of India.

As regards the channels navigable by small country boats, but having potentialities of being used by power propelled vessels, the distribution is none too even. Of the 5,600 km. of such channels, Tamil Nadu alone shares about 50 per cent, U.P. nearly one-third of the remainder leaving only 1,600 km. to be shared by the rest of the country. A detailed breakup of the navigable channels is given in Table 3.5.

I. Comparison

Before we conclude this chapter we must see as to how far the conditions of Inland navigation prevailing in other countries of the world compare with those in India. Inland waterways may be grouped into two main classes: (i) those which are navigable by ocean going ships; and (ii) those which can accommodate only

Table 3.5: Statement Showing the Length of Inland Waterways in India

(In miles)

Sl. No.	*River with navigable stretches*	*Usable by*	
		Steamers	*Country Crafts*
1.	*River Ganga system:*		
(i)	Allahabad to Buxar	—	231
(ii)	River Ganga from Buxar to Goalpara	435	—
(iii)	Bhagirathi (in rains) and Hooghly	330	—
(iv)	River Bhagirathi (in dry season)	—	180
(v)	River Ghaghra-Behrampurghat to confluence with Ganga	97	180
(vi)	River Rapti: Gorakhpur to Barhaj	—	75
(vii)	River Gandak-Bagaha to Patna	—	154
(viii)	Upper and lower Ganga canals	—	239
(xi)	Sone canals: Patna-Buxar	—	134
(x)	Odisha coast canal	—	95
(xi)	Midnapur canal	—	72
(xii)	Kolkata canals	—	145
2.	*Brahmaputra system:*	—	—
(i)	Brahmaputra: Dubri to Dibrugarh	460	—
(ii)	Tributaries of Brahmaputra	75	300
(iii)	Surma valley	85	—
(iv)	River Dharla in Cachar	50	—
3.	*Mahanadi system:*		
(i)	River Mahanadi at mouth	—	14
(ii)	River Baitarni	25	8
(iii)	River Brahmani	—	30
(iv)	River Matai	—	25
(v)	River Karsua	—	11
(vi)	River Hansua	—	11
(vii)	River Maipara	—	23
(viii)	River Mahanadi-Mansua	—	30
(ix)	Mahanadi canals	—	101
(x)	Odisha Coast canal	—	9
4.	*Peninsular waterways:*		
(i)	River Godavari	—	283
(ii)	River Krishna	—	52
(iii)	Godavari canals	—	562
(iv)	Krishna canals	—	342
(v)	Kurnool-Kudapah canal	—	78
(vi)	Buckingham canal	—	258
(vii)	Vedaraniyam canal	—	35
(viii)	West Coast canal	—	90
	Total	1,575	3,587

steamers and country boats. There are, however, not very many rivers except, of course, the St. Lawrence and River Amazon which are navigable by ocean going ships for long stretches. A number of them, including River Ganga, are, however, partly navigable by such vessels at their mouths. Rivers Parana and Paraguay are of the same type. In River Amazon, average size sea-going vessels can penetrate as far as Iquitos in Peru, about 1185 miles from its mouth while any ocean liner can navigate its channel up to Manaos.

River St. Lawrence was navigable by ocean liners up to Montreal, 859 miles upstream; recent channel developments have extended the navigability to the Lakes. River Parana is navigable by ocean liners up to Rosaria, 240 miles upstrem, and River Hooghly in India, 117 miles upstream. There are many other rivers which are in the category of being navigable upstream from their mouths to short stretches.

All these rivers which are navigable by ocean liners are easily recognizable as in such cases the ports are located in the interior and not on the coast. These rivers present a draught of at least 30 ft. as the vessels with the dead weight tonnage of 4,000 to 22,000 require a draught of 20 to 30 ft.

Rivers under the second category are not deep enough to allow ocean liners. Special types of vessels built, in conformity with the navigational limitations are needed. River Rhine is the best example of such rivers, and is navigable up to Basel situated at the Swiss frontier. The upstream trade is in consumer goods such as oil and raw material such as iron ore. Downstream go the finished goods. This aspect of the Rhine trade is unique in the sense that probably this is the only big river wherein manufactured goods flow down stream. For this purpose, the barges which can navigate shallow draughts had to be constructed.

Rio de la Plata and Parana give quite a different movement pattern of cargo. The downstream flow is made up of raw materials and grains while the upstream go the manufactured goods. So is the case with Amazon and many other rivers. Rivers Mississippi and Ganga are a different class by themselves. Their basins are so developed both agriculturally and industrially and so densely populated that the manufactured and consumer goods move both ways.

The fall of River Mississippi from Memphis to its mouth, a distance of about 825 miles is 4.5 inches per mile whereas in the next stage of about 420 miles it rarely exceeds 2.57 inches per mile. The fall between St. Louis and Memphis does not exceed 1.5 inches per mile. As regards Ganga, the gradient from Allahabad to Varanasi (139 miles) amounts to 6 inches per mile, from Varanasi to Colgong (326 miles) 5 inches per mile, Colgong to Bhagirathi (135 miles) 4 inches per mile and from the delta head to Kolkata (200 miles) about 4 inches per mile and from Kolkata to the sea 1 to 2 inches a mile depending upon the tide. The average fall from Allahabad to Kolkata amounts to 4.75 inches per mile. The average speed of currents is 3 miles an hour in dry season and 6 miles an hour during the rains.

The drainage of Mississippi with a coverage of 12,40,000 sq. miles, for exceeds that of Ganga, Brahmaputra and Meghna put together, i.e. 7,52,000 sq. miles; its discharge of water is almost equal to that of the Ganga system. At the Red River Landing, 20 miles up New Orleans, the discharge of Mississippi is 2,24,000 c.ft. in low and 16,00,000 c.ft. in high water. These figures compare favourably with 2,07,000 and 18,00,000 c.ft. for the Ganga. Still Mississippi gives a navigable channel of 3,950 miles whereas the Ganga can hardly provide 600 miles. All these comparative figures lead us to conclude that there are considerable opportunities for development of waterways in India and that waterways are not a primitive means of transportation as many tend to think.

References

1. S.P. Chatterjee (editor), *National Atlas of India* (Hindi edition), Kolkata: National Atlas Organization, 1957.
2. Government of India, Ministry of Shipping and Transport, *Report of the Inland Water Transport Committee,* October 1970.
3. *Report on Inland Water Transport* (*Gokhale Commitee Report*) 1959-60.
4. S. Daggett, *Principles of Inland Transportation,* 1955.
5. *Statesman Yearbook,* 1971.
6. *United Nations Statistical Yearbook,* 1971.
7. B.C. Law, *Mountains and Rivers of India,* Kolkata: National Committee for Geography, 1968.
8. *Encyclopaedia Britannica,* 1970.

4
Navigable Channels of the Ganga Plain

Ganga the mightiest river of India flows through the States of U.P., Bihar and West Bengal which are densely populated and agriculturally rich. Rising from Gangotri (13,800′ above sea level) at a point 33° 55′ North and 79° 7′ E and hardly a few yards in width, this river grows in size as it rushes down through a zigzag route and collects materials, both liquid and solid, brought down by innumerable riverlets emerging from the ice covered peaks and ranges all-around. Initially known as Bhagirathi, it changes its name to Ganga at Devaprayaga, where it receives the waters of Alakhnanda and retains its second name until it reaches the borders of West Bengal, where it recovers its lost name Bhagirathi again. The behaviour of the river in the mountains is marked with the characteristics of adolescence and youth—a fierce flow, a roaring drop, a blow on the left and a blow on the right, a crash, a rise, a fall; it seems nothing can stand in the way of Ganga. It is so, till it grades down to Hardwar where its water is diverted the upper Ganga canal, making it sobber and near mature.

The Ganga is further robbed of her waters at Naraura head-works, 143 miles down stream from Hardwar, which diverts its water to the Lower Ganga Canal. From this point onwards to 34 miles, it flows gently along one of the two banks, squeezing itself to mere riverlet at least in the dry summer till it is replenished by the waters of one of its feeders of the Ramganga. Here onwards it is no more disturbed by man. It assumes its largeness once again at Allahabad or Prayagraja as the Hindus call it, where its milky waters meet the blues of Yamuna, the river far less mature than Ganga in valley formation.

From Allahabad, Ganga flows through the towns of Mirzapur, Varanasi, Ghazipur and Patna and collects the waters of Gomati, Ghaghra and Rapti, Gandak, Burhi Gandak and Kosi from the north and Tons, Son and a few minor rivers like Phalgu and Paimar from the South. Ghaghra is by far the largest tributary of Ganga during its whole length of 1557 miles. From Patna onwards to the point where Bhagirathi the most westerly of the three Nadia tributaries takes off, the river is marked with the absence of any great city except Munger, not a big city by any standards.

Nearly four centuries back the river used to flow through the existing Bhagirathi channel and entered the Bay of Bengal *via* the so-called Adi Ganga channel, east of Kolkata. About a century back, it burst through a hard clay belt which up to that time had arrested its eastward progress, so that, the existing Jalangi and Matabhanga channels became the main channels one after the other. This slow movement of the river to the east soon assumed speed and broke through the deltaic depositions of its own to meet Brahmaputra at Goalundo, leaving the three Nadia tributaries almost dry except in rains.

River Ganga has been a great highway of transport and communication in northern India from time immemorial. The causes for the decline of navigation have been discussed in earlier chapters. To recapitulate them, they are the neglectful attitude of the Government, superiority of other means of transportation over Inland navigation of eighteenth and nineteenth centuries and the withdrawal of large quantities of water from the rivers making them unfit for navigation.

The existing navigable channels of Ganga system may be studied under two heads (1) riverways and (2) canals.

A. The Riverways

1. Ganga

The River Ganga, as it emerges from the mountains, has an estimated discharge of 7,000 cubic ft. per second. The Hardwar mountainous course is marked with steep gradient and hence, i.e. is unfit for navigational purposes. This course is, however, extensively utilised for timber rafting and crores of rupees worth of sleepers are floated down from the upstream forests to the plains and picked up near about Hardwar. It is doubtful whether in the absence of this means of water transport, the inaccessible forests of the Himalaya would have assumed that economic significance that they possess now.

From Hardwar to Kannauj, situated near its confluence with Ramganga, the river sometimes becomes fordable in dry seasons. At important river crossings, ferry services flourish, but the general longitudinal navigability is almost nil. Ramganga itself is a small river of shallow draught and can hardly accommodate boats of 2 to 4 ft. draught that too only in certain stretches. The waters of Ramganga and certain other feeders of local importance keep Ganga alive till it reaches Allahabad, where it is replenished by the waters of Yamuna. From Kannauj to Allahabad, the Ganga is navigable by country boats of 10 ton capacity during monsoon season and small country boats during dry periods of the year.

From Allahabad the river becomes large and navigable. With some training, it can be made navigable by steamers of 50 tons capacity during monsoons and by steamers and large country boats of 15 to 20 ton capacity during dry periods. Up to Buxar, a stretch of nearly 231 miles, it affords navigation by large country boats of 4 ft. draught. There are no steamer services plying on this route. From Buxar to Rajmahal, a stretch of 350 miles, Ganga is navigable by steamers of 100 ton capacity all the year round. Country boats of 60 ton capacity still ply on this route, but the steamer services have been discontinued since January 1958 on the plea of non-availability of cargo and inability to compete with the parallel running railway and road.

From the junction of Bhagirathi, the main channel of the river known as Padma flows through East Pakistan and is navigable throughout its length by vessels drawing 5 to 7 ft. Frequent changes of the channel witnessed year after year and strong bores often rising in Meghna estuary through which it flows, are the two drawbacks of this channel, but the draught is so deep and the other modes of transportation in the region so poorly developed that this waterway still remains the main highway of transportation in the region.

The three Nadia rivers, i.e. Bhagirathi, Jalangi and Matabhanga flow through West Bengal and finally discharge in the Bay of Bengal through Hooghly. Before the close of the eighteenth century, the Bhagirathi used to be the main channel through which Ganga discharged its waters in the Bay of Bengal. Gradually, it started releasing more water in the Padma-Meghna channel. By the end of the nineteenth century, the discharge in Bhagirathi became almost seasonal making through navigation between Kolkata and upper reaches of Ganga difficult. Extensive dredging of the channel resorted to by Kolkata Port Authority proved to be only a temporary solution.

To solve the problem of the navigability of Bhagirathi and Hooghly, a barrage is being constructed at Farakka, a place just below the bifurcation point of Bhagirathi from the main channel of Ganga. With the completion of this barrage the Bhagirathi-Hooghly channel will become navigable by steamers between Kolkata and the lower reaches of Ganga.

2. *The Tributaries of Ganga*

Yamuna is the first principal tributary of Ganga. It passes through important cities like Mathura, Agra, Etawah, Kalpi, Hamirpur and finally joins Ganga at Allahabad. It was navigable by large country boats even up to Delhi, but now except for the small country boats sailing for short distance up and downstream there is no significant navigational activity in the river.

Yamuna has a catchment area of about 3,17,870 sq. km. wherein average rainfall ranges from 40 to 80 centimetres. Its main tributaries, all carrying from the south-west, are Chambal, Sindh, Betwa and Ken. They are too small rivers coming from too dry lands to afford navigation, but they can form effective links in an integrated plan for national waterways. Yamuna can be made navigable by steamers from Allahabad to Agra for six months in a year.

Gomati is the next important river meeting the Ganga from the left. It is a shallow river, but can be made navigable by large country boats from the point it meet the Ganga to Lucknow, the capital of U.P. Gomati passes through an agriculturally rich area, and the development of navigation on it will indeed go someway in relieving its catchment area of the infrastructural problems it suffers from. Further east of the junction with Gomati, comes Ghaghra, the most important tributary of Ganga. Replenished and well fed by many feeders taking their rise in snowy Himalaya, this river descends the mountains to the plain through Kheri and Bahraich districts of Uttar Pradesh. In the plain, it is reinforced by Girwa, Suheli, Dahawar, and Sarda, all perennial throughout the

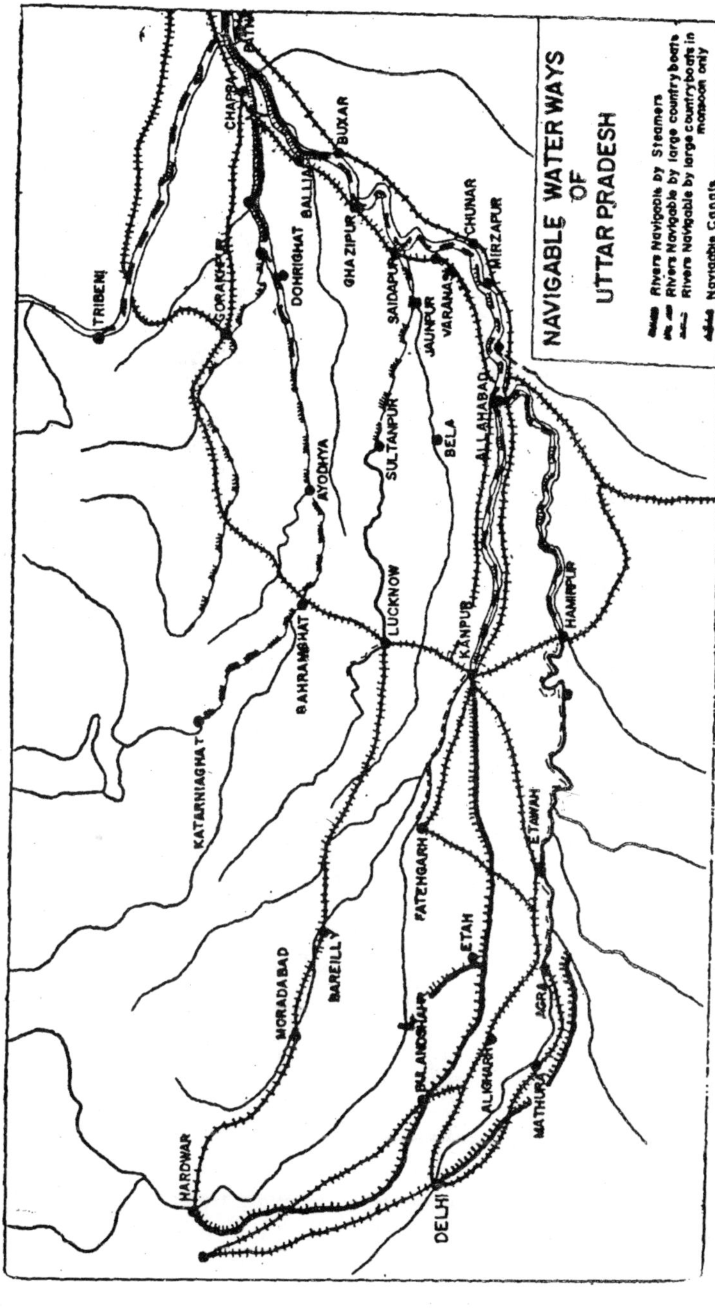

Fig. 4.1: Navigable Waterways of Uttar Pradesh

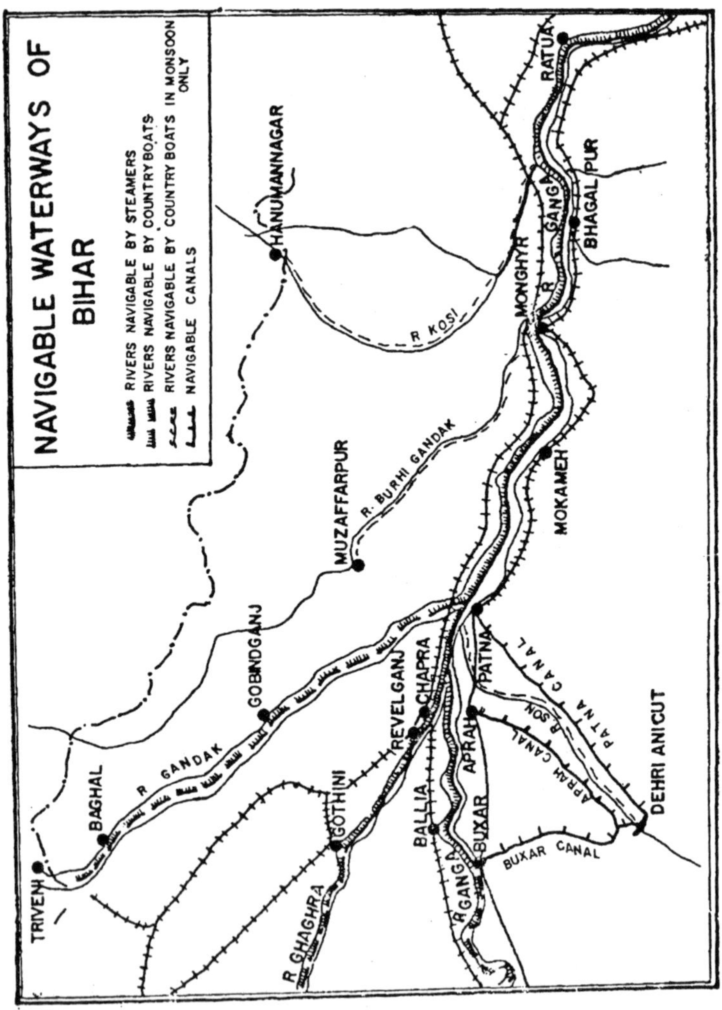

Fig. 4.2: Navigable Waterways of Bihar

year. Up to Behramghat, the junction of Chaluk (a branch of Sarda), the river is navigable by country boats of 3 ft. draught during dry seasons and 4.5 ft. draught during monsoons. Down stream, from Behramghat to its junction with Ganga, it is navigable by modern power propelled vessels.

The physical condition of the Ghaghra channel is not very favourable to navigation. The bed is wide and amenable to frequent shifts and changes. The average fall being moderate, i.e. 6 to 6.5 inches a mile, the river is able to maintain a deep channel to allow navigation by vessels of 4 to 5 ft. draw. Formerly, this river was extensively used for navigational purposes and steamer services used to ply up to Behramghat and even above. There is still considerable traffic on this river by country boats carrying rice and timber from as far up as Katarniaghat. The traffic between Ayodhya (Faizabad) and Patna is still large.

Before we proceed to the next tributary of Ganga, we may discuss the navigational possibilities on Rapti, a feeder of Ghaghra meeting it at Barhaj. This river though small and winding, passes through a region which is rich in agricultural resources and is perhaps the greatest supplier of unskilled labour to the Kolkata industrial region. It flows through Gonda, Basti and Gorakhpur, the three U.P. districts of poverty and natural calamities. It is navigable by country boats throughout the year, but the existing State of navigation is not very satisfactory. Regular cargo traffic can be seen between Patna and Gorakhpur, but beyond Gorakhpur, the traffic is local and small.

Son, the only great feeder contributing to the waters of Ganga from the south rises at Amarkantak in the Maikal range of Central Indian Plateau. Its course, about 485 miles long, passes through the hilly tracts of M.P., U.P., and Bihar. The discharge of the river is generally so poor that leaving aside the few months of monsoon rainfall when even the minute riverlets of northern India assume tremendous size, this river is not fit for navigation. Nevertheless, it serves as the feeder to the Son canal which was constructed in the early seventies of the last century and is navigable even today and permits small boats up to Dehri-on-Son in rains.

At Patna, Ganga is fed by the last navigable tributary worth mention here. It is the great Gandak, the greatness of which is manifest all along the river. It is really a great river, having a minimum discharge of 10,300 cusecs in dry season at Tribeni the place it descends to the plains. It is even more than that of Ganga at Hardwar. It is navigable throughout the year for a distance of more than 180 miles starting from the Indo-Nepal border to its junction with Ganga near Patna. Modern vessels of 4 to 5 ft. draught and 10 to 40 ton capacity can navigate it up to Lalganj 25 miles above its confluence with Ganga. Beyond Lalganj and up to Gopalganj (75 miles it can accommodate country boats of 40 ton capacity in monsoon, and 15 ton capacity in dry periods. Further north up to Tribeni, it is navigable by country boats of 30 ton capacity in monsoon and 5 to 13 ton capacity in dry periods. The great drawback of the channel of the river for navigation is that its bed has risen higher than the surrounding country and hence, it has no tributaries which can feed it mid-way. The drainage is not towards it, but rather away from it. The bed is silted and ill defined. In olden days, it was extensively used for navigation and in 1868 total export through this river amounted to 8 lakh maunds in four months.

Burhi Gandak, comparatively a very small tributary of Ganga takes its rise in the Nepal mountains and is navigable by country boats of 45 ton capacity from Muzaffarpur to its mouth during monsoon. Then comes Kosi the last, but not the least important river meeting Ganga from the north. It is a very large river having a course of a mile or so wide and shows deltaic conditions soon after it emerges from the mountains. The last 80 miles of its course is probably the most destructive and compares well with the Yellow river of China. It shifts its course in each monsoon not by feet and yards, nor even by furlongs, but by miles, scouring new channels through fields and villages. It has done more destruction than any single river of India and hence is remembered as the 'River of Sorrow'. Its abandoned channels are nothing more than heaps of sand spread ununiformly. Even the existing courses are marked with sandbanks and overnight changes. The river has, therefore, been of little navigational consequence nor does it have any bright future in this regard even after the construction of the Kosi barrage. It is, however, used by boats of 15 ton capacity during monsoons. Lastly comes Mahanan which is navigable all the year round by small country boats of 3 ft. draught. The lower reaches of this river being in Bangladesh, navigational the importance of the river is limited.

Of the Bengal rivers meeting the Hooghly at its left bank Damodar is the largest. Above this, two small rivers Dwarka and Mayurakshi meet Bhagirathi. They are navigable by country boats up to Belun and Panchthupi respectively during monsoons. Damodar itself is navigable in monsoons throughout its stretch by vessels of moderate draught. It is also navigable by steamers up to Raspur, 2 miles above Amta. This stretch is affected by tides. During dry weather the upper part of the river shrinks to too small and narrow a channel to afford navigation. Its fall is also too steep to efford safe navigation. It is as much as 3.5 inches per mile below Amta. Due to the opening of Damodar canal, the water supply is still more restricted and hence, it is navigable to hardly 20 miles up from its junction with Hooghly all the year round.

Rupnarayan, south of Damodar, is open to steamer services between Ghatal and Geonkhali—a distance of about 52 miles. Its depth in this course is between 10 to 15 ft. Darakeswar, a tributary has a draught of 24 ft. and is navigable by country boats for about 100 miles during rains. The other navigable channels of West Bengal are Jalangi, Ichamati, Churni, Jamuna, Haldi, Cossys, Selye, Teesta, Torsa, Kalindi, Jilla and Malta rivers. The draught of these rivers is sufficient to allow large country boats all the year round.

Lastly comes the Sundarban steamer route which connects Kolkata with Assam. The Sundarban or the Delta of Ganga and Brahmaputra is a swampy tract full of evergreen forests intersected from north to south by rivers estuaries. These estuaries are interconnected with an intricate series of branches and channels, so that, the whole tract is a tangled network of streams, rivers, water courses and artificial canals, the navigable length of which amounts to 1127 miles out of which 47 miles are artificial. These channels generally run in the east-west direction and are subjected to constant change due to silting caued by the tidal waves. There are three alternative routes, all leading to Barisal from where the boats as well as steamers either follow the Padma-Meghna route or Madaripur route which is a short-cut. The vessels bound for Tripura or South-eastern part of Bangladesh invariably follow the former course. The first two routes starting from Kolkata are used by country boats whereas the last route is used by steamers as it follows more open channels of the Sundarban.

B. Navigable Canals

1. *Major Canals*

Starting from the north, we encounter a network of canals in the alluvial deposits of Ganga and its tributaries. U.P. had taken a lead in this respect, but from navigational point of view very few of the U.P. canals are now significant. All these canals except perhaps the Upper and Lower Ganga Canals and Yamuna Canal are primarily meant for irrigation purposes and had never been important for navigation. Upper Ganga Canal takes off from Hardwar at the foothills of the Himalaya. It was constructed in the middle of the nineteenth century as an irrigation-*cum*-navigation canal. Till 1933-34 it was navigable throughout its entire length of about 213 miles but gradually the navigability dwindled to the extent that at present it is no more than 5 miles from its take off at Hardwar. The minimum width of the canal is 200 ft. with 108′ × 16′ locks at several points. Vessels of 5 ft. draught can ply in the canal if the existing impediments created by the power houses are by-passed.

The Lower Ganga Canal takes off at Naraura; it is 130 miles long and terminates at Kanpur. This canal was also constructed for the double purpose of navigation and irrigation. In the beginning navigation dominated the scene. Gradually, the latter won and navigation became of secondary importance. At present, it is navigable by country boats from the headworks to about 70 miles. Although designed for navigational purposes, the middle course is no more open for navigation. The Yamuna Canal taking off from Okhla near Delhi and running up to the mouth of Chambal was also navigable in the past. Navigation on this canal is now totally extinct.

Next series of canals are: (1) the Main Western Canal, (2) Main Eastern Canal, (3) Buxar Canal, (4) Arrah Canal, and (5) Patna Canal, of which the latter two are navigable by small steamers and either self-propelled vessels. The Main Western Canal and the Main Eastern Canals are navigable by small country boats for 12 and 5 miles respectively. The Patna canal taking off from the Main Eastern Canal is navigable by large country boats in its entire length of 79 miles. It is also navigable by small steamers in its stretch between mile 16 and 78. The Arrah Canal takes off from Main Western Canal, and is about 63 miles long of which the first 52 miles are navigable by steamers and the rest by large country boats. The Buxar canal also takes off from the Main Western Canal and is navigable by country boats in its entire length of 45 miles. The average depth of Arrah Canal varies from 8 to 19 ft. and vessels of 130′ × 18′ can be accommodated. Buxar Canal maintains an average depth of 7 ft. and vessels like country boats, motor launches, steamers and timber rafts can easily ply. The average depths of Main Eastern Canal, Main Western Canal and Patna Canal are 10′ to 3.5′, 10.5′ to 2.5′ and 6 feet respectively. All these canals take off from River Son at Dehri-on-Son and have an aggregate length of 218 miles. They meet river Ganga at Buxar, Arrah and Dinapur. Traffic on these canals has never been very heavy.

Damodar Valley Corporation's irrigation-*cum*-navigation canal takes off from the Durgapur Reservoir town and runs along its left bank *via* Burdwan and empties itself in Hooghly *via* River Kunti at Tribeni, 35 miles north of Kolkata. Its maximum discharge during monsoon period is about 9,400 cusecs. The width of the canal at bed varies from 60 feet to 172 feet with 2 : 1 side slope and a constant draught of 9 feet. These dimensions are sufficient to accommodate vessels of the size of 125′ × 16′ with 300 ton capacity and 6 feet draught. All the three types of locks, i.e. Champlu, Basin and combined have been used according to requirements. The discharge of the canal being different in monsoon and dry seasons, provision of locks at close intervals has become necessary to maintain navigable draught of 9 feet with an allowance of 1 foot for siltation. There is provision for as many as 22 locks of 286′ × 20′ size in a length of 85 miles one lock at every 4 miles, on an average. This would ultimately tell upon the efficiency of navigation as the vessels plying in it would need too much of turn-round time. The sides of the canal being unlined, the speed of the crafts would also have to be restricted to avoid bank erosion. There is total absence of continuous tow-paths to facilitate shore traction by mechanical mules necessitating tieing up of a number of small tugs in the canal for traction of barges between the locks. Despite its limitations, this canal can, however, meet a great felt need of the industrial belt of South Bihar and West Bengal.

From river Kangsabati takes off another important canal of West Bengal that is still used for navigational purposes.

Constructed between 1800 and 1871, Midnapur canal is also an irrigation-*cum*-navigation canal connecting Midnapur town with Ulubaria on the Hooghly. Its total length is 72 miles; it crosses both Damodar and Rupanarayan rivers on its way. The maximum discharge of this canal is about 1500 cusecs and it is navigable by steamers in rains. Hijli tidal canal and Odisha coast canal at the mouth of Rupanarayan are pure navigation canals. The latter is navigable by large country boats throughout its stretch in West Bengal while the former is navigable by steamers. With virtual abandoning of the stretch of Odisha coast canal felling in Odisha state this canal has lost its significance although it may be mentioned that it had never paid its maintenance cost even in the past.

2. *Drawbacks of Canal Navigation*

Almost all the existing navigable canals of the Ganga system, except of course, the Damodar Valley Corporation canal, were constructed before the railways were completed in India. In those days navigational canals, although primarily constructed for irrigational purpose, played an important role in the regional economy. But, as in the case of the riverways, canals too could not compete with the railways. The causes for this decline are not far to seek; they are identical to those applicable to riverways. The inherent drawbacks associated with navigable canals are, however, far more serious. This is specially so, if they are constructed for multipurpose use. Without extraordinary care and attention the navigational, irrigational and power generation functions cannot be coordinated and navigation is often the casualty.

The disadvantages that are inherently found in irrigation-*cum*-navigation canals from navigational point of view are many. Firstly, an irrigation canal traverses rural areas where agriculture requires water for irrgation. Navigational canal, on the other hand flourishes only if it passes through such industrial and commercial centres which can exchange goods with each other and their umlands. Navigation on a canal passing through rural areas can, therefore, have only a limited prospect for development. Secondly, an irrigation canal has to maintain a certain fall as it moves forward. It runs across the contour lines avoiding excessive rate of flow by artificial falls and weirs. This is a distinct disadvantage for navigation. A navigational canal needs uniform slope of gentle gradient, so that, the water currents are slow and the number of falls requiring locks is least. Thirdly, an irrigation Canal is generally unlined and hence the waves generated by power operated vessels scour the banks and increase maintenance costs. Fourthly, the water supply in an irrigation canal depends upon the demand in the area it serves and the discharge of water has to keep to the requirements; nothing more and nothing less. As against this, the navigational canals need perennial supply of water at a certain uniform draught to keep the regularity of trade flow. Lastly, the charges levied on vessels navigating in multi-purpose canals are usually far more than those in purely navigational canals, mainly because of the fact that trades other than agriculture are taxed more heavily particularly in regions of subsistence agriculture. Thus, except in special circumstances where the whole project is designed to serve both irrgation and navigation and where the region is well developed agriculturally, multi-purpose canals do not prove a success. They are suitable for those regions where other means of transportation are lacking. It must, however, he kept in mind that with the increasing mechanization and commercialization of agriculture leading to large scale urbanization and industrialization, the above drawbacks will diminish in importance and it is just possible that a multipurpose canal might give fillip to urbanization and industrialization along its banks.

C. Steamer Services

One of the main causes of the decline of Inland water transport in India had been the late and slow mechanization of the vessels plying in the waterways. The advent of railways with superior organization and efficiency was the other main cause. But, if judged from the point of view of comparative economics of the two systems, it would not be difficult to conclude that the superiority of railways lay to a considerable extent in speed. Had the Inland water transport received the same care from the administration that the railways received and was allowed to improve its competitive position, it would have prospered in India as it did in other countries of the world.

Although the coming of the railways did reduce the importance of river navigation on Ganga, certain private concerns took up steam navigation in Ganga and Brahmaputra to meet the transport requirements of jute and tea industry of North-East India. As stated earlier river Ganga was previously navigable as far as Garhmukteswar by steamers. By the end of the century, a steep fall in the level of Ganga during summer resulting mainly from the opening of the Upper Ganga Canal, closed the upper reaches of the river for navigation. Business of the steamer companies, however, continued to flourish despite this limitation and in 1899 Indian General Steam Navigation and Railway Company Ltd. was registered to operate services on Ganga and its feeders. Subsequently, it entered into a working agreement with the River Steam Navigation Company and the Bengal-Assam Steam Navigation Company for the operation of steamer services as Joint Steamer Companies and continued to render useful service by supplementing railway transportation in the eastern States until its closure in 1958. Since, January 1958, on account of non-availability of sufficient cargo mainly resulting from decline of trade with East Pakistan, and the non-navigability of River Bhagirathi (involving an extra distance of 400 miles *via* East Pakistan to reach Kolkata), the existing power propelled vessel services are confined to ferrying work between Sakrigali and Maniharighats, Samaria and Mokamahghat, Paleza and Mohendraghat, and Monghyr and Monghyrghats.

D. Problems of Navigation

The problems of Inland navigation on River Ganga may be studied under the following heads:

1. Maintenance of channel,
2. Suitability of crafts, and
3. Traffic potentials.

1. Maintenance of Channel

The principal problem of Inland Navigation in Ganga is the intense bank erosion the river undergoes after monsoons. Its meanders, large and winding as they are, are cut from beneath by the fast currents, forcing the river to shift its course. This activity of the river is sometimes so devastating that the ghats and shelters erected to facilitate the handling of cargo disappear over night creating serious problems for navigation. It leaves the sandy, but sometimes well-layered old deposits of clay stand precipitously 10 to 20 feet above water level making the loading and unloading operations extremely costly and problematic.

Although bank erosion takes place in all the seasons, that occurring during August-September is most extensive and destructive for navigation. After the final rise of the river at the end of the rainy season, water level falls very abruptly, e.g. 9 to 12 feet per day. This sudden fall creates several meanders which gradually develop in size and depth. In this period the behaviour of the river is such that the meanders developed overnight, silt up in no time or dig as deep as 50 feet in hours. This is mainly due to the sandy and water saturated loamy character of soil in the river channels and consequent intense erosion.

These changes in the river bed act as great hinderance to safe navigation, particularly in cases of those vessels which are not frequent visitors and the crew of which are not accustomed to the habits of the river. It is only the local boatmen who can judge correctly the course they should follow as they know beforehand the possible changes in the channels to be followed. This is probably the most serious problem of navigation by country boats as these services are so unorganised that they cannot afford to keep the navigable channels marked by regular and periodic surveys to avoid the locking up of their vessels in unknown shoals. The traffic under such circumstances, has got to be limited and confined to short and familiar stretches.

Allied to the problem of bank erosion and meanders is the draught of water available in different stretches of the river. Generally speaking the sharper the meander, deeper the draught of water available. But, as soon as the river emerges from the bend and straightens its course, the draught becomes shallow and the bed far wider. It is these shallow courses which limit the navigability of the stream more than anything else.

The river training devices to be applied to Ganga can be classified into two: (1) checking of the bank erosion and (2) deepening of the shallow channels. No systematic research has yet been carried out to ascertain the relationship between the discharge of the water and development of meanders. It is true that erosive capacity of water depends much upon the extra meterials it carries with it, but leaving aside the load carried by water, what is the relationship between normal water and bank erosion at bends is not yet specifically known. If this relationship can be found, this aspect of the problem of Inland navigation in Ganga can be resolved more satisfactorily. As regards the bank erosion, several methods have been in use in countries like the U.S.A. which can be profitably used in India. It has been reported that Amercian engineers have almost succeeded in checking bank erosion, particularly in Mississippi-Missouri river system. In India, no serious attempt has been made to tackle this problem.

The river training methods applied in Ganga and its tributaries, have been crude, inadequate and unsystematic. The Navigational Authorities carry out seasonal surveys of the channels used by the steamers soon after the rains when the rivers are in the process of forming several spill-channels to adjust to the dwindling supply of water. Their purpose in carrying out such surveys is to ascertain as to which of the several spill-channels would suit navigation most. They select the one which can be expected to last longer after careful surveys of all the other available channels. After a channel is selected, the river training devices are applied to feed the selected channel at the cost of the rejected ones. The method applied is called *bandalling* (pinning of bamboo poles). Despite its cheapness, the work of river training is so extensive and large that India had to spend nearly Rs. 1,50,000 each year on erecting 50 to 60 thousand feet of *bandals* in Ganga alone during the nineteen fifties. Financial problems apart, *bandalling* is not suited to all channels. According to Pointon, it suffers from serious limitations in Indian rivers where bunds to prevent the flooding of adjoining areas neutralise the action of the *bandals*, and deposit large quantities of silt in the river bed. Dredging is probably the only wayout where *bandalling* fails.

The greatest empediment to navigation on Ganga is the non-perenniality of river Bhagirathi. This river was once the main channel of Ganga. The partition of Bengal made even the detoured route connecting the industrially developed region of Hooghly banks with the potential markets of U.P. and Bihar, difficult and the steamer companies did not find it economic to operate regular services *via* Sundarbans involving an extra coverage of 400 miles. The opening and maintenance of a navigable channel either through Bhagirathi itself or through a diversion canal will rehabilitate the old navigability of Ganga. It may be noted that the non-navigability not only hinders a natural connection between the coalfield and iron foundaries of Bengal with the industrial areas of Bihar and U.P., but also renders river Hooghly (Bhagirathi in lower reaches affected by tidal action is known as Hooghly) subject to intense siltation involving frequent and costly dredging. The problem of siltation has increased to such art immensity that if no early action is taken to redirect a part of the water of Ganga to Hooghly, the latter would not remain open to ocean going ships within 50 years. A ship canal connecting Kolkata with Diamond Harbour would become essential. This project would not only involve a sum of over Rs. 109 crore or so, but would also create a counter-problem of drainage. The low lying areas in this part of Bengal, are already waterlogged. Apart from these, the progressive extinction of Bhagirathi would permit Hooghly to greater tidal action and would increase its salinity which is already too high. This will certainly affect the water supply of Kolkata and Howrah.

The problem of Bhagirathi is not merely a problem of conventional river training for navigation. As the water level of Ganga drops down by 20 to 30 feet in the dry periods of the year, the Bhagirathi channel stands at too high a level. Here lies the need of a barrage on Ganga at Farakka, now under construction which is designed to divert the water of Ganga towards Bhagirathi, to give this river a permanent lease of life.

The problem of opening Bhagirathi for navigation and the construction of the Farakka barrage have a long history. Rennel made a survey in 1764-65, but without any results. Soon after, in 1777, John Gowan put forward a plan in his regard, but it was not carried out. Again in 1783 Wildord resurveyed the area and concluded that due to great fluctuations in the water level, it would not be possible to maintain a canal diverting the water of Ganga to Bhagirathi. In 1794, under the aegis of the East India Company another attempt was made which resulted in the recommendation by the Surveyor General to have a cut-off nearly 6 miles and 20 feet wide and 15-20 feet deep between Hurdum and Ichamati. Rennel, however, did not agree with the proposal and commented: "Nature seems to have adjusted matters very nicely, in respect to the capacity of rivers, beds and levels; so that, any tampering with them in delicate cases (particularly when there is so great a periodical swelling and velocity of current) may be productive of much mischief". Rennel's opinion was accepted by the Company's Court of Directors and the proposal was discarded. Since, then several sporadic attempts were made to impress upon the Government to take suitable action in this regard, but without any practical results. After the Independence of the country, the demand for damming river Ganga at Farakka increased to such an extent that the Government could not resist it any longer. During the Third Five Year Plan, the project was sanctioned despite protests and objections from the Government of Pakistan.

With the diversion of large amount of water to the irrigation canals, the marking of navigable channels for the guidance of the power propelled and sailing boats has assumed considerable importance. The usual method applied in India is the pinning of bamboo poles (*bandalling*). It is a cheap and efficient means provided that constant attention is paid to its maintenance and supervision. The poles are generally 12 to 15 feet long and are hammered into the sandy and marshy bed of the river. The pins mark the inner edge of the shoals on both sides of the main channel. To improve the visibility in moon light they are painted white. There are several other expensive methods applied in foreign countries to mark the navigable channels. But due to shallowness of rivers and the sandiness of beds, the bamboo pin markings have been found to be quite suitable in these rivers.

2. *Suitability of Crafts*

Given certain minimum depth of water, any water channel can be made navigable by the application of the following two methods. First is the deepening of the channel to permit crafts of required size and draught and the second is to adopt such vessels which can be accommodated in the channels without resorting to expensive deepening and dredging. It is true that at many places deepening of the channel by dredging and other conventional methods such as *bandalling* etc. cannot be ruled out altogether, the selection of suitable vessels to suit the different channels would go a long way in rehabilitating the navigability of river Ganga and its tributaries in their upper reaches. For example, river Ganga can be made navigable by crafts of 3.5 feet draught in all seasons. Although a regular dredging would make it navigable by crafts of

5 to 6 feet draught, the cost involved would be much heavier than the returns. In such cases redesigning of vessels to suit the channel

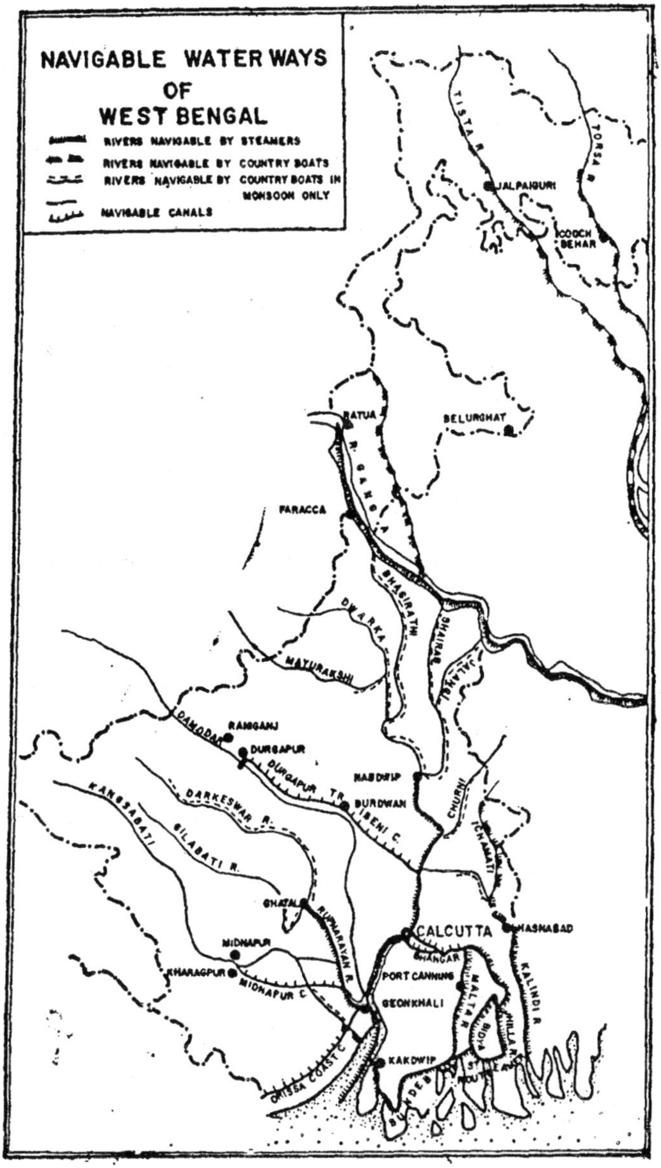

Fig. 4.3: Navigable Wateways of West Bengal

seems more logical and economic. This method has been successfully applied in Europe.

While tackling the problem of selecting suitable vessels for the draught available in different stretches of Ganga system of rivers one cannot ignore the question of examining various types of vessels fitted with different types of bottom components and designs. The selection is among the three types, i.e. vane-wheel, screw-wheel and stern-wheel tugs. All the three can be made shallow draught vessels. Yet they cannot suit all the channels. The nature of the river bottom, amount of silt in suspension and the effect the groundings of vessels in shoals has on the wheels are important considerations in the selection of vessels. In shallow draughted navigation and groundings, the spoon-bow and balanced rudders which do not fall below the bed are considered to be more suitable from technical as well as economic points of view. Most of the navigation companies in India use old fashioned stock anchors for their dumb crafts and stockless anchors for power crafts. Both of them have now become antidated and hardly conform to the present day requirements of quick despatch as they take longer time for launching.

In India, the methods of towing barges are unique in the sense that quite contrary to the practice in other countries, they are towed alongside the towing steamers. In Europe they are towed by exerting pull from the front in other words in line-stern. In the United States of America, the method applied is just the opposite and the barges are pushed from behind by the tugs. A systematic research is needed to find out as to which of the three methods in use in different parts of the world is more economical and suitable for India.

Apart from the question of power propelled vessels, there still exist hundreds of country made boats plying on Ganga and its tributaries. They are of various sizes although the design is limited to only a few types. They vary from hollow trunks of trees to large sailing boats capable of facing even the worst storms. There are frequent local services between the towns of Kanpur, Allahabad, Varanasi and Patna. Very often they have to detain themselves waiting for favourable wind while going up-stream. These services are few and far between, but during slack periods of the year, when the village folks are free from agricultural operations and enjoy visiting fairs, *melas* and gatherings for religious and social purposes, they assume great local importance. The boats deployed on such services are generally multipurpose, and can carry any consignment in full or small including passengers. While taking up the question of improvement of these services, the design of the vessels has got to be kept in view.

3. *Traffic Potentials*

Scientific studies to determine the traffic potentials of the Ganga system of waterways have not been conducted. What is, however, clear is the fact that the Ganga and its tributaries pass through an agriculturally rich area and link the dense population of the valley with the industrial and mineral belt of the east. Agricultural commodities moving down stream can be carried by steamers and on their return journey they can carry coal, ores and finished industrial goods.

A traffic survey conducted by the National Council for Applied Economic Research during the fifties in the stretch of Ganga between Buxar and Rajmahal and in Ghaghra between Chapra and Darauli totalling 400 miles revealed a traffic potential of nearly 2,00,000 tons per annum on these runs of the rivers. Passenger traffic was estimated at 80,000. The survey also states that about six million people in Bihar and 3.5 million in U.P., all of whom live within 12 miles of the rivers, will take advantage of river transport. It would also benefit industries in western Bihar, eastern U.P. and the districts of Santhal Pargana, Mongyr and Saharsa.

Emphasising that Bihar will continue to be the transport cushion for road and rail transit traffic to U.P., Assam and Nepal, the survey says that if both road and rail routes become congested, the escape will be by the river route.

In Uttar Pradesh, there is considerable scope for traffic in fodder, foodgrains, sugar, potatoes, oilseeds, building materials, coal, handloom cloth etc. With the location of various industries along the banks of the Ganga and its tributaries, the traffic potential will further increase. The Transport Research Division of the Ministry of Transport, in its traffic survey of 1968, found that between Allahabad and Rajmahal, a traffic of the order of 4.45 lakh tonnes per year is likely to go to Inland waterways, if dependable services are developed.

Bihar has apparently greater traffic potentials than U.P., Bihar is not so well-served by rail and road transport as U.P. is. River Ganga bifurcates the state into two parts—North and South. There is only one bridge on Ganga in Bihar which links these two parts by land transport. In U.P. there are six bridges on Ganga, the last one being at Varanasi. The distance between Varanasi and Mokamah is 315 km. This leads to long-haulage through a circuitous route between northern and southern parts of the State.

Table 4.1 indicates the advantages of Inland water transport in regard to distance as compared to road and rail.

Table 4.1: Route Distances Between Selected Riverside Centres in Bihar

From	*To*	*Distance in km.*		
		By rail	*By road*	*By water*
Patna	Chapra (M)	314	268	80
Patna	Ballia (V)	379	407	130
Patna	Dighwara (M)	283	248	40
Buxar	Chapra (M)	327	405	105
Buxar	Dighwara (M)	358	385	145
Buxar	Ballia (V)	262	251	55
Buxar	Ghazipur (V)	193	182	65
Bhagalpur	Karagola (M)	132	205	70

(V) = *via* Varanasi; (M) = *via* Mokamah

Source: Report of the Inland Water Transport Committee, Government of India, October 1970, p. 85.

The Transport Research Wing of the Ministry of Transport and Shipping suggested that the quantum of traffic to be carried by Inland water transport in Bihar will be of the order given in Table 4.2.

The traffic potentials in West Bengal rivers will increase rapidly after the completion of the Farakka barrage. In the mean time, the emergence of Bangladesh as a friendly nation has given scope for the movement of over 2 lakh tonnes of goods through the existing waterways connecting the two countries.

The Gokhale Committee on Inland water transport has recommended the joint booking of cargo to divert a certain volume of goods to waterways. But there is a limit to which traffic on this route can be increased. The parallel running railways and roads on both sides of the river extend an efficient carriage of goods and passengers. It must be admitted here that there is no question of developing waterways at the cost of rail and road services waterways have a unique place in transport industry of a country by dint their of cheapness, suitability for bulk carriage and relative slowness. They are most suited to certain bulky and cumbustible goods which cannot be carried by other modes of transportation efficiently. In the absence of a developed water transport line, many of the potential goods remain stagnant as their movement by rail or road would make the landed cost much more than what would attract, the customers. Waterways have thus to attract such goods which are not being moved due to the absence of a cheap means of transportation. They have simultaneously to cooperate with the railways and roads to divert such cargo which are more suited to carriage by waterways yet are being carried by railways.

Table 4.2: Traffic Potential on River Ganga in Bihar

From	*To*	*Distance by river km.*	*Quantity in tonnes*
Patna (S)	Chapra (N)	80	7,022
Patna (S)	Dighwara (N)	40	4,505
Chapra (N)	Patna (S)	80	7,654
Patna (S)	Ballia (N)	130	25,949
Buxar (S)	Dighwara (N)	145	8,624
Buxar (S)	Chapra (N)	105	8,624
Bhagalpur (S)	Karagola (N)	70	59,100
Karagola (S)	Bhagalpur (S)	70	47,300

N = North Bank, S = South Bank.
Source: Report of the Inland Water Transport Committee, p. 87.

The industrial development of the Ganga valley is of great importance to Inland water transport. A cheap transport to carry the raw materials and finished goods to and fro will in turn lead to more rapid industrialization in the valley. As a matter of fact industrialization and development of means of transportation go hand in hand and since the States of U.P. and Bihar are backward and are planning to imbark on industrialization both on manufacturing and agricultural fronts, the development of water transport in the Ganga system of rivers should form an integral part of regional development planning for these states.

References

1. J. Johnston, *Inland Navigation on the Gangetic Rivers*, 1946.
2. Rennel, *Memoirs of Hindusthan.*
3. Gokhale, B.K. *Report on Inland Water Transport*, Ministry of Transport and Communication, 1958-60.
4. *Report of the Inland Water Transport Committee*, 1970.

5
Navigable Channels of Assam and Sundarban Delta

After crossing the Rajmahal hills on the way to the eastern states of India, one comes into a flat deltatic plain of Ganga-Brahmaputra. This plain is torn into pieces by multitudinous riverlets coming from the north and frequently joining each other on their way to the Bay of Bengal. The gradient of the plain is so delicate that these rivers break through the unbroken parts of the plain during the rains, creating new channels and leaving the old ones in almost near-marshy state. The rainfall is torrential and incessant for over eight months in the year. Cyclonic storms are as common as the torrential rains. During the floods; the whole region presents a picture of an unending sea with innumerable 'islands'. The soil is clayee and saturated with water to the top. The slope being too gentle, the low-lying areas become marshy lands in no time. With heavy rainfall, the railway tracks are breached. The road building materials like stones are conspicuously absent in the area. Unmetalled roads are washed away faster than they are built. The only dependable means of transportation and communication in this region are the waterways. Probably this is the only region of the Indian sub-continent where geography had been so favourable to the waterways that other modes of transportation cannot challenge them. The role of the waterways in the transport system of this region is so great that, despite the mechanical and organizational superiority of railways and roads, they have failed to displace them.

The partition of the country into India and Pakistan in 1947 left much of the province of Assam, and the, whole of the princely states of Tripura and Manipur in India, while Bengal was partioned into East Pakistan and West Bengal, the latter becoming a part of the Indian Union. The eastern States of India are linked with the rest of the country through a narrow strip of territory just only 20 km. wide at its narrowest point. The partition dislocated through railway services between Assam and the rest of India. In 1950, Assam rail link was constructed through Indian territory, but it is so vulnerable to the vagaries of nature that each year it remains dislocated at least for a few days during the rains. The waterways, in such, times of emergency help ease the situation.

The Brahmaputra river had been the major waterway of Assam. Its valley traverses the States of Assam and East Pakistan now Bangladesh. In the pre-partition days, the jute growing regions of the above states were linked with the jute factories on the Hooghly bank and with Kolkata the major exporting port of jute and jute goods. Even after partition, Brahmaputra continued to be the major transport line of Assam, but its lower reaches being in Pakistan creating several international trade and transportation problems. In the absence of any reconciliation between India and Pakistan, the future of the Brahmaputra route was bleak. But the emergence of Bangladesh as an Independent nation friendly to India brings a new hope for the future.

A. Important Channels

1. River Brahmaputra

Brahmaputra the main channel of Inland navigation in Assam, takes its rise in the Tibetan plateau and is known, as Tsangpo. It descends to the valley of Assam through Dihang or Siang. From Pasighat it takes the name of Brahmaputra and then Jamuna in the plains of Bangladesh. Near Sadia, the eastern most large town in the Assam valley, tributaries like Sesar, Dibang, Luhit and Noa Dehing meet Brahmaputra from both sides. Among these Noa Dehing is navigable by country boats during the monsoons. From Pasighat on Siang, and Sadiya on Ruhit, Brahmaputra is navigable by power propelled vessels of 4 feet draught up to Deshangmukh, 46 miles down stream from Dibrugarh. From Deshangmukh to Tezpur, the channel has an operational draught of 6 feet from June to October and 5 feet to 5.5 feet from November to May. Downstream from Tezpur the draught increses to 6.5 feet during June-September and 5.25 feet during October-May.

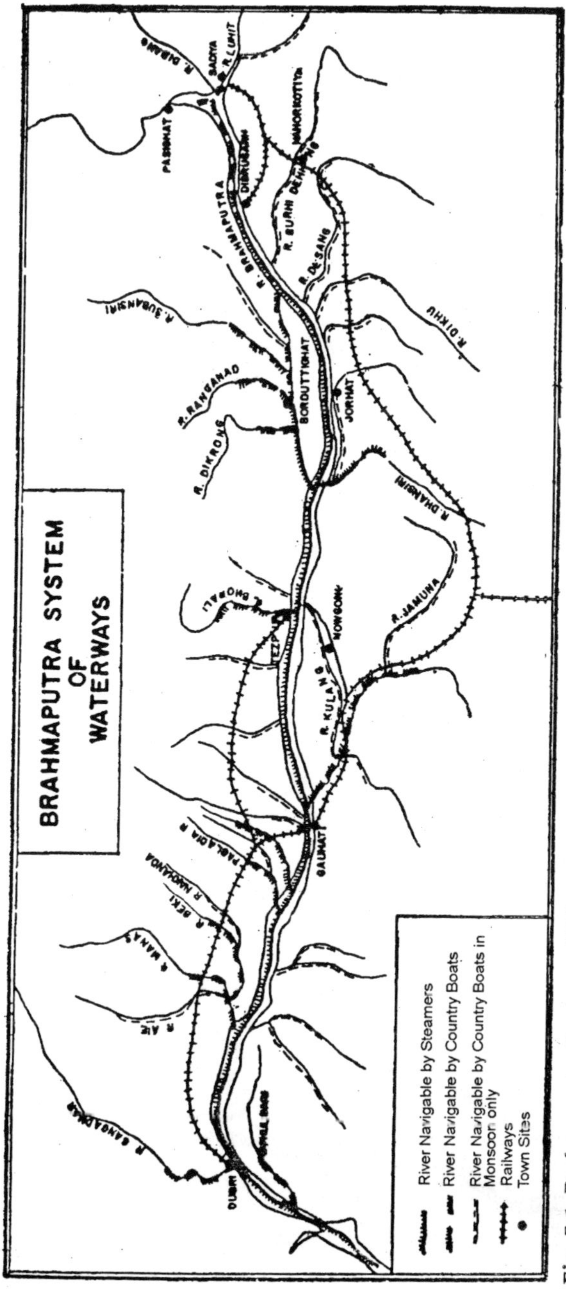

Fig. 5.1: Brahmaputra System of Waterways

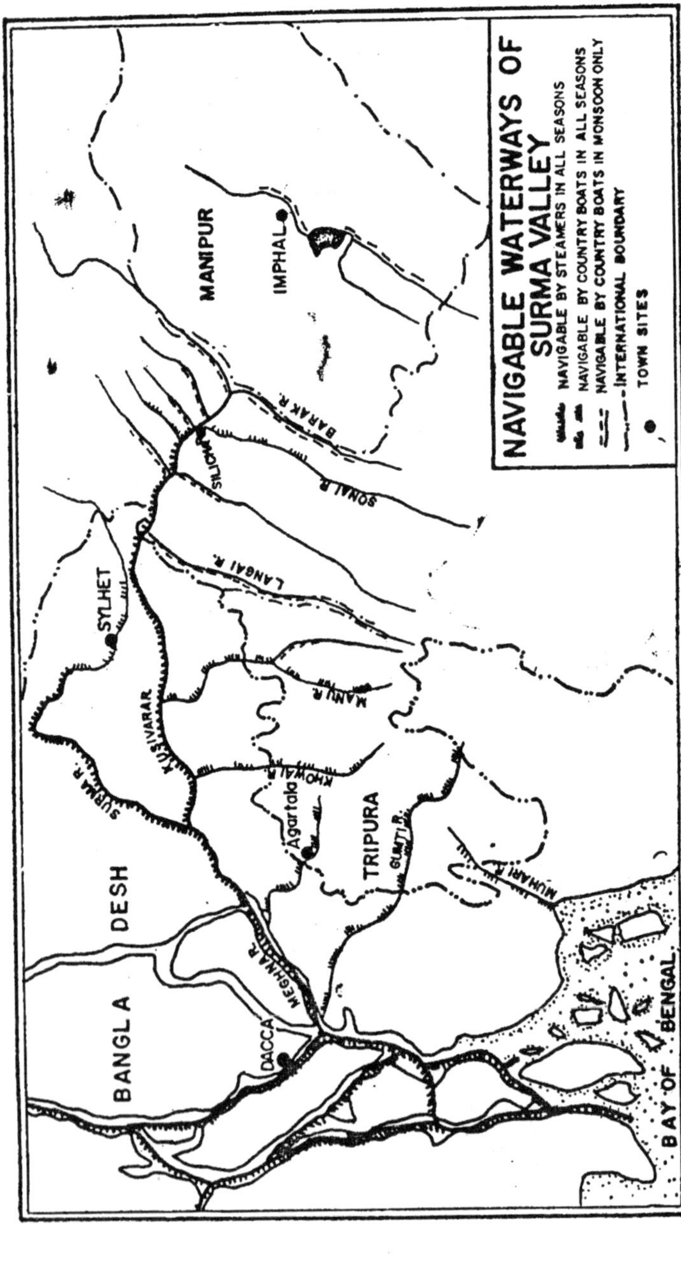

Fig. 5.2: Navigable Waterways of Surma Valley

The main channel of Brahmaputra has a total length of 450 miles in Assam. The discharge of the river and the level of water vary considerably between monsoon and dry seasons. A seasonal fall of 30 feet in the water level is not an exception. During the dry periods, the currents are no faster than three miles an hour. But in monsoons, they assume tremendous speed. The monsoon water is loaded with silt, debris and fallen trees and creates serious navigational problems such as bank erosion, washing away of wharves, ghats, and river conservancy devices.

Before 1950, Brahmaputra afforded a working draught of 6 feet during monsoon and 5 feet during dry seasons up to Sadia and Pasighat on rivers Lohit and Siang respectively. The earthquake of 1950 caused considerable change in the topography of upper Assam and raised the upper part of the Brahmaputra valley. As a result of this, the 6 feet draught of the channel ends at Deshang, 46 miles west of Dibrugarh. The 4 feet draught available upstream is not enough to accommodate steamers which require a minimum of 5 feet draught. The main channel suffers from several natural drawbacks such as the existence of shoals and bank erosion.

Of the dozens of tributaries of Brahmaputra a few such as Burhi Dehing, Desang, and Subansiri have a minimum draught of 4 feet. On such rivers, feeder services of the Joint Steamer Companies ply at suitable intervals. Other feeders, namely Jaidhol, Ranganad Dikrong, Bhovalli, Gabru, Dhansiri Pagladiya, Buki, Manas, Her and Gangdhar from the north and Noa Dehing, Dikhu, Jhanji, Bhogdoi, Dhansiri, Kullong, Jamana, Kopilli, Killing, Boko, Singara, Dudnai, Krishani and Jingiram from south, are navigable by country boats of various dimensions.

2. *Surma and Kusivarar Channels*

The Surma and Kusivarar channels have a draught of 5 to 6 feet all the year round. These rivers serve Sylhet district of Bangladesh, the Silcher district of Assam and the States of Tripura and Manipur. After collecting the waters of Jatinga Madhura, Chiri, Jiri, Barak, Sonai and Longai, river Kusivarar flows through Silcher and Karimganj and meets with Surma coming from the north. Before its junction with Meghna, it collects the waters of Manu, Khowai, Madra, Gumti and Munari, all navigable and passing through Tripura. All these aforesaid tributaries of Kusivarar are navigable by country boats and have great navigational potentialities.

3. Sundarban Channels

The importance of Brahmaputra channel is considerably reduced without a connecting link between the estuaries of Meghna and Hooghly. Jute and tea, the two main products of Assam having international market are destined for Kolkata, the largest river port of India. These products pass through the Sundarban creeks an idea of which has already been given in the previous chapter. There are three different routes, two of which pass through the lower reaches of Matla, Bidya and Jhill. These routes lead to Kolkata through two different navigable canals. Matla is navigable by power propelled vessels up to Port Canning from where a canal leads to Kolkata. Kalindi with Jamuna and Ichamathi forms another route available from a point 35 mile north-east of Kolkata. The main channel, however, passes through numerous creeks of the deltaic deposits of Sundarbans. This is known as Sundarban steamer route. All the vessels passing through this route are destined for Barisal from where they move either to Brahmaputra *via* Jamuna or to Surma and Kusivarars *via* Meghna.

B. Steamer Services

Navigation by power propelled vessels in Brahmaputra and Sundarban channels has been in the hands of the Joint Steamer Companies composed of India General Navigation and Railway Company Limited and the River Steam Navigation Company Limited, both incorporated in England with Sterling capital. Besides these, there are ten Indian compains registered in Kolkata.

1. Calcutta Steamers Ltd., Kolkata.
2. Bengal-Assam Steamship Co. Ltd., Kolkata.
3. East Bengal River Steam Service Ltd., Kolkata.
4. Pioneer Shipping Co. Ltd., Kolkata.
5. Assam-Bengal River Service Ltd., Kolkata.
6. Indo-Swiss Trading Co. Ltd., Kolkata.
7. Indian River Transport Co. Ltd., Kolkata.
8. Bengal River Service Co. Kolkata.
9. The Indian Shipping Co. Ltd., Kolkata.
10. Neptune Navigation Co. Ltd., Kolkata.

Financially, the Indian companies were week in comparison to the Joint Steamer Companies. Leaving aside Neptune Navigation Company and the Indo-Swiss Trading Company, data regarding which are not readily available, the total authorised capital of the 8 Indian companies amounted to Rs. 1.50 crore only whereas that of the Joint Steamer Companies amounted to Rs. 1.80 crore in 1955. Likewise the subscribed and paid up capital of the said Indian companies were 1.03 crore and Rs. 0.59 crore respectively as against Rs. 1.70 crore and Rs. 1.60 crore in case of the British companies.

In respect of the traffic handled and the vessels owned, the Joined Steamer Companies were the foremost carriers on this route. The Indian companies owned about 400 vessels:

1.	Steamers	61
2.	Flats	61
3.	Pontoons	2
4.	Barges	204
5.	Steam Launches	15
6.	Steel Cargo Boats	1
7.	Wooden Boats	53
	Total	**400**

As against this, the Joint Steamer Companies owned 549 vessels of following description:

1.	Steamer	81
2.	Feeder Steamers	16
3.	Tugs and Launches	28
4.	Motor Boats	2
5.	Running Flats	148
6.	Cargo Boats	110
7.	Feeder Barges	28
8.	Oil Carrying Flats	4
9.	Oil Carrying Barges	3
10.	Miscellaneous	52
11.	Receiving Flats and Pontoons	72
12.	Coal Flats	5
	Total	**549**

The volume of traffic both cargo and passenger handled by different companies of Indian origin had also been far less in comparison to that of the Joint Steamer Companies. A statement showing the total volume of cargo and passengers handled by each company in mid-fifties is given in Table 5.1:

Table 5.1: Traffic Handled by Steamer Companies in 1954-55

Sl. No.	*Name of Company*	*Route*	*Cargo in maunds*	*No. of passengers*
1.	Calcutta Steamer Ltd.	Kolkata-Assam	n.a.	189
2.	Bengal-Assam Steamship Co. Ltd.	Kolkata-Narayanganj-Kolkata	15,65,387	nil
3.	East Bengal River Steam Service Ltd.	Kolkata-East Pakistan	13,35,000	nil
4.	Assam-Bengal River Service Ltd.	Sundarban river route-Hooghly river route	12,75,000	nil
5.	Indian River Transport Col. Ltd.	Local	15,401	nil
6.	India General Navigation and Railway Co. Ltd.	Ganga Despatch Service; Assam-Sundarban Despatch Service	2,72,83,014	1,98,540
7.	Bengal River Service Co. Ltd.	India-Pakistan	27,08,000	nil
8.	Indian Shipping Co. Ltd.	Kolkata-East Pakistan	24,05,012	nil

One of the advantages, the steamer services had in this region is the availability of cargo on both ways. The companies have agencies at places like Dibrugarh and Pondu to book the goods and passengers, apart from similar arrangements at almost all steamer stations. For the convenience of the people, a through-booking system with the railways *via* Shalimar C. Shed, Dhubri, Pondu, Amigaon, Tezpur, Silhat, Neamati, Karimganj, Maniharighat, Paleza, and Dibrugarh is also done. Table 5.2 shows the main traffic movements over the Joint Steamer Companies services from and to Kolkata from 1951 to 1955.

The cargo going to Assam originates at Kolkata which is a meeting ground for all modes of transportation—railway, roads,

Table 5.2: Traffic Handled by the Joint Steamer Companies

(In maunds)

From Kolkata

Year	*To Assam (India)*	*To Cachar (India)*	*To Ganga (India)*	*To East Bengal and Tripura*	*Total*
1951	1,17,17,136	19,94,031	13,68,009	44,74,629	1,95,53,805
1952	1,03,87,440	19,43,136	9,62,010	40,62,663	1,73,55,789
1953	55,24,767	12,54,960	6,71,760	27,94,257	1,02,45,744
1954	81,83,214	13,76,703	11,32,110	26,18,136	1,33,10,163
1955	1,03,22,505	16,08,606	7,88,859	27,91,881	1,55,11,851
1962*	7,700,000	—	—	—	—
1964*	8,500,000	—	—	—	—

To Kolkata

Year	*From Assam*	*From Cachar*	*From Ganga*	*Total*
1951	1,04,29,371	10,42,740	86,103	1,15,58,214
1952	85,42,638	10,45,467	2,11,761	97,99,866
1953	1,00,37,763	10,04,076	1,57,383	1,11,39,222
1954	83,22,453	11,67,588	37,987	95,30,028
1955	81,18,225	11,65,563	4,833	92,88,621
1962*	6,700,000			
1964*	68,00,000			

* Report of the Inland Water Transport Committee, 1970, p. 72.

airways, Inland waterways and ocean liners. It has a great railway junction, airport and seaport and it is the terminal of the Grant Trunk Road, the longest and oldest modern road of Northern India. Kolkata, being the greatest industrial centre of south Asia, is the busiest port of Inland navigation. In return for the raw materials supplied to the factories of Kolkata, the people of eastern India and now to a certain extent of Bangladesh depend on the Hooghly side factories for, the manufactured goods nearly 3.5 lakh tons of raw materials used to move down the Brahmaputra channel to Kolkata port. The main products of Assam consisted of mineral oil, jute, tea and timber. About 93 per cent of Assam's tea and 90 per cent of jute used to come to Kolkata *via* the riverways. The quantity of tea exported from Kolkata and the foreign exchange earned was indeed large.

Table 5.3: Export of Tea from Kolkata

Year	Quantity in 1000 lbs.	Value in 1000 rupees
1953	5,00,655	10,42,173
1954	4,77,960	13,07,523
1955	3,67,523	11,36,132
1956	5,25,557	14,28,240
1957	4,42,651	12,33,858
1958	5,07,600	13,74,000

Note: When the services operated by the Joint Steamer Companies were at their peak, about 93 per cent of tea and 90 per cent of jute used to move to Kolkata by river. The traffic gradually declined and by 1965, tea traffic by river to Kolkata was reduced to 65 per cent and jute to 25 per cent only.

Of the total imports of 11,08,110 tons, and total exports of 8,90,750 tons from Assam, Cachar and Tripura, the riverways handled 5,98,130 tons of export and 4,15,820 tons of imports as against 5,09,980 tons of exports and 4,74,930 tons of imports handled by the railways. By 1965, the imports were reduced to 1,97,000 tonnes and exports to 1,17,000 tonnes.

C. Problems of Assam Waterways

1. Physical

Unlike the Ganga system of rivers, the Brahmaputra and its tributaries have adequate supply of water for navigation. They, however, suffer from shoal formations which obstruct navigation. There are hundreds of shoals in the Brahmaputra, but leaving aside a few major ones, they can fee easily side-tracked by the vessels. The major shoals that obstruct navigation are Banaria and Bangamati, upstream from Tezpur, and Kurwa, Kholabanda, (Goalpara and Noonkhowa downstream from Tezpur. In the second week of April 1958, as many as 70 vessels with 30,000 tons of essential cargo were held up at Noonkhowa shoal near the Assam-Bangladesh border. Nearly 10 per cent of the carrying capacity of the Joint Steamer Companies was lost each year due to shoal obstructions.

The Surma and Kusivara channels also suffer from shoals such as those between Karimganj and Silcher. The Kuttagong shoal often proves to be most troublesome. In recent years, the supply of water to these rivers; during dry periods has been progressively diminishing. Being rain-fed rivers, their perenniality depends upon the capacity of the basin to trap the rain water and, to obstruct it from flowing down the flooded valleys. Forest covered basins are able to hold the water for longer periods. Deforestation of the river-basins during the last thirty years or so, has led to excessive flooding during the rains and shortage of water during the dry periods.

Bank erosion is another problem of navigation in Brahmaputra and its tributaries. Now, it assumes serious magnitudes affecting the navigability of the streams and inflicting considerable economic loss on the people by washing away standing crops, villages and even cities. The destructive flood of 1954 which washed away part of Dibrugarh town is still fresh, in the memories of the people of Assam.

To tackle these problems, river conservancy and training methods such as *bandalling*, dredging and aforestation, in the catchment area, are essential. Special attention needs to be paid to the removal of snags and shoals wherever they exist. The objective of all these measures should be to minimise the uncertainty with regard to the depth of the channel. A draught of 6 feet for the main services and 4 feet for the feeder services is the minimum that must be maintained. Unfortunately, the data regarding the change in the river courses from year to year and its relationship with the formations elongation of shoals is not available. Unless such data are collected, effective conservancy and training methods can hardly be planned. Aerial photography of the river beds at the start of the dry period followed by systematic hydrographic surveys both in the dry and flood seasons would yield considerable useful data.

The improvement of the Brahmaputra system of waterways involves the following:

1. Maintenance of a single main channel by closing the subsidiary ones,
2. Deepening of the channel at shoals,
3. Removal of other obstructions,

4. Straightening of the sharp bends, so that, the currents may not gain sufficient force to push the vessels off the course,
5. Construction of dykes and spurs,
6. Protection against bank erosion, and
7. Construction of dams, weirs, lateral canals and hicks for maintaining sufficient draught.

2. *Navigation*

(i) *Handling Facilities:* There are several Inland ports on river Brahmaputra. Important among these are Dibrugarh, Neamati, Tezpur, Guwahati, Pandu, Jogighopa and Dhubri. None of these were, however, provided with modern cargo handling and warehousing facilities. Most of the facilities were temporary ones and the handling of the cargo was manual. To remedy the situation, Pandu was developed as a modern Inland port. Later on Jogighopa was also developed. With the stoppage of Inland water services between Kolkata and Assam in 1965, facilities available at Pandu became superfluous. Jogighopa was developed to handle traffic destined to Kolkata and Bihar, U.P. centres *via* North-East Frontier Railway. It, however, could not attract expected amount of traffic. Now, that the traffic potential of the region has increased, further development of the Inland port facilities is necessary.

The construction of permanent sheds, warehouses, jetties, landing stages and gangways for discharging the cargo, small cranes, mechanically operated trolleys and fork-lift trucks for loading the cargo, will be needed as traffic increases. Apart from these, the maintenance and opening of approach roads connecting the Ghats with the hinterland has also to be taken up.

The Gokhale Committee on Inland Water Transport recommended the provision of the following navigational facilities on these waterways:

1. Construction of an Inland port at Pandu near Guwahati, with adequate terminal facilities for heavy lifts etc. by the end of the third five year plan (1966);
2. Pitching of foreshore and the provision of parking space for lorries at Guwahati;
3. Maintenance of approach roads;
4. Preparation of plan for the construction of a port at Dhubri;

5. Preparation of plan for provision of port facilities at Kusiyara river; and
6. Provision of mobile transit sheds at Neamati and other places where permanent structures cannot be errected.

Kolkata, Jogighopa and Pandu being the chief terminal stations for Inland navigation in North-East India, the cargo handling facilities available at these ports have a great bearing on the efficiency of the services. There are four important sheds with ghats in Kolkata. The Jagannath ghat is the largest and handles the major part of the cargo carried by steamers. It is situated near the Howrah bridge and has good warehousing and jetty facilities. With the increasing pressure on railways of the region, it has assumed considerable importance. It handled 5,38,596 tons of export and 602,000 tons of imports in 1950.

The next in importance is the Armenian Steamer Ghat which handles the export and import cargo bound to or coming from upper Cachar section of the Assam route. This Ghat, however, suffers from heavy silting and the lack of dredging equipments has hampered the movement of cargo. In 1950, it handled 10,500 tons of exports and 30,000 tons of imports. If no immediate steps are taken to dredge this Ghat, it may get silted to such an extent that it would have to be closed down.

The tea transit sheds which handle the incoming tea boxes from Assam are owned by the Joint Steamer Companies. The capacity of the sheds amounts to over 1,00,000 chests (each chest of 50 kg.). Approximately 75 per cent of the tea exported from Assam is handled by these sheds. The operations are still manual. The 'C-sheds' of the King Georges Docks are the last of the important Ghats where Inland water transport vessels deliver and receive cargo. It has an Inland water transport berth inside the dock basin.

(ii) *Safety Measures:* The vessels plying in Brahmaputra system of waterways are old and ill-equipped and lead to accidents involving lives and property. The Sundarban route is subjected to the tidal influences and hence its navigability depends upon the weather conditions prevailing in the Bay of Bengal. During the storms, the route becomes unsafe and unless the vessels are in the mid-stream, they have every chance of being thrown off and wrecked. Even in normal conditions, the vessels in distress, due to leakage or other unexpected occurances, cannot hope to receive help from outside. With a view to remove these difficulties, two immediate steps are called for. Firstly, an effort should be made to replace the old crafts and to modernize the fleet; and secondly, arrangements should be made to provide radio-telephone communication service, which would keep the vessels and their owners in touch with each other. In all advanced countries where Inland navigation is developed such as the U.S.A., West Germany, U.S.S.R. and France, such services are liberally available to transport companies engaged in Inland navigation.

(iii) *Night Navigation:* The companies provide hurricane lanterns to the steamers in night service. Although cheap and used for quite a long time, they require constant attention particularly in stormy weather. They cannot be kept alight during storms forcing the crafts to halt at night. This causes considerable delay affecting the scheduled delivery of cargo. To avoid these contingencies, it would be advisable to try lighting arrangements used by steamer companies in other countries. The 'Aga' automatic flashing beacon operated by gas contained in replenishable cylinders have been found to be suitable. These can be operated for several months without replenishing. Apart from this, the illumination of the relatively unsafe and difficult stretches of the channels by automatic beacons is also urgently called for. This will avoid frequent grounding vessels.

(iv) *Servicing of Vessels:* The servicing facilities for the crafts operating in Ganga-Brahmaputra waterways are sufficient if considered in relation to their capacity. The small country boats do not need much specialised labour and are repaired locally all along the channels. In the case of power propelled vessels with high tonnage capacity, the navigation companies are fairly well equipped to carry out maintenance and repair works. At Kolkata, the focal point of Inland waterways of north-east India, there are several well equipped workshops. Facilities have now been created at Pandu in Assam. The Garden Reach Workshop can undertake any docking and repairs job. They can handle 25 vessels to be shipped or decked at a time. The afloat repairs on deep sea vessels are also undertaken by them. The Workshop is equipped with mobile cranes and wheeled transport, and employs about 4500 men. The Rajabagan Dockyard an important yard of Kolkata, also extends repair facilities to Inland navigation vessels.

The repairs and maintenance facilities are, however, limited to Kolkata and Pandu ports and are scarcely available at other places on the route. This means that vessels going out of order hunderds of miles from these ports have to be brought to Kolkata or Pandu for repairs. It would certainly be desirable to extend these facilities to a few other places also, although Kolkata and Pandu have to remain as the main centres for this purpose. Initially, it would be advisable to have a few floating workshops, such as the one based at Guwahati, to meet the immediate requirement. Gradually, the provision of docking facilities including dry docks and slipway with ancillary provisions may be taken in hand.

(v) *Polical:* A scheme was prepared to link Kolkata with the Brahmaputra through a system of navigable channels passing through Indian Territory. It would provide a navigable channel, from the Ganga upstream of the barrage being constructed at Farakka along River Mahananda and Kosi canal up to Chatragorge. From there the channel would run along Tiesta canal up to the Jalpaiguri Barrage on the Tiesta. From this point a new canal would be constructed to join Brahmaputra at Dhubri. Preliminary investigations for this scheme have been completed, but no concrete steps have so far been taken to implement the scheme. Although the scheme looks very ambitious, it is not in anyway impracticable. If completed, it would not only solve the problem of sea-route to Kolkata and then from Kolkata to northern India, but will also, (with the Tiesta dam and barrage scheme coming into operation) connect Kolkata with Assam and North Bengal by navigable waterways. The cost involved is, however heavy and in the changed political circumstances in the region the scheme has to be considered afresh. It would be cheaper and more efficient to attempt a coordinated development of the Ganga and Brahmaputra system of waterways in cooperation with Bangladesh than to develop a new route at a great cost, at least in the immediate future.

6
Navigable Channels of South-Eastern States

A. Odisha

The State of Odisha forms part of a region of India which is very poorly served by modern transport network. Most of the railways and roads are confined to the coastal areas and run from north to south. The vast plateau that lies in the catchment area of river Mahanadi is still to be opened up economically and socially. Mahanadi river has acted as the main line of transportation from east to west through the centuries. In the deltaic region, numerous navigable canals taken out from Mahanadi supplement the railways and the roads.

1. Navigable Rivers

Mahanadi itself is the main navigable channel of Odisha. During the monsoons, it is navigable by country boats as far as Sambalpur from its mouth. In the dry periods of the years, the navigability is, however, limited to the stretch between its mouth and Dholpur. The river as a whole has a total length of about 300 miles in Odisha. The stretch between Sambalpur and Dholpur measures about 95 miles and is marked with rocky bed, swift-currents, and numerous rapids, making navigation in the river unsafe. From Dholpur, starts the sandy reach measuring 100 miles which ends at Cuttack. This stretch suffers from sudden shifts in the river channel, minor shoal formations, and bank erosion. From Cuttack to sea, is the deltaic reach of the river that divides itself into numerous spill-channels. This stretch of 65 miles is most important from the navigational point of view.

In 1951, the Government of India invited a French Mission of five engineers to study, among others, the navigational prospects in river Mahanadi. The mission suggested that the river could be made navigable up to Hirakud dam by suitable river training devices. They recommended that (1) a laboratory test should be carried out on a model of Mahanadi mouth; (2) detailed studies suggested in the main report should be conducted immediately; (3) the channels at the mouth of Mahanadi should be protected with backwaters; and (4) the proposed Paradip port should be located on river Mahanadi. The above suggestions are being carried out gradually, but no concrete step has so far been taken to improve the navigability of the river.

With the construction of the Hirakud dam 13 km. upstream from Sambalpur, the water supply in the river has been fairly regulated at 8,000 cusecs. Due to the absence of river conservancy and training, the draught available during dry periods of the year is no better than 3 feet. Boats of only 1.5 to 2 feet effective draught and 3 to 5 ton capacity can ply in the middle reaches of the channel. During rains, the effective draught increases and big country boats of Sambalpur type with 3.5 ft. draught and 8 ton capacity can navigate the channel. From Cuttack to the sea, Mahanadi is navigable by steamers. The Kendrapara and Taldana canals are linked with the tidal reaches of the river and are open to small launches and country boats.

The other navigable rivers of Odisha are Brahmani, Baitarni, Dharma, Subarnarekha, Burabalang, Matal, Karsua, Hansua, Maipara and Mahanadi-Hansua. River Brahmani is navigable by country crafts of 3 to 3.5 ft. draught for a stretch of 55 miles from its mouth throughout the year. River Baitarni has quite a deep estuary which allows coasters of 12 feet draught up to Chandbali, a distance of 25 miles from its mouth. It is open to country boats of 6 tons capacity for 15 miles from Chandbali. Like Baitarni, Dharma is also open to coaster steamers and country boats of 12 feet draught for a stretch of 16 miles from its mouth all through the year. Rivers Subarnarekha and Burabalang are navigable by country boats of moderate size and tonnage up to a distance of about 20 miles from their respective mouths. Other rivers, such as Moyapura, Hansua, Devi and several other interconnected creeks form parts of a system of tidal waterways measuring 134 miles. These are navigable by country boats and small steamers of 3 to 6 feet draught. Nature has endowed this region with a network of waterways through these estuaries and connecting cross channels comparable to Sundarbans of Bengal.

2. *Navigable Canals*

Odisha is the only State where canals are more important than rivers as navigable channels. These canals have served the transport requirements of the coastal plains of Odisha for over a century. Among the important canals are shown in Table 6.1.

Table 6.1: Important Canals of Odisha

1.	The High-level Canal Range I	5 miles 2750 feet
2.	The High-level Canal Range II	Non-navigable
3.	The High-level Canal Range III	18 miles 900 feet
4.	Kendrapara Canal	74 miles 2780 feet
5.	Taldana Canal	56 miles 3280 feet
6.	Odisha Coast Canal	9 miles
7.	Jaypore Canal	6 miles 2640 feet
8.	Gobri Canal	15 miles 2170 feet
9.	Gobri Extension Canal	6 miles 550 feet
	Total	**210 miles 4510 feet**

The High-level canals and Kendrapara and Taldana canals connect the town of Cuttack with the port of Paradip which has acquired great importance in recent years. These are irrigation-*cum*-navigation canals and are, therefore, financially sound. The High-level Canal Range I connects Cuttack with Jevapur on Brahmani while Range III connects Bhadrak on Solandi with Baitarni channel. The Range I canal has 3 locks of 150×20 feet dimensions and a minimum depth of 6 feet as designed originally, but the effective depth is now much reduced due to the silting of its bed. The Kendrapara Canal takes off from the Birupa anicut lake and falls in Jambo river about 10 miles west of Paradip port. It thus connects Cuttack with Chandbali as well as False Point Harbour. The existing depth of the canal varies from 4 to 5 feet, although the original design was adopted to provide a depth of 7 feet. There are 8 locks of 100 × 17 feet dimensions. Before the advent of the railways, the canal was the main artery of transportation; regular steamer services used to connect Cuttack with Chandbali Port *via* Kendrapara and Gobri canals and Brahmani and Baitarni rivers. These are linked with regular boat services to Kolkata *via* Matai Nallah and the Odisha Coast Canal. The Taldana canal starts from the right bank of Mahanadi near Cuttack town. Its outfall is in lower reaches of Mahanadi about 9 miles east of Paradip port. It has seven locks of 150×20 feet.

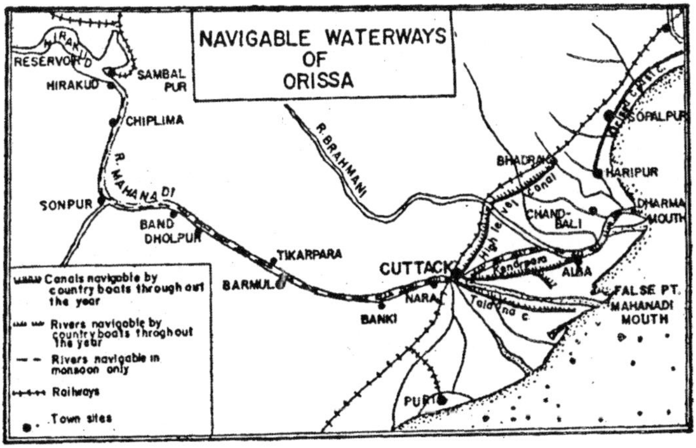

Fig. 6.1: Navigable Waterways of Odisha

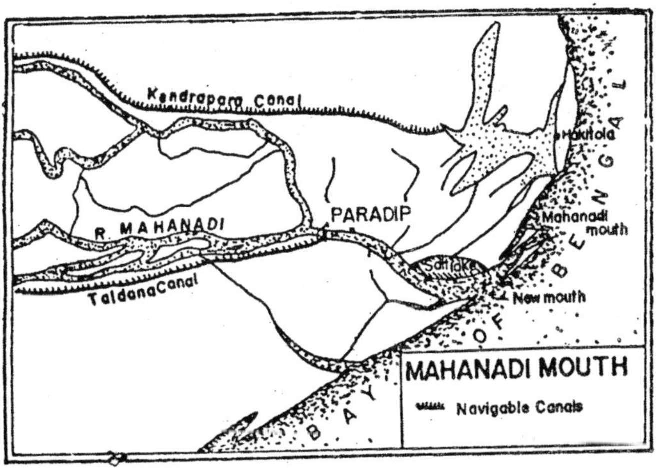

Fig. 6.2: Mahanadi Mouth

The Odisha Coast Canal connects Geonkhali on Hooghly with the Matai Nallah of Odisha. It was constructed in 1880 and is known as Hijli Tidal Canal between Hooghly and Rasulpur rivers. With the introduction of railways, the importance of the canal as a transport artery diminished considerably and a part of it measuring 37 miles is now left abandoned. The traffic on Hijli Tidal Canal has increased recently, but the navigational facilities are miserably poor. The lock gates are old and leaky and the toll charges are excessive. The toll rate in 1955 was Rs. 4.75 for 100 maunds of cargo. In 1952-53, the canal carried 19,000 tons of cargo whereas in 1955-56, it carried 46,975 tons, roughly 2.65 times increase in 3 years.

3. The Problems

Waterways are the chief modes of transportation in the deltaic districts of Cuttack, Balasore and Puri. But there are several drawbacks such as the silting of canals and poor organization of services which hamper the growth of traffic. A traffic survey conducted by the State Government in the fifties revealed these drawbacks and suggested the following measures to improve the situation:

1. Development of Inland water transport along the Paradip Port;
2. Development of canals and roads in such a manner that they play complementary and supplementary role with the railways;
3. Improve of the Delta canals;
4. Setting up of a Water Transport Corporation and through-booking with the railways; and
5. Development of a shipyard at Paradip.

The development of Paradip port as a major port is likely to have great bearing on the Inland waterways in Odisha. The minor port of Chandbali can only cater to ships up to 400 tons capacity. The region is full of natural wealth such as iron ore, manganese, coal, copper etc. A port capable of accommodating ocean liners will help in the exploitation of these resources. Simultaneously, with the development of the Paradip port, the canals and natural channels converging on it from all directions should be widened and deepened and if possible brick lined. These steps would make these channels fit for power propelled vessels as well. The navigability of Mahanadi in its sandy stretches between Dholpur and Cuttack should also be improved. The tidal creeks such as Brahmani and Baitarni which are navigable by sea-going liners and large steamers should also be improved by dredging and hydrographic surveys. The existing locks over the canals in Odisha are too narrow and limit considerably the size of the vessels that can navigate them. It would be desirable to adopt a uniform dimension of say 250 × 30 feet for all the canals. The opening up of Odisha Coast Canal between Matai Nallah and Subarnarekha will enable the movement of agricultural commodities between Odisha and West Bengal.

The traffic potentialities in the region are by no means small. Mahanadi alone may carry a traffic of about a million tons by 1985. At present it handles traffic consisting of bamboo, stone and agricultural produce to the tune of 1,25,000 tons.

B. Andhra Pradesh

I. Navigable Rivers

Godavari and Krishna are the two main rivers of Andhra Pradesh which along with their numerous tributaries debauch in the Bay of Bengal. These rivers have little similarities with those of the north and north-east Indian rivers. The sandy character of bed and large scale bank erosion are conspicuously absent here. The rocky and stony bed except of course in the lower reaches and particularly the deltaic parts, does not permit the shift of the course that is often witnessed in Ganga-Brahmaputra system of rivers. Being rainfed, the discharge of the river in extra-monsoon period is meagre and hence, a hindrance to navigation. The deltaic part of the river bed is criss-crossed by numerous irrigation-*cum*-navigation canals and the two deltas are interlinked by these canals form a simple network of navigable channels.

Godavari is the largest river of the Peninsular India. It rises in the Western Ghats at Triambak near Nasik. The total length of the river is about 1,500 km. It is navigable by crafts drawing 3 to 4 feets of water up to Chandrapatla, a distances of about 188 miles.

It is navigable by power propelled vessels such as steamers and launches for a distance of 100 miles. From there, it is open only to country boats up to Venkatapuram. From Venkatapuram, the river is navigable in rains alone. In dry months of March to June the navigability by large country boats and steamers is often confined to the stretch ending at Gannavaram, 90 miles upstream from, Dowlaishwaram anicut. The river has a number of rapids near Dummagudem anicut (183 km. above Dowlaishwaram). A by-pass canal with locks helps the crafts to circumvent this stretch of the river. No such facilities are however available at Dowlaishwaram anicut. River Sabari, a feeder of Godavari, coming from the north has its junction at Kunavaram. It is open to country boats of 2 to 3 feets draught during the monsoon up to Kumta. The catchment area of Godavari and its tributaries particularly of the Sabari and Sileru is immensely rich in mineral resources. The deltaic stage of the valley of Godavari is below Dowlaishwaram anicut. Thereafter, the river divides itself into several channels among which Gautami and Vasista are navigable in the stretches affected by tides. Both are navigable by crafts requiring 3 to 4 feets draught for 17 and 27 miles respectively. Other channels of navigational importance are Vyanteyam and Venamadura drains, both being navigable by small country boats for 16 and 10 miles respectively.

The Krishna is the second biggest river in south India. Rising from Mahabaleshwar, it has a course of 1,408 km. Its course is hilly. River Krishna is navigable by power propelled vessels and country boats up to 60 km. from its mouth throughout the year. From its anicut near Vijayawada, it is again open to mechanised vessels for about 15 miles throughout the year and thence to another 45 miles during the monsoon season. The river runs midway between the Vijayawada-Kazipet and Vijayawada-Guntakal rail lines of the Southern Railway Except Vijayawada there is no big industrial centre on this river. It can, however, be utilised economically and gainfully for transporting lime Kankar from Chintapalli, 44 miles upstream of its present navigable limit.

2. *The Delta Canals*

The deltaic plains of Godavari and Krishna are well served by irrigation-*cum*-navigation canals. These canals connect Kakinada and Masulipatnam, two important ports of the region with the industrial town of Vijayawada. Although not navigable by power propelled crafts, they form an important adjunct of the transport system of the area. Being the principal Carriers of cargo to the ports of Masulipatnam and Kakinada, the Masulipatnam and the Ellore canals are the busiest among them, The former handles about 2,50,000 tonne of cargo and the latter about 3,50,000 tonnes of cargo each year, a major portion of which is iron ore. The region being well served by other means of transportation, there is a coordinated movement of cargo. The Cannanore canal connecting the Krishna delta canals with the Buckingham canal in Tamil Nadu is also a useful link.

The details of the canals, their length, depth and the types of vessels plying on them is given in Table 6.2.

In addition to the delta, canals, there are two others which are sufficiently old and are of moderately long stretch. These are Kurnool-Cuddapah and Buckingham canals. The total length of Godavari and Krishna canals amounts to 904 miles (562 miles + 342 miles). The Kurnool-Cuddapah canal meaures 78 miles and the Buckingham canal 258 miles. The former takes off from river Tungabhadra, a tributary of Krishna a few miles upstream Kurnool town and meets river Pennar near Cuddapah. Originally, it was navigable all along its total stretch, but now, it is used for navigation only for about 15 miles west and 35 miles east of Kurnool town. A new canal known as Tungabhadra irrigation-*cum*-navigation canal has now been completed. This canal flows along the left bank of river Tungabhadra and is 127 miles long.

The canals of Godavari and Krishna systems suffer from several drawbacks as a result of which they are not able to see their full development as transport arteries. Constructed primarily for irrigational purposes, the supply of water depends upon the demand for it by agriculturists. They are virtually closed for about two months in summer. The effective depth of the canals is also limited to 3 to 4 ft. and hence even small country boats have to navigate them only partly loaded and the tonnage of crafts does not exceed 40. Under such circumstances power propelled vessels, if any, are confined to the tidal zones of the rivers and have no place in the canals. Certain canals like Kurnool-Cuddapah canal suffer from the disadvantage of not serving any important trading centre.

Table 6.2: Navigable Channels of Krishna and Godavari System of Rivers

Name of canal	Length in miles	Depth in feet		Types of vessels plying
		Head	Tail	
A. Godavari Eastern Delta Canal:				
1. Main canal	4	8	6	Country crafts and cargo vessels
2. Samalkota canal	33	7	6	
3. Cocanad canal	31	8	6	
4. Bank canal	40	—	—	
5. Mandapila canal	13	8.5	6	
6. Coringa canal	22	7	4.8	
7. Injaram canal	11	6.9	7.5	
8. Kovvur Manjoir jn. canal	9	7	3	
B. Godavari Central Delta Canal:				
1. Main canal	8	9.5	8.5	
2. Bank canal	35	8.1	7	
3. Gannavaram	37	7.6	6.55	
4. Amalapur canal	30	7.6	6	
5. Bendamur Lauka canal	2	6.5	6.3	
C. Godavari West Delta Canal:				
1. Main canal	6	10.7	8.7	
2. Kankarapara canal	10	9	7.5	
3. Bank canal	2.5	6.5	4	
4. Narasapur canal	30	7	4.5	
5. Ellore canal	40	8.7	5	
6. Attili canal	16	7	4	
7. Jn. canal	3	5.5	3.5	
8. Venkyya & Weyyaru canal	32	8.5	5	
9. Unpi canal	20	6.5	5.5	
10. Old Weyyaru canal	5	3.6	—	
D. Krishna Delta Canal:				
1. Eastern Delta main canal	0.5	8	—	
2. Ryves canal	22	6	—	
3. Ellore canal	40	9.6	51	
4. Masulipattnam canal	49	10.3	4.2	
5. East Bank canal	11	5	—	
6. Lower Pulleru canal	13	8.5	8	
7. Jn. canal	0.5	6.8	—	
8. Bantumilli canal	26	7.2	5.5	
9. Polraze canal	26	7	4.5	
10. Campbell canal	23	12	—	
11. Western Delta main canal	13	7.5	4	
12. W. Bank canal	46	6.8	—	
13. Connanur canal	58	5	4.5	
14. Nizamapattna canal	28	7		

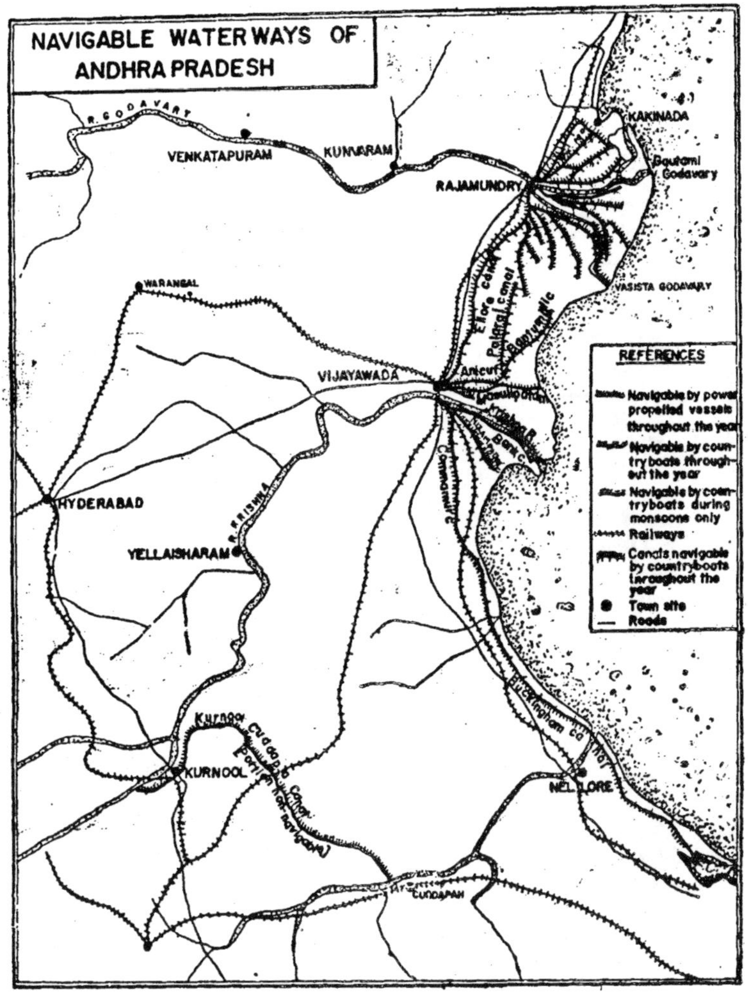

Fig. 6.3: Navigable Waterways of Andhra Pradesh

Prior to the construction of a railway line connecting Bailadilla with Visakhapatnam, bulk of iron ore was handled by two ports of Kakinada and Masulipatnam. The Ellore and Masulipatnam canals through which this ore moved to the ports are, however, primarily irrigational and remain closed for navigation for about 3 months. If the draught of these canals is increased by 1.5 feet their capacity to carry cargo would be doubled. With the lining of

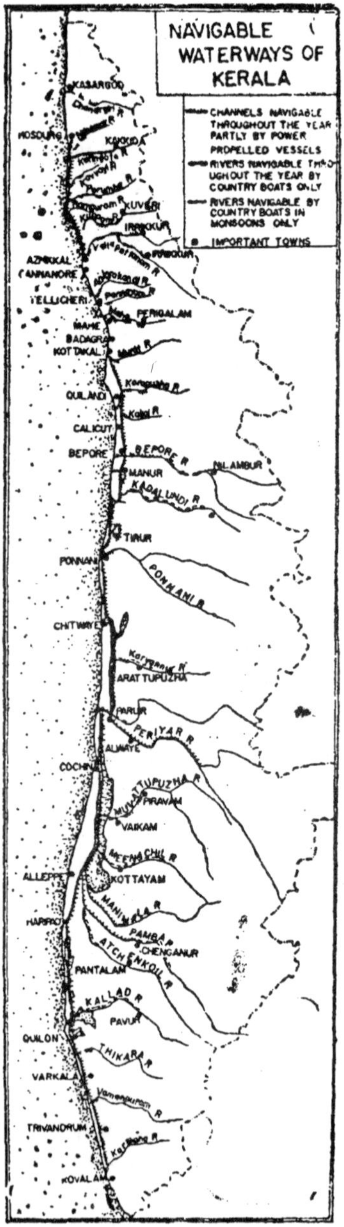

Fig. 6.4: Navigable Waterways of Kerala

the canals, it would be possible to use them for navigation by mechanised crafts also.

C. Tamil Nadu

Topography and climate have made Tamil Nadu almost devoid of natural channels for Inland navigation. There are no backwaters or lagoons in the State. Artificial canals are the only channels of Inland navigation.

1. Buckingham Canal

The Buckingham canal connecting Markannam backwaters in South Arcot (66 miles south of Chennai) with the canals of the Krishna and Godavari deltas is one of the oldest and longest navigable canals of the world. A short sketch of its historical background has already been attempted in Chapter 2. The canal follows the Coromandel coast for a distance of 262 miles, of which 160 miles lie in Andhra Pradesh and the remaining 102 miles in Tamil Nadu. With the Krishna and Godavari delta canals, it makes a continuous navigable stretch of about 400 miles from its southern tip to the port of Kakinada. The rivers of Tamil Nadu and Andhra Pradesh discharging in the Bay of Bengal, pose serious problems of maintenance of navigable depth in the canal. They fill the canal with

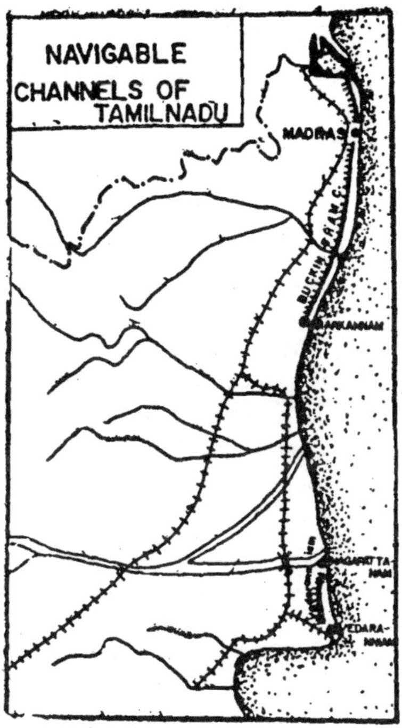

Fig. 6.5: Navigable Channels of Tamil Nadu

silt. There are 19 such crossings. Many of them dry up during summer and are navigable only at the tail end and that too during high tides. The Pennar river crossing is the most serious of all and requires desilting to the tune of over 7,00,000 tons every year. There are 28 locks in the canal, 21 in the northern section and 7 in the southern section. These are of 150×20 feet dimensions. A draught of 3 feet is available in the north canal and of 2 feet in the south canal.

The canal remained neglected for a longtime except for some intermittent repairs here and there. During the Second World War when the traffic increased and the railways, and roads failed to cope with it, greater attention was given to this canal. In 1943-44, it carried a peak cargo of 4.86 lakh tons. Since, then the traffic has tended to decline.

Table 6.3: Traffic on Buckingham Canal

Year	*Total Traffic hadled (Tonnes)*
1938-39	2,30,000
1943-44	4,80,000
1952-53	2,16,000
1953-54	1,21,003
1955-56	1,83,000
1956-57	2,71,000
1957-58	2,87,000
1965-66	2,00,000
1967-68	1,57,000

In view of the important role this canal plays in the transport economy of the States of Tamil Nadu and Andhra Pradesh, the former formulated a scheme to improve the navigability of the canal. The scheme contained several proposals but due to financial limitations, none of them could be taken up.

The proposals were:

1. Construction of wharfs and additional landing place between Barbar's Bridge and Mylapur Bridge in Chennai at a cost of Rs. 4.57 lakhs;
2. Improvement of existing inlets and outlets and construction of a few new ones at a cost of Rs. 85,000;
3. Improvement in the amenities of stall employed in the management of the canal at a cost of Rs. 60,000;
4. Revetting of slopes of the canal between Adyar and Cooum rivers in Chennai City at a cost of Rs. 3.01 lakh;
5. Revetting slopes in other places at a cost of Rs. 10.02 lakh;
6. Construction of quarters for lock establishment at a total cost of Rs. 1.27 lakh;
7. Raising and strengthening of canal banks at a cost of Rs. 1.55 lakh;
8. Purchase of 3 dredgers for the north canal at a cost of Rs. 3.10 lakh; and
9. Linking of Buckingham canal with the Vedaranyam canal in Tanjore District at a cost of Rs. 25 lakh.

From the point of view of navigation, the canal can be studied in three parts: (1) north of Chennai, (2) south of Chennai, and (3) the Cooum river which connects the two. The stretch of the canal north of Chennai city is known as North Buckingham canal. It is 316 km. long, 58 km. of which are in Tamil Nadu. Southern stretch is called South Buckingham canal. It is 102 km. long. The width of these canals varies from 20 to 30 ft. The minimum draught of the North Buckingham is 3 ft. and of S. Buckingham 2 ft. From its junction with the Connanur canal to the Swarnamukhi river, a stretch of about 120 miles, the North Buckingham canal can be safely depended upon for navigation by country boats of 3 ft. draught. In this stretch, the canal is well locked and the sea bars hardly assume serious proportions. The stretch between Kothapatnam and Mudigudi rivers, however, is narrow and silted.

In this stretch the banks are low and considerable quantity of fine clay is blown in causing siltation. The maintenance costs amount to over Rs. 7000 per mile as compared to the normal cost of Rs. 2,000 per mile in other closed reaches of the canal.

The second part of the canal south of River Swarnamukhi, is not in good condition. Numerous sea bars which obstruct the entrance for 4 to 6 months in a year, and the want of double locks at junctions with the east-west river channels, pose insurmountable problems for navigation. Although boats of 3 ft. draught can ply in this stretch also, the speed has to be slow and the movement cautious. Within the limits of Chennai City, the condition of the canal is very deplorable. The canal passes through the heart of the city collecting all the sewage and storm water of the city into the Cooum river which is the junction between the northern and southern canals. The outlet of the river being blocked for several months, the sewage of the city remains stagnant in pools polluting the canal and its environs. Recently, the Tamil Nadu Government took up the development of the river Cooum and the canal mainly with a view to clean them of the stagnant sewage. The banks of the canal are being paved and beautified. These developments will not only make the surroundings of the canal hygienic, but will also make the canal a better channel for navigation.

The southern canal offers a draught of 2 to 2.5 feet only and hence is not fit for cargo services. It is better suited to passenger traffic. Fortunately on this very stretch falls the famous religious township of Thiruporur which attracts thousands of people from the city of Chennai for monthly Krithigai festival. Here also are situated the seven Pagodas and the Vishnu temple, which are visited daily by the people of the nearby districts. In Covelong, there is a Church and a Mosque and both are frequently visited by the people. The southern canal offers passenger services to these pilgrims.

From the economic point of view, Buckingham canal is a losing concern and a drain on public exchequer. It passes through a region which is sparsely populated and the dense population to the west of the canal looks more to the parallel running railways and roads for carriage of goods and passengers than to it. Lack of proper approach roads has depopulated many coastal villages and driven the people to settlements in the interior and west of the canal. For example, the Ennore town once an attractive summer resort, has now lost its charm. The unkept bunglows along the canal bear testimony to this.

The non-availability of two way traffic is another drawback of the cannal. Chennai City is the focal point for boats coming from north and south loaded with rice, paddy, building materials firewood and other unfinished consumer goods. But Chennai itself has very little to offer to the returning boats. It must, however, be added that this canal is an essential link between the northern and southern parts of the eastern coast. It has assisted the region in tiding over the transport bottlenecks during wars and famines, and can, of course, play a similar role at the time of emergency in the future.

At present there are about 1300 locally made country boats of teakwood measuring 77×7 feet and 3 feet draught plying in the canal. They employ several thousand people. Further neglect of this canal would render it unsuitable for navigation. This in turn will lead to the unemployment of the people and greater pressure on the coastal railways and roads. To improve the navigability of the canal, at least to the present requirements of traffic, it should be thoroughly dredged to provide an effective year round draught of 4 feet. It should be connected with the Chennai Harbour to allow the boats to deliver goods on coasters, if need be. Special attention needs to be paid to the maintenance of channel at the river junctions. Construction of approach roads and a good tow path and adequate supply of fresh water at the locks will improve the efficiency of the canal. In addition to these, freight rates should be made more favourable and adequate terminal facilities such as transit sheds and warehouses should be built along the route. The problem of providing sufficient head-room under Park Station Railway Bridge near Penitentiary and the Railway Plate Girder Bridge at Elephant Gate should also be considered. An independent corporation should be set-up to carry out the development and maintenance of the canal.

2. *Vedaraniam Canal*

Vedaraniam canal, named after the town of the same name at its southern trip, takes off from the mouth of river Kudavayyar, a deltaic branch of Cauvery near Nagapattinam port. A look into the map of the region gives the impression that the objective of the planner of this canal must have been to provide ultimately a navigable channel from Nagapattinam to Markannam, the southern tip of Buckingham Canal. The existing state of the canal is rather miserable. It is silted up in several reaches. A number of straight drainage cuts and tidal inlets allow the flood water to enter the canal. These inlets bring considerable quantities of silt and deposit in the canal. A lock was provided at Karungani with a view to save the standing crops below the lock from flooding when the canal is in high floods. But the drainage cuts have made the lock now redundant and gates are permanently kept open except for a few weeks during summer when the drainage water is diverted to Nagapattinam port.

The canal was primarily meant for the movement of salt, fuel and rice. At present there are over 100 licensed boats, with carrying capacity of 7,000 tons of cargo, plying in the canal. In its hay day as many as 1000 boats used to ply. A regular dredging to maintain a depth of 5 ft. and an effective draught of 3 ft. for country boats would considerably improve the situation. In view of the cost involved, and the potential traffic diversion to the canal, it does not seem very alluring to connect the Buckingham with Vedaraniyam canal. This proposal had been put forth several times, but was always shelved on these two grounds. The Central Water and Power Commission has again revived it as a part of their scheme to have an interlinked canalised waterways all along the eastern and western coasts *via* Cape Comorin. The water transport Committee appointed by the State Government in 1967, estimated the traffic potential of 6 lakh tonnes by 1975-76 and 12 lakh tonnes by 1981.

7
Navigable Channels of South-Western States

A. Kerala

Geography has endowed Kerala not only, with ample opportunities for the development of Inland navigation, but has also placed several restrictions on the expansion of other modes of surface transportation. This is the reason why Kerala waterways have always played an important role in the transport system of the State.

The State has forty one west flowing streams—medium and small—and all of them are navigable by large country boats at least to a few kilometres from the sea. The gradients of these rivers in the tidal stretches is very gentle. Interconnecting these streams, are numerous lagoons and backwaters. They are linked with each other by artificial canals. All these together offer a well-knit system of waterways in the State, the total length of which is about 1,700 km.

The entire system of waterways of the State can be divided into three sections: the northern, the middle and the southern. The Vembanad lake (200 sq. km.) forms the centre of Kerala's Inland waterways. The southern limit of the northern section is Ponnani. From Ponnani to Quilon extends the middle section and from Quilon to Trivandrum and beyond, the southern section. The main north-south artery of Inland navigation is the West Coast Canal.

Unlike the eastern coast, the coast of Kerala is densely populated. Much of agriculture and industry is along the backwaters. The inadequacy of rail communication is an added advantage to the waterways. Due to dense population, being one of the highest in India, mass education (over 60% literacy), and plantation agriculture, the mobility of the people and the goods is very high. The waterways are important carriers of both. Their most famous traveller, in the past, was Pierre Loti who took a French decoration to the ruler of Travancore and travelled through the waterways.

The backwaters of Kerala have the same economic and social significance for the region that Ganga has for northern India. It was here at Anjengo, now a deserted place, that the first settlement of the East India Company on the west coast was started. Here was built a fort which commanded the spice trade for many decades. There was indeed a time when it was only second to Mumbai on this coast in matters of trade and commerce.

An idea of the existing navigable channels and their characteristics can be had from the list of the waterways given in Table 7.1. Unless stated otherwise, all the channels mentioned in table are navigable by motor-boats, Vallams and barges suitable for cargo and passenger services.

The portion of the West Coast Canal connecting Hosdurg with Azhikkal is known as Sultan Canal in its lower reaches. The Azhikkal port located at the tail end of this canal handles about 30,000 tons of cargo. The general condition of the canal has considerably deteriorated due to lack of maintenance. Although effective draught available is still sufficient, the lagoonous conditions prevailing on both sides of the canal make it unwelcome to the boatmen. Handling facilities are conspicuously lacking all along the canals specially at Azhikkal port. From Azhikkal to Badagra, a distance of 29.5 miles there is no navigable channel at present.

Calicut and Beypore are the other two important ports on Badagra-Baypore section of the canal, which together handle nearly 30,000 tons of cargo annually. From Beypore to Cochin, the navigation is handicapped in several ways. This stretch has a narrow lock of 50 x 12.5 feet dimensions at Payoli. The road bridge at Ponnani has a head clearance of 6 feet only, making the passage of large Vallams and country boats difficult. The depth of the channel in different stretches is also inadequate for Vallams of 10 to 12 ton capacity. The Conolly canal, the name given to the waterway in this area, is too narrow for Vallams.

Alleppy is the most important Inland port of Kerala. From here radiate four major routes to the north, west and south *via* Vembanad lake in the north, Pamba and Pantalam rivers in the

Table 7.1: Navigable Waterways of Kerala

1. *Trivandrum-Shorapur (Length in miles)*	*(T.S.) Canal (178 miles)*	*Depth in feet*
0-40		4
40-45	Ashtemudi lake	7
46-48	-do-	4
49-59	do and backwaters	7
60-67	Kayamkulam lake	5
68-74	Thrikunnapuzha river	8
75-78	Karithodu	4
79-88	Pamba river and Vadaikayal	6
89-111	Vembanad lake	8
112-123	do	8
124-132	Waterways	12
133-148	Vambanad lake	7
149-173	Enamakkal	5

2. *Branches from T.S. Canal*	*Length in miles*	
	Depth	*in feet*
45th mile to Pattakadavu	9	6
60th mile to Kayamkulam	5	4
83rd mile to Ambalapuzha	4	3
88th mile to Changanacherry in Pamba R.	35	5
via Vattakayal and in Pamba R.	19	6
to Kottayam	18	7
to Shertallai	11	7
111th mile to Kottayam	18	4
to Upanchira	10	4
to Neendur	12	3
123rd mile to Shertallai	14	5
to Kuthiathodu	9	3
132nd mile to Kottapuram	20	6
to Varapuzha	8	10
to Narkal Bunder Canal	8	6
to Cheriapatti	14	8
to Kundoor	22	8
Kalado river from lake to mouth	4	6.5

3. *Pamba River*	*Length in miles*	*Depth in feet*
From Kuthiathodu to Vembanad lake *via* east of Thalavadi, Pulikeezhu, Chakolam, Edathua Champakulam, Munnattamulkkam and Kaina-karya etc.	31	4
From Chakolam to Vembanad lake *via* Muttar,		

3. *Pamba River (Contd.)*	*Length in miles*	*Depth in feet*
Kidangare, Palimkunnu, Monkombu and Munna, the Kubhom and Kuttamangalam.	21	4
Kidangara to Vembanad lake *via* north of Velianadu and Kavalam etc.	15	3
Kidangara canal from Changanacherry to Pamba river at Kidangara	5	3
Kottayam Puthen Thodu-from Kottayam boat jetty to Vembanad lake at Vettikad	5	4
Erakkodi canal from Ambalapuzha to Pamba River	1.5	3
Alleppy-Ambalapuzha canal	7	3
Pullincunnu Puthenthodu to Kavalam Junction	3	4
Kavalamputhenthodu from Kaimakari to Kavlam	6	4
Kainadithodu from Kavalam junction to Vembanad lake	4	4
Kottayam Changanachrry canal via Pallam	12	4
Kumarkom canal	2	4
Kumarkom canal Athirampuzha	8	6

4. Other navigable channels	*Length in miles*	*Width in feet*	*Negotiable by*
Muvathipuzha		3	Vallam only
Arithodu	3	4	-do-
Pennarthodu	5	4	-do-
Puchakal canal	1.25	3	-do-
Muhamma canal	1.5	3	boat and Vallan
Changadam canal	1	4	-do-
Main backwater from Edacochin to Ernakulam	10	40	Ships and others
Rivers and canals from Cherai to Puthussery	12	8	motor boats etc.
Rivers and canals from Parur to Mala	16	8	Motor boats etc.
Rivers and canals from Narkal to Eloor	8	6	-do-
Rivers and canals from Olloor to Kundoor	10	8	-do-

west and the backwaters to the south. With further development of Cochin Port, it has recently lost its importance at least partly. It now handles nearly 20,000 tons of cargo as against 100,000 tons handled earlier. At present there are over 100 power propelled vessels plying on 8 different routes in Alleppy. They are all local passenger services. The Alleppy-Shertallai canal has silted down to a great extent and the State Government is attempting to further develop it. At present petroleum is being transported annually between Cochin and Quilon *via* this route and the oil companies expect this traffic to further increase through time. If the draught of Quilon-Trivandrum channel is increased, the movement of oil to Trivandrum would become easier. The Verkalla tunnels poses a serious problem here as their head room is inadequate for big barges. The width of the tunnels is also only 14 feet unsuited to large country boats and barges. South of Trivandrum, the 6.5 miles of canal is utterly neglected.

The Government of Kerala has a plan to develop the Inland waterways of the State. This includes the maintenance of sufficient depth and width of the north-south channel from Trivandrum to Badagra and Azhikkal to Hosdurg, and the construction of a link canal between Azhikkal and Badagra.

The Gokhale Committee on Inland Water Transport recommended the following measures to improve the navigability of the waterways of Kerala State.

1. Both the locks at Thotapalli on Alleppy-Shertallai canal should be operated to avoid delay in traffic movement.
2. Narrow stretches of the channel should be provided with navigation aids such as lights fixed on mooring posts.
3. The Irriyad-Quilon waterways should be dredged deep to provide an effective draught of 6 ft. at normal water level.
4. The busy side of Quilon jetty should also be dredged and adequate terminal facilities should be provided at Quilon, Alleppy and other places.
5. Tow-walls on the sides of canals at Alleppy and other places should be repaired.
6. The earth dams between Ponnani and Chetwai should be replaced by locks of 150x20 feet dimensions.
7. The existing locks north of Cochin should be replaced by 150x20 feet locks.
8. The stretch between Cochin and Badagra should be maintained to provide an effective depth of 5 feet in normal water level and a bed-width of 30 feet.
9. Road bridges should have a minimum head-room of 16 feet.
10. The proposed extension of canal from Badagra to Male should be designed to have a minimum bed-width of 30 feet and effective draught of 5 feet.
11. Same standard of 30 feet bed-width and 5 feet effective depth should be applied to the stretch between Quilon

and Trivendrum also. In rocky areas the width may be reduced to 20 feet.

Over four million tonnes of goods move annually on over 20,000 crafts plying in Kerala waterways. Some of these crafts are mechanized. During the last few years, the number of country crafts has increased, while the number of mechanized crafts has declined. With the industrialization of the State, prospects of Inland navigation have further improved. Such industrial products like fertilizers, cement, tiles, bricks, hardware, petroleum, timber, coir products, sugar etc. now being produced in the State can be handled by the waterways more efficiently. There is a great scope for the development of passenger services in the water-locked areas of Central Travancore stretching from Ernakulam to Quilon, Alleppy-Kottayam, Changanacherry, Chengannur and Mannar.

B. Karnataka

Unlike the continuous stretch of Inland waterways in the Coastal strip of Kerala, the coast of Karnataka State between Mangalore and Karwar is conspicuous by the absence of any through communication system. With the construction of the West Coast Highway, the situation has improved. The West Coast rivers of Karnataka are short and violent, and rush from heights of 2 to 3 thousand feet without any interruption of gradient till they come close to the coast. They do, however, form a few lagoons and backwaters which afford easy navigation. A scheme was chalked out by the State Government to construct a canal between Coondapur at the mouth of river Haladi and Mangalore, but it had to be abandoned partly because of the construction of the West Coast Highway and partly because of the lack of provision for such a channel in the Mangalore Harbour Project.

The following are the important rivers and creeks of the State which are navigable by country crafts.

1. Kalinadi
2. Gangavalli
3. Aghanashini
4. Sharavathy
5. Venkatapur
6. Bhatkal
7. Baindur
8. Kollur
9. Chakranadi
10. Kubjanadi

11. Haladi
12. Sitanadi
13. Swarnanadi
14. Udyavar
15. Mulki
16. Pavanje
17. Gurpur, and
18. Netravati

There are over 4000 crafts plying in the creeks and rivers like Kalinadi, Gangavalli, Aghanashini and Sharavathy, employing about 6000 people in north Kanara District. In Kalinadi, there are 10 boats of 7 tons berthen each carrying both cargo and passenger, and about 300 small doneys of less than 3 tons each used mainly for fishing. In Gangavalli, ply 40 large boats and 80 small doneys transporting mainly timber. Aghanashini is navigable for 81 miles from its mouth. This river is famous for fishing and as many as 1000 small doneys of average dimensions of 16x2 feet are in operation in the creek and the adjoining high seas. Their approximate tonnage would be about 2000. Sharavathy, the last but one big river of the Western Coast of Karnataka (the last being Netravati) has an extensive entrance and a brisk trade. The river is sufficiently deep to be navigable up to Gersoppa, a distance of 18 miles. Vessels of 100 ton berthen can enter the port of Honavar and take shelter at about 200 yards off the bar where the depth of the river is 40 to 50 feet.

Karnataka State has built an irrigation-*cum*-navigation canal recently. The canal takes off from Tungabhadra reservoir in Raichur district and runs for a total length of 225 km. The navigable stretch starts at 38th km. and ends at 160th km. The canal is 16 metres wide and carries a depth of 3 metres at full supply level. Known as the Tungabhadra Left Bank Canal, it passes through an agriculturally rich area. The existing traffic on the canal is of the order of 2.5 lakh tonnes. By 1980, the traffic is likely to treble.

C. Goa

Goa, though small in area, has 555 km. of Inland waterways. Only one-third of this is, however, navigable. Two major rivers Mandovi and Zuvari, together with Cumbarjua canal form the main channels of Inland water communication. The hilly terrain of the State, makes the construction of railways and roads difficult and costly. With the increasing flow of minerals specially iron ore to the Marmugao port for export, the demand for new transportation facilities has increased. In this context, the role of the Inland waterways has to be reassessed.

Mandovi, with its tributaries, provides 88 km. long navigable channels. Mandovi itself is navigable for 62 km. and can accommodate barges of 300 ton capacity up to Usgaon, 41 km. upstream from its mouth. Zuvari is 145 km. long, of which 64 km. are navigable. It also takes barges of 300 ton capacity. The barges can go up to Sanvarden where iron ore loading jetties are built. The depth of Sanvarden is, however, shallow and hence, the loaded barges have to wait for high tides to navigate it.

The Cumbarjua canal links Mandovi and Zuvari rivers. It take off from Tonca on Mandovi (about 11 km. from Panaji) and runs for 17 km. in north-south direction to connect with Agacaim on Zuvari.

The iron ore mines of Goa are located in close proximity to the navigable channels. Both Mandovi and Zuvari are used for ore traffic. Mandovi's mouth, however, has a bar called Aguada which hinders the movement of larger vessels. The traffic has, therefore, to pass through Cumbarjua canal. The canal is, however, navigable by 500 tons capacity barges only during the high tides. The first five miles of the canal from Mandovi is very narrow. Widening of the canal to 35 metres and further deepening of it to 3.5 metres would make it an excellent channel for Inland navigation.

About 60,000 dead weight tonnes of shipping is in operation in Goa's Inland waters. Many of the vessels are old and need replacement. The Chowgule & Co., have started manufacturing 1,000 tonnes barges in the yard at Sirigao. The Government also has a workshop for the repairs of their vessels at Betin.

8
Navigable Channels of Western States

A. Maharashtra

Maharashtra State has numerous minor ports on the western coast between Goa and Bassein creek in addition to the major port of Mumbai. This region is very poor in communications, and coastal steamer services are the only means cf transport and communications. There are a number of streams and creeks which penetrate into the Konkan coastal plain for 4 to 40 km. The tidal limits of these rivers permit the coasters to enter Inland. Regular passenger service is maintained by the Mumbai Steamer Navigation Company Ltd., between Mumbai, Rewas and Dharmavatar port on the mouth of River Amba.

There are as many as 44 tidal rivers and creeks having a total length of 929 km. Important among these are Auranga, Vaitarni, Ulhas, Thana, Panvel, Patal Ganga, Amba, Kundalika, Savitra, Vashishti, Shashtri, Ratnagiri, Purnagad, Jaitapur, Vijayadnag, Devgad, Karli and Terekhol. Among the creeks, Thana and Bassein are the important ones.

In the absence of any other means of transportation steamer services originating at Mumbai are the main means of communication for the coastal settlements. The rivers and creeks of this coast assume, therefore, special importance, even though they might appear very insignificant from the national point of view. The details of the navigational services rendered by these waterways are given in Table 8.1.

Apart from the rivers and creeks of the Konkan coast there are two lakes in Poona district that have acquired some navigational importance. Lake Whiting at Bhatgar provides water connection between Bhatgar dam and Basarapur, Harnas, Pasure, Masuli, Rajghar, Karandi Bank, Walwandi, Kambre, Nanavade,

Table 8.1: The Navigable Waterways of Maharashtra Coast

	Name	*Length from mouth (in miles)*	*Depth in spring tide (in feet)*	*tonnage of crafts*	*Remarks*
1		2	3	4	5
1.	Kelwa creek	1	3 to 4	Small crafts	Local knowledge necessary
2.	Vaitarni River	1	Shallow	do	-do-
3:	Bassein creek	1	12	-do-	-do-
4.	Manori creek	8	8	20	At high tide only
5.	Vasava Malad creek	1	15	200	-do-
6.	Mahim Bandra creek	1	8	45	-do-
7.	Thana creek	8	10-25	200	-do-
8.	Panval creek	6	6	30	-do-
9.	Dharmavatar creek	1	25	300	-do-
10.	Awas creek	1	Shallow	Fishing boats only	-do-
11.	Thai creek	At mouth only	8	8	Only at high tide
12.	Varsoli creek	-do-	5	Small crafts	entrance is rocky
13.	Theron-Pada creek	2	20	100	at high tides
14.	Theroh-Pada creek	at mouth only	6	Small -do-neys	-do-
15.	Kundalika River	4	12	100	Sand bar
16.	Kal River	2	12	40	high tide only
17.	Savitri River	2 & 26	12 & 8	70 & 25	sand bar
18.	Kalshi creek	2	9	30-	
19.	Ada creek	2	5	15	
20.	Paj creek	3	6	15	—
21.	Vashishti River	7	11	75 to 100	
22.	Jaigad creek		2,4 & 8	30, 20. & 10	100, 200 & 20 Steamships
23.	Varada creek	1	10	25	
24.	Ganpattipula creek	2	7	Fishing -do-neys	
25.	Nevra creek	—	—	not available	
26.	Kalbadevi creek	1	15	50 not deep	
27.	Rajiwad creek	2.5	19 to 15		
28.	Ranpar creek	—	—	—	Not navigable
29.	Pamagad creek	12	8 to 10	30 to 40	
30.	Jaitapur creek	2	10	50	
31.	Vijayadurg creek	3 & 20	12 &5	750	Small crafts
32.	Deogab, creek	7	12	100	Safe harbour
33.	Mubri creek	—	—	—	Not navigable
34.	Mitbhav creek	—		—	Not navigable
35.	Achra creek	2.5	10	25	At high tides
36.	Kalvali creek	4	8	8	In fari season
37.	Mobar creek	5 & 12	18&8	75 & 10	
38.	Kochra creek	4	6	8	
39.	Kulus creek	—	—	—	Not navigable
40.	Vengurla creek	3 & 4	5	5	largo ships anchor in the sea
41.	Mochemad creek	—	—	—	Not navigable
42.	Redi creek	1.5	6	8	At high tides.
43.	Tenekhol creek	20	7	10	At high tidds

Male, Bhotanda and Sangli all adjoining the lake, the depth of which varies from 50 to 143 feets. Country boats and launches ply in the lake. The total distance of the above mentioned villages from the dam site is 168 miles. In the Mulshi Lake, bank to bank services are available for both cargo and passengers. The traffic is, however, mostly limited to passenger services. Launches and barges as well as ferry boats are available during the day.

Navigation in the rivers and creeks of the Western coast (from Kanyakumari to Mumbai) is considerably handicapped by the sand bars formed at their mouths and the unusual silting of their tidal limits. The rivers being small, navigation has naturally to be coastwise. If these rivers are open, the vessels can easily enter the Inland coastal plain and meet the communication needs of the people. A few of the rivers have rocky entrances. In such rivers, the vessels have to wait for high tides before they enter the creeks and that also only with the help of such people who know the behaviour of the rivers and the tides locally. For efficient navigation and development of this industry, the dredging of the large shoals, sand banks and bars is necessary.

The boatmen of this coast are unorganized. The system of one man one boat prevails and hence they generally compete against each other. It would be advisable to organise boatmen's co-operatives which could not only initiate systematic and organized work of transporting goods and of fishing, but also arrange for the collection of fish caught by the individual boatmen and selling it in market at favourable prices. In the recent past several such cooperatives have come up, but still a large number of boatmen have no real links with them.

B. Gujarat

Gujarat has two major navigable rivers, Narmada and Tapi, in addition to a number of smaller ones like Mahi, Mindhola, Purna, Ambika, Auranga and Par. They together provide navigable channels of 312 km. in the State. Narmada is navigable by steamers in its tidal stretch of 66 km. Thereafter, it is navigable by sailing vessels for about 100 km. Tapi is navigable in its tidal reaches—a distance of 25 km. Purna is also navigable for about 15 km. from its mouth.

Narmada was navigable by 12 feet draught vessels upto Bharuch in the past. The channel is now silted and several bars are formed between the sea and Broach. The main shoals are at Kukarwara, Samari, Meghaum, Dasan, and Warva. These sand-bars-shift their position. Tapi also has some bars between its mouth and Surat. The main bar of 3 km length is close to the mouth of the river.

There are serious problems in the development of Inland navigation in Narmada and Tapi, specially in the reaches beyond Broach and Surat. The gradient of the valley is steep and there are rocky outcrops making navigation unsafe. The water level also fluctuates too drastically between the monsoon and dry seasons. Vessels take 5 days to navigate 48 km. from the mouth of Narmada to Broach.

In the past, both Narmada and Tapi were navigable channels of international importance. Broach and Surat, the two river ports of western India had a unique place in the maritime trade of the country. But today no more than 25,000 tonnes of cargo is handled by these ports. A new Inland port has been constructed at Magdala 10 km. downstream of Surat and about 15 km. from the sea. Magdala has a 350 feet long RCC jetty, three mobile cranes of 5 tonnes capacity each and three warehouses. It also has other facilities such as water, electricity and approach roads to important centres like Surat. It is equipped to handle 60,000 tonnes of cargo annually. The traffic potentials of this port are likely to go up to 200,000 tonnes by 1975, provided that some of the sand bars are dredged out.

The Gulf of Khambhat separates the Inland Gujarat from the Kathiawar peninsula. Dahej at the mouth of Narmada is being developed as a lighterage port. The distance between Dahej and Ghogha (near Bhavnagar) is only 50 km. by water, but 443 km. by rail. There is a great, potential for the development of ferry services between these two points.

C. Jammu & Kashmir

The length of navigable waterways of the State of Jammu & Kashmir is about 200 km. Jhelam is the principal waterway. Water transport is, however, developed only in the Khanabal-Baramula stretch of the river. The other rivers important for navigation are

Vishow and Sind, Dal, Manasbal and Wular lakes have their own significance for Inland navigation.

There are over 4000 boats plying in Kashmir lakes employing over 10,000 people. In addition to these, there are about 2,500 'Khatchurs' (cargo barges) employing about 10,000 people. As the recreation facilities in Kashmir improve and the exploitation of natural resources such as timber takes place, the traffic potentials of the Inland waterways will further improve.

9
Rehabilitation of Inland Waterways

Rehabilitation of Inland waterways in India involves action in many directions. The development of a self-paying water transport system requires systematic and effective river training and conservency measures, canalization in areas unserved by rivers, introduction of modern vessels suitable for draughts available locally and a well-knit administrative machinery to coordinate the multiple agencies engaged in this and other modes of transportation. Thus, the problems and issues related to the rehabilitation and development of Inland waterways fall under four heads—physical, technical, administrative and economic.

A. Physical Problems

For purposes of navigation, there are certain physical requirements of channels that must be fulfilled. These are: (i) sufficient depth of water, (ii) absence of violent currents, and (iii) stability of water in the channel. The depth of water depends mainly on the nature of the watershed and on the width of the river bed. A catchment area devoid of vegetation, cannot hold water long and hence such rivers are subjected to violent gust of water during rains and almost trickling flow during dry seasons. Likewise, the rivers whose channels are narrow, are apt to have deeper course than those which have several parallel channels in the bed or have a very wide channel. The speed of the currents depends upon the gradient through which the river flows. In the hilly tracts where gradient is too steep and where the gradient is interrupted by falls and rapids, the currents are violent and fast whereas in plains where gradient is gentle, they are moderate. The speed of the current also depends upon the discharge of the river. During rains when the rivers are flooded, the speed of currents in the Ganga often increases four times. Thus, the devices which can hold the water from flowing down to the lower reaches would not only ensure sufficient-depth of water in the channel but would also ensure to a certain extent a non-turbulant flow.

Stability of the water channel depends upon the erosive capacity of the river, the supply of water from the source and tributaries, and the nature of the river bed itself. In the absence of stability, the main channel of the river shifts from bank to bank and instead of maintaining one deep channels, it maintains multitude of channels all too shallow for navigational purposes. It is more so during the dry seasons and is probably one of the greatest problems of river navigation in Ganga and its tributaries.

The above mentioned problems are far less difficult in such channels as that of Amazon in Brazil, where ecological balance is not yet disturbed appreciably. Unfortunately, this is not so in India. In India of Vedic and even *Ramayana* times, almost every part of the country was covered with forests. At that time, Ganga must have been in the same natural condition in which Amazon, probably is now, the duly major river of the type is at present. The climate at that time and until the forests were felled must have been temperate as recorded by Fa-Hien. The general flow of the Ganga was, at that time, controlled by these forests. Gradually, the cultivable virgin land was opened up for crop raising. As the forests were cleared off, the balance that was maintained in the nature was disturbed and the floods and droughts started visiting the valley frequently.

Thus, to tackle the physical problems of navigation through river training and conservancy, we have first of all to try to re-establish the ecological balance in nature. And since, in view of the social and economic conditions prevailing now, it can be done only in the long run, we have to adopt certain immediate measures to tackle the problems. These measures are discussed later. Here, we will go into further details of the natural balance, the establishment of which will not only help navigation, but will also lead to the general prosperity of the country as a whole.

The immediate result of deforestation is soil erosion which brings in a multitude of problems for Inland navigation. Disastrous floods in rains and just a trickle of water during the summer are the direct consequences of the heavy denudation of the soil in river a intracts. In areas where vegetation in its luxurious forms still exists, the soil is saved from exhaustion and denudation. Vegetation not only keeps the water arrested, but also enables the soil to absorb it. The ground water thus created comes up on the surface during the succeeding dry season by capillary action of the soil. It also raises the water table which ultimately supplies water to the rivers through numerous pores and springs not only at the head of the river, but also on its way.

The absence of vegetation cooperates with the torrential rains to remove the surface soil. As the water gets muddier, the capacity of the soil to absorb it further declines and hence, it flows down the slope collecting more and more silt. The silt ladden water gains still more strength to corrode and erode the soil. It rushes through gullies that it forms while moving down, and greater the slope, greater the power it possesses to form gullies and collect the silt. On gentler slopes, the water runs in sheets instead of gullies and causes sheet erosion. Along the steep slopes, the silt-ladden water strikes the softest strata of the soil, collects the loose earth and gushes down to strike other obstacle on its way. Thus, the land on both sides of the valleys present a picture of desolation, devoid of any vegetation, natural or man-made, and a topography suited more to wild animals and anti-social elements of the society like robbers, dacoits and thieves than to the civilized men.

The silt ladden water as it flows into the river, disturbs the peaceful flow of the stream and strikes against the banks at every possible bend. The water becomes still more muddy and hence erodes faster. As it flows down, more and more water pours in from many tributaries and its volume and velocity increases. And as the velocity increases, the carrying capacity of the river also increases. The river thus collects more and more silt desolved in water. When the slope becomes gentle the velocity decreases, these materials get deposited in and along the stream bed.

Geomorphologically, the course of a river can either be young mature or old. In its young stage of valley development, the river is torrential and violent, cutting across anything that comes in its way. The gradient is steep and is marked with frequent occurrences, of falls and rapids. In its mature stage, the valley becomes gentler. The volume of water increases, but the velocity is not fast enough to erode the banks or the bed. The channels of such rivers are deep narrow and meandering. In its last stage, velocity of water slows down and the volume of water and the width of the river course increases. The erosive and corrosive power of the river is reduced. As the velocity decreases, the materials kept by the river in suspension start settling down, layer after layer, the coarser materials form the bottom layers.

Indian rivers are marked with all the three stages of valley formation. But the main problems of navigation are confined to their last stage. If the velocity decreases too rapidly, the deltaic conditions develop miles above the actual delta. In such rivers, navigation without river training involving dredging or *bandalling* is impossible. The total mass of mud brought down to the sea by the Ganga and Brahmaputra rivers annually is nearly 2,500 million tons, of which at least 1,500 million tons are brought down to the delta and deposited in the Bay of Bengal discolouring the water for about 750 miles from the coast.

For the last 200 years or so, Indian rivers, particularly those of north arid north-east India, become very violent in rains creating an unending chain of floods. The main cause of this is not far to see. The indiscriminate felling of forests in the upper reaches of the rivers is the fundamental cause for this change in the behaviour of rivers. Forests protect the soil from being eroded in many ways. They do not allow the drops of rainwater to strike the earth surface directly by providing a protective cover of fallen leaves. The grasses growing under them and their roots also protect the soil from erosion. By protecting the soil from the direct rays of the sun, they also helps the soil retain its accumulated moisture.

The forest wealth of India was destroyed due to three main reasons. Firstly, the invaders from the north-west in the early part of our history burnt the forest indiscriminately to have their way clear for further penetration. Secondly, the growing population compelled people to fell the forests for cultivation, and thirdly, the administration did not pay much attention to the protection of forests. In fact, at times it became party to the destruction of the forest wealth. Up to 1750, deforestation was resorted to for cultivation alone, but since then great demand for Indian timber in foreign as well domestic markets encouraged indiscriminate felling of trees. The advent of railways opened up new forest areas hitherto left virgin for commencial exploitation.

Williams in his memoir of the Doon mentions that during 1837-1843, "everyone continued to hack and hew away at trees as he pleased, only paying certain dues to the farmer, in the event of the wood being exported. Reckless waste was inevitable and the fine *sal* forests began to disappear rapidly. The absence of conservancy was absolute. The district still abounded in fine trees 100 to 200 years old and upwards. All these fell before them and probably the rest would have gone with them had the roads been a little better." So was, the case with the whole of India.

Unless the previous balance of nature between rainfall and vegetation is at least partly, restored, the erosive power of the running water cannot be substantially checked and unless the latter is done effective river training will not only be costly, but also undependable. In the interest of navigation and of general public welfare a forestation seems to be essential and must not be delayed any more. First of all, steps should be taken to a forest the areas in the upper reaches of the rivers which are hilly and desolate and of little consequence to agriculture. If the catchment area is covered with vegetation, the floods would be reduced, velocity of river decreased and hence the erosive power also decreased. But a forestation in the catchment areas alone would not solve the problem. The banks of the rivers and the adjoining areas are equally affected by erosion. Devoid of vegetation, the river currents strike the banks and erode them from the bottom leading to cliff formation and making the river water muddier. To check this, a forestation along the banks is essential.

The idea behind the preventive methods to stop soil erosion or to conserve the soil is to reduce excessive run-off of rainwater. This cannot be achieved by a forestation alone, although it would probably go a long way in solving the problem. Soil conservation methods like contour ploughing of fields, restricted grazing of grass land, terracing, contour hedging and ditching must supplement the afforestation measures. It must, however, be added that all these measures alone cannot eliminate floods altogether. They only allow that much soil, run-off which nature can bear without any loss of soil fertility.

Post-independence trends in forest development are indicative of the fact that the Government and the people of India have become alive of the irreparable destruction being-done by incessant run-off of soil. Systematic afforestation schemes have been launched in the hilly tracts of U.P. and Himachal Pradesh with particular attention to the Siwaliks and their foothills where soil erosion poses serious problems. The present position of forests in

India can be guaged from the fact that per capita forest area in India is only 0.2 hectares as against 3.5 hectares in the U.S.S.R., and 1.8 hectares in the U.S.A. Not only the forest area is proportionately smaller in India, but it is also most unevenly distributed, so that, in many regions, there are hardly any forest. The total area covered by forests amounts to 2.81 lakhs sq. miles or 12.54 crore acres which is about 22 per cent of the total geographical area of the country. Afforestation in the hitherto barren and uncultivable lands amounting to 8.75 crore acres, in permanent pastures and grazing lands amounting to 2.83 crore acres and in cultivable waste amounting to 5.42 crore acres, is quite feasible.

B. Technical Problems

The technical aspects of the question of rehabilitation of Inland waterways, have to be viewed in two parts. Part one relates to the technical aspects of river conservancy and training, while part two to the technical aspect of the vessels plying on the waterways.

1. *River Training*

There are several methods of river training and conservency apart from the ones we have already dealt with earlier. Most of these come purely under engineering devices. Some of these are discussed below:

(i) *Bandalling: Bandalling* is an indigenous method of river training widely used in India and Burma. "A Bandal is a system of lightly erected bamboo and bamboo-mat spurs, the main function of which is to stop sands moving and thus to build up and consolidate small sands and help the river to contract its channels and deepen and scour out the resulting river bed." The process is something like this. Bamboo staffs about 20 feet long are pegged down into the sand in a row on both sides of the channel to be kept navigable. The rows are ganerally 150 to 250 feet long and the distance between them is less towards the flow of the stream. After these rows are ready, thinner bamboo poles are lashed and strutted horizontally which give support to thick mats made of local materials. Several *bandallings* are errected through which the river is forced to flow. As the width of the channel is narrowed, the velocity of flow increases, the bed sand is scurred and the channel deepened. As the tail ends of the bandalled channel is narrow, water gushes through it in force and drops out the collected sand behind the *bandals* to create sand banks.

This method of river training has been used in Ganga and its tributaries for quite a long time. In certain other countries also such as Iraq, this method was used successfully on river Tigris. It, however, has its own limitations and cannot be used everywhere with advantage. At places where the bed of the river is already too narrow, the currents are so fast that bundalling becomes almost ineffective. It is most effective in courses which are sandy, shallow, and wide. It is, however, possible that an improved method of *bandalling* using wire-nets can became more effective.

(ii) *Buoyage and Scour:* Once the water level goes down after rains, rivers like Ganga develops several narrow shallow, and sluggish channels traversing the whole river bed from bank to bank. Gradually, only one or two channels survive and the rest become extinct channels. All these obstruct navigation.

To overcome these difficulties, it is suggested that the vessels plying in the riverways should follow only a set course. This stirs the bed sand as the vessels pass and helps maintain a uniform depth. If the reduced supply of water is accompanied with increased depth of the channel, much of the problem will get resolved. This method of maintaining the depth of the channel is called buoyage. Scouring is the process by which the bed of the river is scratched by the waves and currents generated by fast moving vessels.

(iii) *Dredging:* In the stretches of rivers where *bandalling* and buoyage fail, artificial dredging becomes necessary to maintain the navigability of the stream. Dredging is an artificial scouring of the river bed using mechanical devices. The dredgers are of two types; one has a number of buckets on a big wheel that keeps moving. It can be well compared with a Persian wheel on a grand scale. The buckets scour the bed, collect the silt and deposit it on the deck. The other type of dredger sucks up the mud scoured and carries up through a huge pipe. This type is called suction dredger while the former is called bucket dredger. It may be noted that both of these are useful only in soft clay or sand and no in rocky beds.

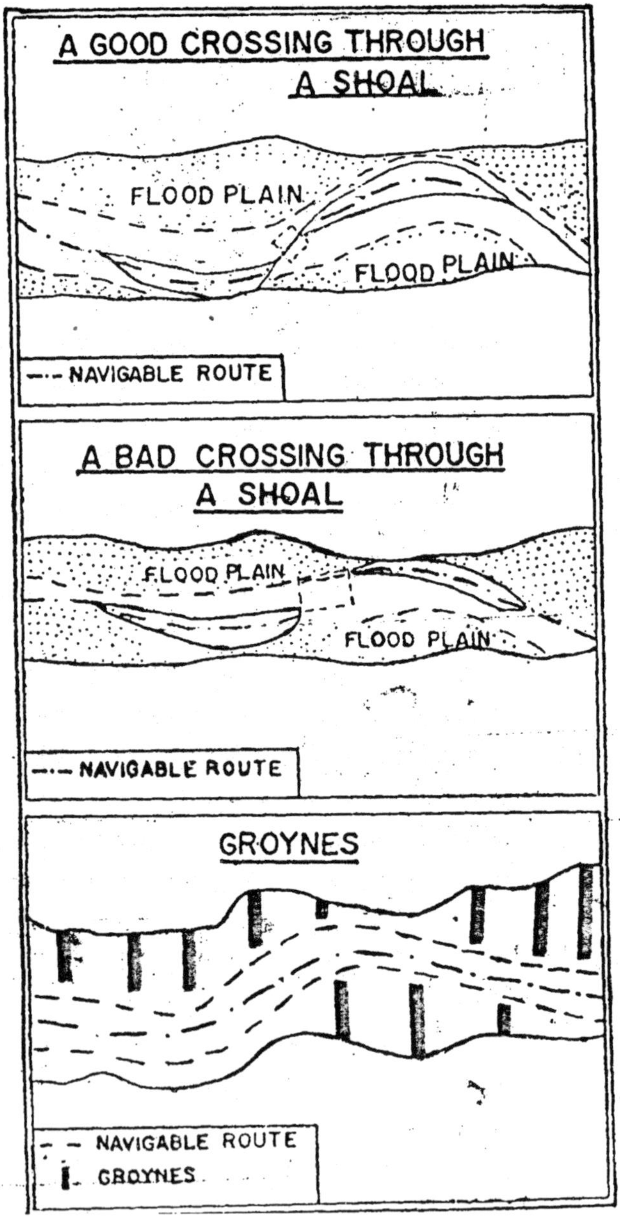

Fig. 9.1: A Good and Bad, Groynes Crossing through a Shoal

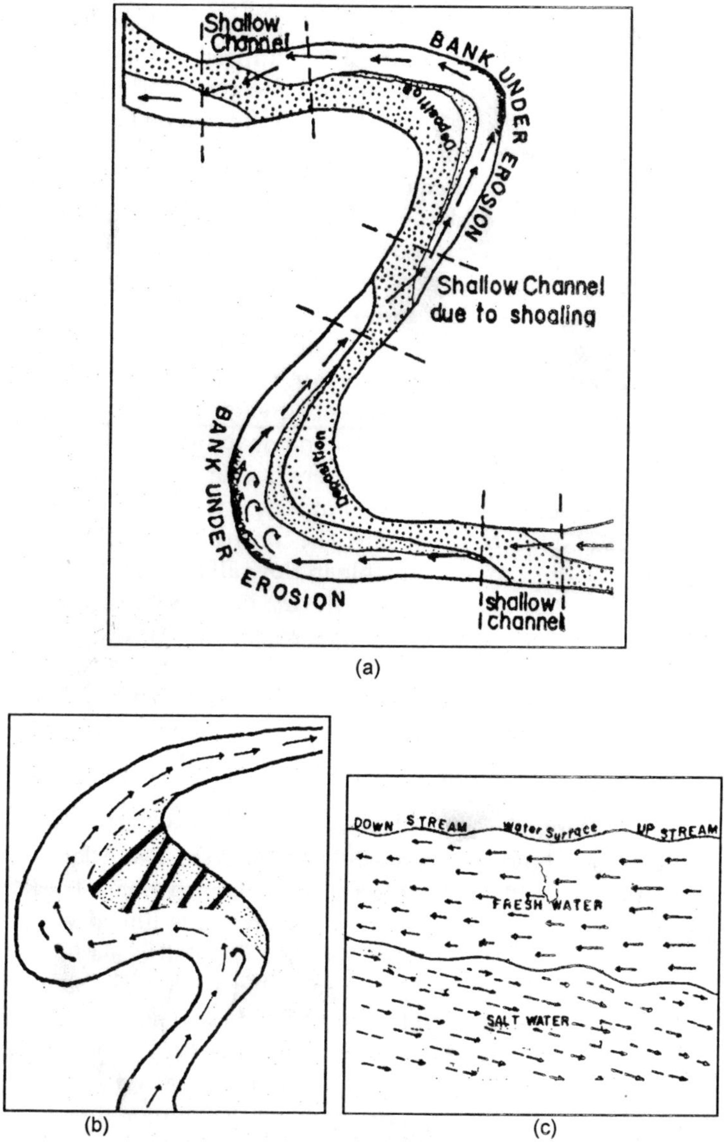

Fig. 9.2: (a) Behaviour of Rivers at Bends, (b) Diagram showing flood repelling spurs, and (c) Movement of water in tidal limits of rivers

J. Johnston suggested that a third type of dredger which can only scour the sand may be profitably utilised in Ganga because this river needs scouring alone and the transportation of the scoured material is done by the river itself. Point on also held this view. He says "as a rule there would be no great difficulty in attracting water into one channel for a time as the shoals, being of sand, are easily operated upon with the assistance of the currents. Such shoals may be deepened temporarily or permanently for the dry season by various methods *viz.*, by bundalling (open or closed), light dredging, jet agitators and stern wheelers, and stern wheelers alone moving over the shoals a number of times. Steamers themselves undoubtedly play a very important role in maintaining the navigability of a channel and hence greater the volume of traffic lessor the work required to maintain navigability. This specifically applies to the spill rivers, where there is a large volume of water in the main river to draw upon or attract.

(iv) *Canalisation and Damming:* The construction of dams across such rivers which are not equable in flow all the year round and become empty or almost empty in dry periods, is essential for navigation. Construction of dams with a multipurpose view including the facilities for navigation is an ideal arrangement. Even if the main purpose of the dam is irrigation, the canals distributing the water can be made to serve the double purpose of irrigation and navigation. This arrangement would probably be most suited to Indian conditions.

Human engineering skill has rendered it possible to construct canals to join rivers, nay seas and oceans even. The Atlantic has been connected with the Mediterranean by French canals. The latter with the Red sea by Suez and the North Sea is linked with the Black sea through Rhine and Danube. The Baltic sea has easy approach to the Black sea by several water routes. The same can be true of India too. Indian rivers can be made navigable for long stretches and wherever they fail to provide this facility, canalisation may be resorted to. The standard European dimensions of 24 metre bed width and 3.5 metre depth capable of accommodating barges of 1350 tons capacity would not suit Indian conditions. The French canals with bed width of 10 metres and depth of 2.6 metres are more appropriate for India. The side slops of these canals are 2:1 to 3:1 and the size of locks 28.5×5.2 metres with head clearance of 3.7m. These canals can accommodate crafts of 280 tons carrying capacity. The English canals are very narrow and are navigable by country boats of 70×7 feet dimensions.

2. Design of Vessels

In India, most of the things are still done as a matter of convention. The Inland navigation is no exception to this. The general shape and design of the country boats plying in Indian rivers, are by and large, suited to certain lock conditions prevailing sometimes back when the rivers contained more waters and canals for irrigation were not many. When they were faced with the problem of paucity of water in the channels, the vessels were reduced in size and hence, their usefulness as long distance carriers of goods and passengers was considerably reduced. Although substantial amount of traffic is still handled by the country boats to warrant improvement in the crafts design, no serious steps have been taken to develop new designs of vessels which suit the available depth of water without reducing their carrying capacity.

There are certain advantages of country boats. Firstly, they are inexpensive and hence within the easy reach of small traders and boatmen. The initial cost of a 50 tonne boat would come to about Rs. 30,000 to 50,000 whereas a steel barge of similar capacity will cost anywhere from Rs. 80,000 to Rs. 1,50,000, depending upon the design selected. Another advantage of country boats is that in areas where self-propelled crafts cannot ply for one reason or the other, they can serve the purpose of trade and commerce. It is recorded that during the period 1937-38, 5.5 million tons were carried by the country boats through the Eastern and Kolkata channels.

At the same time the limitations of the wooden country boats are obvious. They become unserviceable soon if well seasoned wood is not used. Their speed is top slow for present day requirements. Their carrying capacity is also limited. Thus, there seems to be a need for mechanically run vessels wherever feasible. But how to judge the feasibility is the main question? We cannot just have self-propelled vessels everywhere, unless sufficient draught is available. Even if this condition is fulfilled, the non-availability of sufficient cargo may render this venture uneconomic. It, therefore, seems necessary to consider these technical and economic limitations and possibilities before a new type of vessel, whether country boat or self-propelled, is introduced in any stretch of Inland waterways.

The following factors must be taken into consideration in the designing of new vessels:

The depth of water available all along the channel, the craft has to ply in the possibility of improvement in the draught and the nature of the river bed must be taken in view.

The cargo to be carried decides the design of the vessel. For example, liquid can be transported efficiently in tankers. Formerly, this aspect of water transport had little if any importance and most of the ships and boats were multipurpose. With the ever increasing trade opportunities, it is now possible to earmark vessels permanently to certain routes, specialising in certain types of cargo, with the result that now, we have oil tankers, wheat and grain ships, colliers, fruit carriers and banana ships.

The volume of cargo to be carried is another consideration that weighs much in designing of vessels. As a matter of fact, the larger carrying capacity of the vessel, more economic it would prove, provided that it sails fully loaded. That is the reason why the availability of cargo becomes an important factor in the selection of a vessel. In case sufficient amount of cargo is not available and the vessel is to be kept standing for some times or has to move only partly loaded, it would soon become a liability rather than an asset. In designing a vessel, it must, however, be kept in view that existing availability of cargo alone should not be considered, The life of a vessel and the possible changes in the pattern of trade should also have some weight. Modernisation for its own sake should not be resorted to. On many routes, the old time country boats would serve the purpose.

The regularity of trade is another aspect to be considered certain goods move during a particular season such as foodgrains, sugarcane etc., while manufactured goods move all the year round. In case of seasonal goods, it is more economic to have several small barges which can easily be utilised during the off season in carrying other goods in smalls, instead of having few large barges, because unless sufficient traffic available to move them all the year round fully loaded, they would become uneconomic.

The nature of cargo to be handled also puts certain limits to the design of vessels. The perishable goods need quick delivery and hence only such vessels which have sufficient speed are suited for them. The economics of transportation is based, on three dimensions (i.e.) ton-mile-hour, although the general tendency is to have it on two dimension, i.e. ton and mile alone. Thus, even though the goods may not be perishable, speed is always an advantage to any means of transportation.

It must not be lost sight of that the design of vessel also puts certain limits on the speed. While in movement, the speed of the vessel is arrested by skin friction. That is, the area of contact between the body of the vessel and the water and, the displacement length ratio, that is the relation of the beam and draught to length. The skin friction resistance may be calculated by the formula:

$$Rf = fSVn$$

where

R = skin friction resistance;
f = co-efficient of the friction of the surface;
S = area of wetted surface in sq. ft.;
V = speed in knots, and
n = an exponent the value of which varies with length and smoothness at the surface.

but may be taken as constant for general purpose. As the variable factor f does not vary considerably in the higher ranges of length, skin friction will vary pretty well in proportion to the square of the increase in length of the vessel for a given speed and as the square of the speed for different speeds.

The resistance generally called wave making resistance or Rw farms only a small portion of the total resistance and increases more slowly than Rf where the ratio of length to speed expressed by the term $\frac{V}{\sqrt{f}}$ less than 1. Above this ratio and up to 1.5, this resistance increases rapidly and becomes the principal resistance to forward motion. The wave making resistance is affected by two factors—speed and the ratio of beam and draught to length or displacement length ratio expressed as $D/(L/100)^3$. Thus lesser the $V/\sqrt{L}$ greater the speed. And since this ratio decreases as the length of the vessels increases, it becomes negligible in modern cargo carriers which usually exceed 450 feet length. It means that a 12 knots speed for a 450 feet W.L. length vessel is less in comparison to the same speed of a 100 feet barge as the $V/\sqrt{L}$ of the former is only 0.57 while that of the latter is 1.2.

Keeping the displacement ratio the same, if the length of a 100 feet vessel is increased to 120 feet, it would require only 400 h.p. to attain a speed of 12 knots in stead of 475 h.p. in the previous case. Thus, a larger vessel carrying 20 per cent more cargo actually requires almost 10 per cent less power to drive her at the same speed. The reason is that the extra length means a drop in the speed length ratio $V/\sqrt{L}$ from 1.2 to slightly over 0.9 with a corresponding very rapid drop in wave-making resistance.

From this, it becomes clear that longer vessels are more economical. But there is another technical matter relating to speed that we must take up here. It is related to the economics of engines used in vessels. Every engine has its own r.p.m. which is most economical. But every engine can be run at its prescribed speed or below or above it according to requirements. Running them at a speed below or above its prescribed speed would prove more costly in the long run. It is, therefore, always better to have an engine of the appropriate requirements of say 10 h.p. instead of having one of 8 h.p. and running it at 10 h.p. on the grounds of economy in fuel. It is equally important to use larger power units instead of several units of low power.

(i) *Crafts for Inland Rivers:* Generally speaking, the feeders and the upper and middle reaches of the main rivers contain too shallow a draught during the dry periods of the year to encourage any large scale navigation even by small country boats, what to say of power propelled large vessels. To ensure navigability all necessary measures discussed above under physical problems have to be undertaken. But even then, it is doubtful if much can be achieved as the existing rate of diversion of water to irrigation canals can hardly be reduced. The only alternative left, therefore, is to attack the problem from two sides. One is the improvement of the channel by a forestation, *bandalling* etc., and the other to design such vessels which can ply in shallow draughts. As discussed earlier, large vessels ultimately prove more economical and must be resorted to in Indian waters.

(ii) *Expert Opinions:* In this connection, it would be worthwhile to recall the view of Otto Popper, an expert on Inland water transportation who visited India in 1950 to investigate and report on the possibility of developing traffic on Ganga from Buxar to

Allahabad, Ghaghra from its mouth to Behramghat, Rapti from its mouth to Gorakhpur, Bhagirathi, Mahanadi and Odisha coast canal, Buckingham canal and Tapi up to Karapara and 50 miles up and on the possibility of improving traffic capacity of the existing, navigational routes. Popper based his recommendations on, the expressed conclusion that "if systematically organised and exploited, the Inland waterways, would become equal partners to the railways in addition to their use for irrigation purpose."

He suggested that at every possible line, steamship services should be started on cooperative basis. Whenever, the introduction of power propelled vessels is not feasible, country boats, may be, grouped into cooperative units. These steps would go a long way in attracting cargo to the waterways, as in the absence of any security of goods offered, no trader would come forward to utilise the services of existing unorganized and privately run boats.

His other suggestion related to the use of mechanical tug-boats to increase the speed of country boats by towing them along the banks. He also recommended compulsory registration of country crafts. He estimated that if all these measures are introduced "the freight of Inland navigation can be brought down to about half *anna* per ton-mile." The Government of India have since amended the Inland Steam Vessels Act of 1917 providing for compulsory registration of steamers, but not much has been done regarding other recommendations.

In 1951-52, a group of experts drawn from South-East Asian countries was sent to U.S.A. and Europe to study the working of the Inland waterways there and to recommend measures to be taken to improve Inland navigatian in India. The group *inter alia* recommended the following steps:

1. The rivers like Ganga and Ghaghra being shallow (1 to 1.2 metres no shoals), for the greater part of the year, it would be cheaper and better to use modern tugs generally suited to these depths. The barges should preferably be made of alluminium alloy to reduce the weight. They suggested that such barges called Thames were in use in English waterways. They measure 24.4 × 6.1 × 1.7/1.4 metres and have a carrying capacity of 90 tons at about 3 feet draught, which is commonly the depth of water available in Indian waterways during summer season. These barges are

comparatively cheaper as well. The steam engines currently used in India do not suit modern conditions and should, as far as possible, be replaced by diesel engines. Although self-propelled barges are more efficient than the towed ones, the present conditions do not warrant any immediate change. Tanker crafts would have better prospects in India;
2. Experiments should be conducted to find out as to which of the three methods, i.e. abrest, pull-towing astern and push-towing would suit Indian waterways;
3. Till conditions so demand large scale mechanization of loading and unloading operations of cargo should not be undertaken. They may, however, be introduced for experimental purposes;
4. Navigation companies being well equipped for maintenance and repairs, immediate efforts should be made to manufacture new vessels; and
5. The Government should take over the river conservancy work.

Soon after, J.J. Surie, an Inland water transport expert from Netherlands, came to India to advise the Government on the projects of using shallow draught vessels in the Ganga and Ghaghra. He felt that these rivers, due to efficient parallel railway services, offer limited scope for the development of Inland water transport. But in view of the possibilities the other rivers offered, he recommended that:

1. A pilot project for shallow draught tugs and pusher type barges should be started in Ganga and Ghaghra with two 250 b.h.p. tugs and eight 100 ton barges at 3 feet 8 inches draught. The size of the vessel would depend upon the results of the cross section surveys of the rivers;
2. Another pilot project with smaller sized tugs and 8 barges (pusher type) of 40 ton carrying capacity at 3 feet draught of barges and 2 feet of tugs should be started; and
3. A third pilot project for one diesel propelled car ferry with a maximum draught of 3 feet to carry nearly 10 cars or 5 lorries and 100 passengers should be started.

(iii) *Choice of Engines:* Most of the self-propelled Inland water transport vessels use steam power. Recent researches have, however, shown that the diesel engines are operationally more efficient. They could not be introduced in India due mainly to the availability of cheap coal. It would certainly be advisable to, change over to diesel power as soon as the finances so warrant. The grounds for this recommendation are the following:

1. The steam engine with boiler is heavier and more expensive than the diesel engine with reduction gear and hence, the former does not suit the small vessels;
2. The diesel engine fitted with reduction gears, has faster speed than the steam engine;
3. The large paddle tug of a steam engine makes it more costly in initial outlay as well as in maintenance;
4. The quantity of fuel consumed in relation to the space covered is more in the steam engine than in the diesel one. The diesel requires less space for storage as well;
5. The strength of the crew in a steam engine is more than in a diesel engine; and
6. The diesel engine, being of high speed, can be directly coupled to screws capable of running at high speed. It can also be put in tunnel to provide diameters larger than the draught would otherwise permit. By the use of Kort nozzels, additional tow rope force for the same h.p. can be achieved in case the speed does not exceed 14 km. an hour.

A word may be added regarding the choice between a towed and a self-propelled vessel. It is possible that in countries where handling of cargo at transhipment points is mechanised, the latter would prove economic and suited to local conditions. In India, this is not the case and much of the loading and unloading is done and will continue to be done manually at least for a few decades. Self-propelled vessels are costly and delay in loading and unloading means idleness of engines during that period. It would, therefore, be advisable to have towed vessels which can be left at transhipment points for loading or unloading while the engines are busy in towing the vessels elsewhere.

(iv) *Wharfage:* The unpredictable behaviour of Indian rivers makes it extremely difficult to construct any permanent wharf for loading and unloading of cargo. Even temporary wharfs such as ones carried on pontoons etc., sometimes fail to be of any avail before the sudden and violent changes in the river bed. Unless proper river training and conservancy measures are resorted to, mechanisation of handling of cargo would continue to pose a problem. In view of the fact that large number of labourers are available cheaply in this country wharfage should consist of those facilities also which are related to handling by human labour. The development of Inland ports and steamer stations with warehousing facilities needs, however, immediate attention.

(v) *Design of Country Boats:* The country boats which carry the major part of Inland water traffic have no organized construction houses or factories. The design of these vessels is old and suited to certain original conditions which have lost currency now. The constructional work is done by local carpenters and blacksmiths who now lack any training of significance which they can utilise in the improvement of the design of vessels. Nor they possess any knowledge of the conditions prevailing in different stretches of the river. They design the crafts only for local ferries.

Effort should be made to impart training to local craftsmen in boatmaking. There should be a machinery for proper checks and inspection of the wood used and the design adopted. These steps would reduce the work of baling, but water from the bed of the boat and also of frequent beaching for recanting. Both of these result from the use of unseasoned wood. The design should, as far as possible, incorporate arrangements for protection of cargo from rain etc.

C. Economic Aspects

The economics of Inland water transport has already been discussed in earlier chapters. In this chapter, we therefore propose to cover only those aspects which have not been touched before. The most important aspect of its economics is its cheapness and capacity to carry in bulk. In a country like India, where poverty is rampant anything that is inexpensive is likely to be popular, provided, of course, that it meets certain felt needs. A great majority of the people in India would still prefer relatively slow, but cheap means of transportation. It is more so where the traffic involves only carriage of goods.

The Inland water transport is not only inexpensive but also most suited to bulky and cheap materials such as ores, grains, timber etc. Because of its capacity to carry in bulk at a nominal cost, it can make many 'immobile' commodities like hay and fodder, move long distances. During the periods of drought millions of cattle die in one part of the country while in other parts huge quantities of hay and fodder remain unused. Such commodities cannot be sent out to long distances by rail or road because the cost of their transportation proves to be prohibitive. They can be carried by the waterways charging only the amount they can bear. Similar is the case with building materials in such alluvial zones as the Ganga valley.

This being the case, there is sufficient scope to develop waterways in India without jeopardising the interests of other modes of transportation in anyway. And this scope is expanding everyday as the economy improves its performance in agriculture, industry and other fields.

The parallelism of the railways and waterways, should not lead to cut-throat competition as the roles of the two are not always the same. In almost all the European countries having significant waterways, the situation is not very difficult, but the various modes of transportation have co-existed with mutual benefits to each.

How can the railways be helpful to waterways, is clear from the following quotation taken from the Counsular Reports to Parliament of Belgium. "It may justly be claimed that in providing the country with a system of navigable and cheap transport, in multiplying the points of contact between road, rail and water transport and thus facilitating transhipment, in rendering the sea ports easier of access and in stimulating the erection of numerous commercial and manufacturing establishments, this work of improvement (of waterways) has been one of the principal factors of commercial prosperity of the country." By an investment of Rs. 120 million in the last quarter of the nineteenth century, the traffic on waterways increased from 225 million ton miles in 1880 to 560 million ton miles in 1900, while during the same period the traffic on the railways increased from 14 million to 40 million ton miles and on the sea ports from 5 million to 17 million tons.

The same was the story in Germany and France. Thompson speaking of France quotes French official circles as sayings that "it is conceded the waterways and railways are destined not to supplant, but to supplement each other. Between the two there is a natural division of traffic. To the railroad the quick transit; to the waterways gravitate the heavy freights of small value which can only be transported when freights are low." Or in the words of M. de Freyeinst "waterways by increasing traffic are rather the auxiliaries than the competitors of railroads. In procuring for manufacture cheap transportation for coal and raw-material, they create freights, whose subsequent transportation gives profit to the railroads."

This brings us to the question of co-ordination among railways, roads and waterways in India.

The term 'transport coordination' indicates the following co-operative efforts on the part of certain agencies playing same, similar or complementary roles in the field of transportation:

1. "Cooperative or joint action by two or more independent operating agencies of a single type in performing acts of transportation."
2. "Cooperative or joint action by two or more independent agencies of different types in performing act of transportation."
3. "Use by a single operating agency machinery or techniques which have, customarily, been independently controlled."
4. "Arrangements or agreements by two or more independent operating agencies of different types for the division of traffic, so that, each will do that work for which it is inherently fitted. The arrangement may cover a field which is already occupied, or a field which it intended to invade."

The objective of coordination in transport system of a country is to provide the consumer with service at minimum cost through the elimination of technically inefficient method to ensure that services which are jointly demanded or complementary to each other are supplied in harmony. As discussed earlier, every mode of transportation has its own merits and demerits and if it operates within the sphere it is most suited for, the question of coordination. hardly arises. But in actual practice, a cut-throat competition sets in and the better organized system invades the sphere of the less organized ones. A situation is thus created in which the transport industry becomes inefficient and inflexible. To avoid such contingencies, coordination is essential.

In India little attention has been paid to this aspect of transportation; in fact, the administration has been instrumental in accentuating bitter competition among the different modes. It had encouraged the railways to capture the business of waterways and allowed the latter to die uncared. As stated by C.N. Sumner, a representative of Inland steamer companies before the Road-Rail Conference, 1933, "gradually the policy adopted by the railways and the Government was that no development of trade towards the rivers, no question of shorter or more natural traffic routes, no consideration of public interest or convenience, no action in making use of natural highways which other countries regard as priceless possessions, must be allowed to interfere with that one all important factor, the interests of the railways too, which may not as yet even be in existence, but which may conceivably be constructed at some future date."

In recent years, a serious problem has arisen because of the powerful competition offered by roads to railways in India. Motor vehicles have started plying on trunk lines from one corner of the country to another and the cargo which was formally under the exclusive control of the railways is now being gradually diverted to roads. But strangely enough many parts of the country, particularly the rural parts are still devoid of good transportation facilities. Such mal-adjustments, created by uncoordinated operation of services, has proved very costly, the financial consequences of which the community ultimately has to bear.

Turning back to coordination between Inland waterways and other means of transport, we must keep in view that within certain limitations to be discussed later in detail, waterways are most suited to bulky and cheap goods such as timber, stone, cement, ores, coal and raw-materials for industries like jute, cotton, and iron and steel. The cost of transportation will depend upon the bulk which is offered for transport. Certain types of cargo such as oil, are by dint of their nature, more efficiently carried by waterways than by rail or road which are not immune from loose shunting. All these cargoes have to be collected from the place of their origin and have to be delivered at the actual place of use. These places would most probably be unconnected by waterways. This naturally creates problems of transhipment, which can be solved much easily if all modes work in cooperation with each other.

Coordination among different modes of transportation would result in the diversion of traffic to the carrier most suited to handle it. The Joint Steamers Companies which were the largest carriers running steamers in Kolkata, Assam, Cachar and Bihar claimed in 1957 that they had a spare capacity of about 150 million tons. Had there been proper coordination between railways and waterways part of the railway traffic could have been diverted to them and thus equivalent rail capacity would have been freed for use in other parts of the country where rail transport facilities were inadequate.

Even allowing a liberal margin for exaggeration, it is evident that there was and still is fair surplus capacity in the waterways of north-east India which can be profitably utilized by proper transport coordination. In this connection it may not be out of place to quote from the report of the Indian Delegation to the Soviet and other European railways:

> "The tariff is not entirely based on the principle of 'what the traffic can bear', but it is also designed to provide comparatively cheaper transport for commodities, movement of which are considered more essential in the interest of national economy and to secure a rationalised use of all forms of transport even if this entails loss of traffic to the railways. Freight rates on railways for certain commodities are higher during summer, so that, traffic may be diverted to waterways which operate only during that season. The tariff, however, aims at recovering on each commoditity at least what they call the self-cost, i.e., the actual cost which includes the field cost of handling the commodity over the required distance."

In India too some such arrangement could be thought of so as to enable maximum use of the surplus capacity. On the Rhine and the Tennessee rivers in Germany and the U.S.A. respectively, bulk of non-perishable goods move on the riverways. It would certainly be advantageous if the oil companies in India avail of the services of river transport and build terminals and bulk storage plants at selected places along the navigable waterways distributing the products by trucks and rail according to need. Sugarcane, coal, ore, pig-iron, timber, fodder, cement limestone, fertilizers, and raw-meterials can also move in bulk *via* the waterways.

Although it is true that by diverting the traffic from the railways to the waterways as proposed above, some relief can be given to the latter, it must not be forgotten that the ultimate solution does not lie here. The railways have come to stay and their growth rate has to be faster than that of the waterways as they have distinct superiority over them. The job of the waterways is to handle traffic, both passenger and goods, which railways cannot handle efficiently. This will not be unbearable to the railways as the loss will not be significant and can be easily made up as the industrialisation makes further headway. Timber in long logs, and oil together with food grains, cotton, coal, fodder and imported machinery are the commodities that railways cannot handle efficiently and cheaply. With the opening of oil refineries in Trombay, Guwahati, Visakhapatnam and other coastal locations, oil can move to different parts of the country through coastal as well as river traffic. Secondly, the waterways should try to attract such traffic which is stagnant and does not move due to prohibitive transport costs. Under this comes fodder both dry and green, sand, bricks, tiles, stones and similar other commodities.

A word must be said about, the prospects of oil and timber industries in India and the possibility of the movement of their products through waterways. In fact oil and timber are the two commodities which the railways cannot handle economically. Probably, the waterways will succeed only where the railways have failed, and hence there are greater prospects in these two fields for the waterways. Tank wagons are limited in capacity and costly. They need stringent precaution against fire, loose shunting, and inefficient storage. To move the oil imported from foreign countries Inland, larger storage facilities have to be created. This can be avoided in case rivers are used for transportation. In case of timber, railway firstly cannot handle very long logs; secondly, the tariff they charge is so high that it becomes prohibitive in cost when carried to long distances.

With the extension of forest areas under several schemes launched by the Government and the increase in the demand for both timber and oil in the country, their transport will assume particular importance. Perhaps on this ground alone waterways should be given a fair chance to develop.

In the end it is worthwhile quoting an extract from the Inter-State Commerce Act of the U.S.A., which gives the outline of a transportation policy that a National Government must follow:

> "It is hereby declared to be National Transportation Policy of the Congress to provide for fair and impartial regulation of all modes of transportation, subject to the provisions of this Act, so administered as to recognise and preserve the inherent, advantages of each; to promote safe, adequate, economical and efficient service and foster sound economic conditions in transportation and among the several carriers; to encourage the establishment and maintenance on reasonable charges for transportation services, without unjust discrimination, undue preferences or advantage or unfair or destructive competitive practices; to cooperate with the several States and the duly authorised officials thereof; and to encourage fair wages and equitable working conditions all to the end of developing, coordinating and preserving a national transportation system by water, highway and rail, as well as other means, adequate to meet the needs of the commerce of the United States, of the postal services and of the national defence. All of the provisions of this Act shall be administered and enforced with a view to carrying out the above declaration of policy."

D. Organizational Problems

One of the main causes why Inland waterways could not sustain the competition offered by railways was the absence of organization which could save them from disaster. The functional aspects of any such organization fall under following categories:

1. Traffic Surveys to find out navigational potentialities;
2. Rationalisation of services which includes adoption of latest methods and equipment suited to local conditions. It should also advise on the question of best operational system in respect to both time and space.
3. Efficient running of the services by way of deepening and maintenance of waterways, construction and repairs of

crafts in use as well as the wharfage whenever necessary and organizing efficient handling of goods and development of trade on the rivers.

Efficient performance of these functions obviously requires sufficiently trained technical and commercial staff; under an authority which has sufficient power to coordinate the activities of all waterways in India irrespective of the States they fall in. Separate action by different states will be of no avail as the States are only administrative units and the waterways do not respect political boundaries. For example, the Bhagirathi channel in West Bengal is perhaps biggest obstacle in the way of steamer services in the Ganga. The Government of West Bengal would hardly be prepared to spend on this as the benefits would naturally go to Bihar and U.P. also. Similar are the cases of other waterways such as the Buckingham canal which passes through the States of Andhra Pradesh and Tamil Nadu and the Odisha Coast Canal which partly lies in West Bengal and partly in Odisha.

Bilateral and multilateral agreements among different States may ease the problem to certain extent, but the consequent disagreements and delays that would arise in the process of deciding over privileges and expenditure etc., would make such an arrangement totally unworkable. This may also lead to undesirable competition among different States. The question of leaving the whole matter in the private hands does not arise, as no such agency can come forward to shoulder the responsibility. We thus have only one choice, that is, a central authority that can coordinate the activities of the States as well as of the carriers.

1. Some Basic Issues

India being a federal-*cum*-unitary form of State, the administration of waterway does not fall wholly within the purview of either of Central or State Governments. The Central Government is responsible for the operation of power propelled vessels and such of the waterways which the Parliament declares to be of national importance. The operation of country boats and the rest of the waterway come within the purview of the State Governments and local authorities such as Municipal Boards, Jila Parishads and Village Panchayats. This being the case, there is no over-riding authority unmindful of the interests of the State and Local Governments. Therefore, it would be better to have a coordinating authority with such powers as essential for proper development and upkeep of the waterways.

It will serve the purpose as far as the development and maintenance of the waterways is concerned. But unless the operational activities also come under its purview, this authority will remain a liability to the Government and can never hope to be self-paying. In fact here lies the crux of the problem. Whether the operation should remain in private hands as it is now or it should be partly or wholly taken over by the coordinating authority mentioned above ?

Supposing that private companies are allowed to function and parallel to them a public sector corporation is also established to function in areas which these companies do not find economic or to compete with them as in the case of Mississippi waterway in the U.S.A. Would such an arrangement be in national interest? It would not, for even though the arrangement may work indefinitely, it will lead to a considerable waste of efforts and fund. Apart from this, the sharing of the wharfage and safety devices which the public corporation must undertake, would entail lot of unwholesome problems suicidal to Inland navigation.

It appears that India will have to go for a Government monopoly in Inland water transportation with modifications necessitated by local conditions. When a channel passes exclusively through one state, it would be possible for that State Government to manage it in its own way. The minor services such as ferries and boat bridges can be managed by local authorities with State Government help. The major waterways passing across two or more States must be treated as of national importance and managed accordingly. Now, we are perhaps prepared to evaluate the arrangements in vogue in India.

At the highest level, the Ministry of Transport is charged with the job of looking after the interests of Inland navigation in so far as they relate to power propelled vessels which are confined to Ganga-Brahmaputra river system. The question of finding out the technical potentialities for development of waterways such as the depth of water, current and channel conditions is dealt with by the Central Water and Power Commission which functions under the Ministry of Irrigation and Power. At the State level, there is hardly any effective organisation with adequate technical personnel and know-how which can work out any developmental plan or take up the maintenance of the existing waterways. Although in a few States there are organizations for this purpose, their work is confined to the desk and has very little to do with the practical side of the job.

2. G.B.W.T. Board

North-eastern India is the only region which has to depend on Inland waterways for about 50 per cent of its transport requirements. In 1951 the Government of India after discussing the problems of transport coordination and improvement of waterways decided to set-up an organization known as Ganga-Brahmaputra Water Transport Board. The Board functioned under the chairmanship of the Secretary, Central Ministry of Transport and Communications and was represented by the participating States of West Bengal, Assam, Bihar and U.P. It had the powers to co-operative representatives of other interests concerned like the Railways, the steamer companies and the Kolkata Port Authorities. It coordinated the activities of the participating Governments and examined their proposals in regard to the development of traffic, maintenance and improvement of navigational facilities in the channels, coordination of administration, registration of Inland vessels, inter-State movement of goods by river, amenities for passengers, fixing the passenger and freight rates and other cognate matters.

In the discharge of its executive responsibilities, the Board was intended to function through the agencies of the participating States. It was financed by a non-lapsing fund made up of contributions made by the Central and State Governments. Certain proposals which the Board made in the fifties were:

1. Controlling and training of Brahmaputra at important points in Assam to minimise floods;
2. Launching of pilot projects both on Ganga and Brahmaputra to discover the navigational potentialities;
3. Registration of country crafts of the capacity of 10 tons or above;

4. Checking the steamer companies from charging undue or excessive freight;
5. Training of Indian nationals as masters and serangs;
6. Preparation of schemes to be included, in Second and Third Five Year Plans; and
7. Amendment of Inland Vessels Act, 1917.

Among the pilot projects undertaken by the Board was the traffic survey on Ganga between Allahabad and Buxar and the use of shallow draught push-tow vessels on this route. A similar project was undertaken on some feeders of Brahmaputra in Assam. A diesel propelled ferry service for vehicles and passengers on Brahmaputra was also included in the project. Subsequently, the Board also took up the construction of an Inland port at Pandu.

3. *Legal Aspects of Inland Navigation*

The administration of Inland navigation is governed by Inland Steam Vessels Act, 1917. Under this Act, the tidal waters were governed by Central Government. The provincial Governments were, however, empowered to define how much of a tidal water should be deemed to be an Inland water for this purpose. Under the Government of India Act of 1935, shipping and navigatian oil tidal waters were included in the federal list. The State Governments ceased to excercise any such powers by reason of consequential adaptation made in section 70 of the Act. But the adaptation did not specify any authority which could prescribe the limits of Inland waters for the purposes of the Inland Steam Vessels Act of 1917. This lacuna was filled in by vesting that power in the Government of India by the Inland Steam Vessel (Amendment) Act, 1950.

Inland Steam Vessels Act, 1917 which regulated the operation of Inland Steam Vessels did not however provide for the registration of vessels. According to its original provisions, all that a steam vessel required before proceeding on a voyage or service was a certificate of survey in force for the period and applicable for the voyage. The Merchant Shipping Act, 1894 contained a provision for the registration of such vessels exceeding 15 tons in capacity but failure to register the vessel was not an offence under the Act. Thus, the Act of 1917 imposed only a limited control over the craft plying on a voyage or service. With a view to ensuring a greater measure of control on Inland crafts plying in Indian waters, the Act was amended in April 1951 to provide for the compulsory registration of all steam vessels. It was also felt that dumb barges, flat, and bigger country boats, not falling under the category of Inland steam vessels, should be similarily registered by the State Governments as such vessels come under their purview.

The Republican Constitution of India is almost in conformity with provisions of the Government of India Act, 1935 in so far as Inland navigation is concerned. It places under the Union List shipping and navigation on Inland waterways declared by Parliament by law to be National Waterways, as regards mechanically propelled vessels and the rule of the road on such waterways. Under the Concurrent List comes "shipping and navigation on Inland waterways as regards mechanically propelled vessels, and the rule of the road on such waterways and the carriage of passengers and goods on Inland waterways subject to the provisions of list I (Union List) with respect to National Highways". The State List consists of "Communications, that is to say roads, bridges, ferries and other means of communication not specified in list I, municipal tramways, ropeways, Inland waterways and traffic therein subject to the provisions of list I and III (Union and Concurrent) with regard to such waterways, vehicles other than mechanically propelled vehicles."

4. Views of Gokhale Committee

The Gokhale Committee on Inland Water Transport in India suggested that the existing sub-committee under the Road and Inland Water Transport Advisory Committee should be upgraded into a full-fledged advisory committee separate from the roads to effect proper and necessary coordination among different Ministries of Government of India, State Governments, private operators, traders and business and different modes of transportation. This committee would function as an advisory body to help the Ministry of Transport and Communication chalk out schemes for the development of Inland Waterways.

For the physical planning and execution of the developmental schemes as well as the maintenance of the existing waterways, the committee suggested the setting up of an Inland Water Transport

Directorate in the said Ministry headed by a Director General with sufficient administrative powers to carryout the schemes expeditiously. Parallel to this, the existing Waterways, Irrigation and Navigation Directorate of the General Water and Power Commission should be upgraded and placed in charge of a Chief Engineer who should be conversant with the problems and requirements of waterways.

The functions assigned to the proposed Inland Water Transport Organization in the Ministry of Transport were:

1. To study the transport requirements of the country with a view to coordinate Inland water transport with other modes for immediate requirements and long-term planning;
2. To set-up a technical organization for promoting Inland water transport in conjunction with the Central Water and Power Commission and to make a careful study of all proposals on a large scale relief model to be set-up;
3. To study modern developments in all aspects such as improved design of craft, navigation aids, terminal facilities and conservancy. Necessary research should also be carried out to draw up standards for classification of waterways, size of locks, clearance under bridges etc.;
4. Setting up suitable training of, (i) diesel mechanics, (ii) Deck and engine room personnel, and (iii) conservancy and technical staff; and
5. To coordinate and guide activities of the State Government and amalgamating the existing organization in the Centre.

The functions assigned to the proposed Inland Waterway Organization in the Central Water and Power Commission were:

1. To study the existing waterways in the country and formulate schemes for their improvement;
2. To prepare technical reports on design of waterways and connected structures;
3. To formulate proposals for extension of navigability of Inland waterways for immediate and short-term implementation having regard to availability of water under irrigation, power, multipurposes projects. Any

special project to be undertaken purely for navigation must also be considered; and

4. To investigate and prepare project report, designs and estimates after carrying out necessary structural and hydraulic model tests for the above, due consultations and coordination with State chief engineers concerned and the organization of Inland water transport to be set-up under the Ministry of Transport.

In regard to the operation of country boats employed in long distance or local services such as ferries, the committee were of the opinion that the excessive tolls and certain restriction put on such services should immediately be done away with. These should be organized on cooperative basis and the existing system of one man one boat should not be allowed to continue any more in the interest of the nation as well as the individual boatman whose economic position is very pitiable. Better design of boats suitable for subsequent conversion into self-propelled vessels, should be introduced. The committee were against the existing practice of auctioning the ghats. They recommended that Governments should run their own ferry services.

With the implementation of these recommendations and the consequent establishment of two powerful organisations at the Centre and one each in every State having navigable waterways, the Ganga-Brahmaputra Water Transport Board would become superfluous and hence, the Committee recommended that it should be disbanded. They also felt that thc time is not ripe for the declaration of certain waterways as National Highways.

5. *Efficacy of Committee's Recommendations*

In the early part of this chapter, we had concluded that unless the operation of the Inland waterways comes under the direct control of a coordinating organisation established at the Central Government would not be able to finance the huge expenditure that is involved in developing this industry in India. This brings to the forefront the question of nationalisation of steamer services. It is rather unfortunate that the committee has totally side tracked this issue probably because it did not specifically fall within their terms of reference. It must not be forgotten that the income earned by the railways and to a certain extent the road services, directly augment the Government treasury whereas the steamer services, being foreign concerns, partly absorb the profits and only a fraction of the total goes to the State. There is very little reason to believe that a Government can ever meet the initial finances involved in the development of an industry purely through taxation measures at the same time no Government can afford to spend huge sums of money on an industry, the profits of which fill some other's pockets.

The point is not, as to whether the companies are National or Foreign in character and origin; the question is as to how far the private ownership of vessels would fit in the overall Government policy and transport planning. After all, these channels are not like roads which are used every day and night even by the pedestrians. Riverways are of single purpose use and have ultimately to pay for the expenditure incurred on them. The grounds on which railways were nationalized are fully applicable to waterways, and there seems to be least justification in leaving the operational side to the private companies while keeping the maintenance of channels and their development on the sholders of the Government.

As regards the question of country boats and ferry services, the field must be left to the states as suggested by the Gokhale Committee. The question of vesting the ferry services in the hands of cooperatives or village panchayats may sound very pleasing and just but it has several implications which cannot be dismissed easily. There is, however, no doubt that the existing arrangement of auctioning the ghats is injurious to public interest and alternative arrangement must be devised to do away with this practice. Probably the time has come for the survey of the service requirements of all river crossings and thereafter to classify them into three classes. The class I crossings would be those which can afford mechanically run vessels and require handling of bullock carts, motor cars and buses daily. They should be run directly by the State Governments or other agencies such as the Ministry of Transport or Railways etc. Under the class II crossings may come those which are on major rivers like Ganga and Mahanadi and which offer sufficient finances to be handled by the State Governments directly in conjunction with the services on class I crossings. The last class would consist of those which have only local importance and can be handled by Village Panchayats or cooperatives.

10
Planning and Development

Planning for the development and improvement of Inland waterways in India starts with the plan proposed by Sir Arthur Cotton in 1874. Sir Cotton suggested a national water grid (with special emphasis on peninsular India). Under which all the major rivers of the country would be linked together and canalized to give an extensive network of irrigation-*cum*-navigation canals. Sir Charles Trevelyan was another eminent administrator of the nineteenth century India who supported the opening of canals on a large scale. Lord Lawrence, despite his staunch advocacy to open irrigation-*cum*-navigation canals could hardly take up planned work for implementation, due mainly to the cold reception his views received in the British circles.

A. Sir Arthur Cotton's Plan

Sir Arthur Cotton suggested a network of waterways for Inland navigation by steam vessels. The following extract from his famous lectures give the principal lines he suggested, for immediate opening in peninsular India:

(a) "The first line would be a very complete one round India, *viz.*, from Bombay, by Ahmedabad, up the valley of India across by Sirhind canal to the Ganges canal, down the valley of Ganges to Calcutta along the east coast to Cape Comorin and up the west coast to the new port of Carwar near Goa. The only impracticable piece of country is that from Goa to Bombay.

(b) Across the peninsula by the valleys of Godạvari, Wardha and Tapi to meet the former line at Baroda.

(c) A second line across the peninsula from Nellore, 100 miles north of Madras, by the valleys of Pennar, Tungabhadra and Kali Nadi to Carwar in the west coast.

(d) From Chennai across the Garnatic and by valleys of Amravati and Palghat river to Ponani on the west coast.
(e) The Wardha line of navigation may also be connected with the valley of Mahanadi down to the east coast line at Cuttack. The Wardha may be connected by the valley of the Veinganga with the Narbada and with the valleys of Chambal down to the Ganges valley line near Allahabad. The Brahmaputra is a very fair line of navigation at present though no doubt it could be greatly improved."

As evident from the above, the plan of Sir Arthur Cotton was commendable particularly because it came out at a time when everyone's attention was diverted towards the railways. Had these schemes been implemented, and they could be implemented at a comparatively lesser outlay than what they would require now, India could have saved enormous sum of money that was lavishly spent on the railways. The fact, however, remains that some of the schemes suggested by him are almost impracticable now, or even if practicable the returns from them would not justify their implementation. There are several reasons for this. Firstly, many of the rivers due to withdrawal of water in canals cannot be made navigable for long distances. Secondly, many of the river valleys are now well served by roads and railways and have no spare cargo to offer to the waterways. Thirdly, the cost involved is so enormous that unless the country attains a self-generating economy and moves up the take offstage of industrial development substantially, such schemes would neither be justifiable socially nor expedient economically. And fourthly, the bases on which the author of the plan chalked, but the schemes are now partly changed. Canalisation has developed fast without any provision for navigation. Economic structure of the country has also changed. Neverthelss many of the schemes suggested by him can still be implemented and have been included in the new plan of the national water grid.

B. The Master Plan for Inland Navigation

After the Independence of the country, a Master Plan for Inland Navigation was chalked out by the Ministry of Irrigation and Power, Government of India. This plan also includes several of the schemes suggested by Sir Arthur Cotton.

The basic idea behind this plan was spelled out in following terms:

> "In the wake of development of industries in the country adequate cheap transport will be essential. The development of communications, *viz.* rail, road and waterways is, therefore, necessary to cope with the future heavy increase in traffic. Extension of railways in a planned way progressed gradually since its introduction. Attention has also been given in developing the national highways for road transport since Independence, but no attention worthy of mention has so far been paid to improve the depleted rivers and to develop new waterways on the rivers and canals which hold *prima facie* navigation potentialities, but at present are not navigable."
>
> "The potential of extension of navigation in the waterways of India is great... It is possible to connect the western and eastern coasts through multi-purpose works on the Narbada, Son, Chambal and Ken, connecting the Narbada with the Ganga river system and also in the Wainganga and Godavari connecting the Narbada with the Godavari system. These rivers are at present not navigable except in their lower reaches. A number of dams, rivers and locks and probably lateral canals will have to be constructed to make these waterways navigable. Other principal features of the development will be flood control in the lower reaches of the rivers, extension of irrigation to millions of acres and generation of huge blocks of power."

The Master Plan was in no way a blue-print of certain concrete proposals. It simply indicated the possible water routes that could be developed in future if the essential requirements are fulfilled. Unless and until all the rivers of the country are surveyed properly and their potentialities known, it is indeed difficult to put forward any specific proposal. The outline plan, however, does indicate the potentialities. If implemented, the country will have a network of waterways which would connect the sugar belt of India with the ports of Kolkata and Mumbai; the cotton belt with the textile industry of Mumbai, Ahmedabad, Kanpur and Kolkata; and Hooghly side jute mills with the densely populated Ganga-Brahmaputra valley. There would be steamer services from Hardwar in the north to Chennai in the south, and Mumbai in the west to Dibrugarh in the east. The plan has five major schemes.

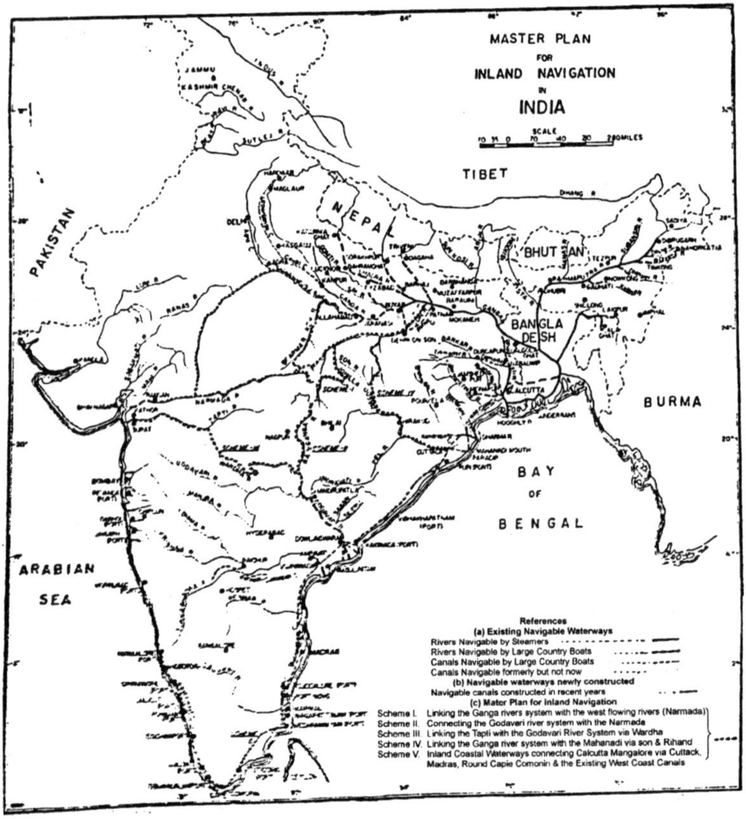

Fig. 10.1: Master Plan for Inland Navigation in India

Scheme I

Linking of river Ganga and its tributaries with the west flowing streams of Narmada and Tapi. This would provide a continuous waterway between the two major ports of India *viz.* Kolkata and Mumbai. This can be achieved only in case the following four proposals prove practicable.

Proposal I. Training the river Son from its confluence with the Ganga in Bihar to that of Johilla in Madhya Pradesh. This would be connected with river Narmada *via* river Johilla and a navigable canal.

Proposal 2. Linking of river Katni Nai, a tributary of river Son to river Hiron, a tributary of Narmada. This connection will give an alternative route.

Proposal 3. Training river Yamuna to its confluence with Chambal and thence of River Chambal which will be linked with river Karma a tributary of river Narmada by a canal.

Proposal 4. Linking of river Ken, a tributary of river Yamuna with river Hiron, a tributary of river Narmada *via* river Bearma, a tributary of river Ken.

Scheme II

This scheme has only one interlinked proposal to connect river Narmada with Godavari *via* various tributaries. River Polda, a tributary of river Ganga will be linked with Banjhar a feeder of Narmada. River Godavari is navigable up to Chandrapatla at its confluence with Indravati. From Chandrapatla, Godavari would be trained up to its confluence with river Pranhita.

Scheme III

This scheme envisages the linking of river Wardha, a tributary of Godavari with river Tapi.

Scheme IV

It connects river Ganga with Mahanadi *via* Son, Rihand (Ganga system) and Genj and Hasdo (of Mahanadi system).

Scheme V

Under this scheme, there are proposals to have interlinked navigable canals on both east and west coasts of India. Starting from Kolkata *via* Odisha Coast Canal, it will pass through Cuttack which will be linked with Lake Chilka by a 45 mile long canal. From Lake Chilka, a 250 mile long canal will join the Godavari Delta canals. The Godavari Delta canals are already connected with Buckingham canal. From Cuddalore, at the southern tip of Buckingham canal, another canal, 105 miles in length, will meet the Vedaranyam canal at its northern most point called

Hegapatram. From Vedaranyam, a point at the southern end of Vedranyam canal, will start a new canal 300 miles long girdling cape Kanya Kumari and meeting the southern tip of the West Coast Canal. The West Coast Canal has two breaks of 35 and 50 miles on the way to Mangalore. The first is between Cannanore and Badagra and the other between Mangalore and Hosdrug. These breaks will be canalized under this scheme.

Although the plan as given above is quite ambitious, the dropping of the scheme of making Ganga and Yamuna canals in Uttar Pradesh navigable does not seem reasonable. These canals pass through an area which is developing very fast and a canal with navigational facilities would be a great stimulant to economic development. The linking of the Gulf of Khambhat with the gulf of Kutch *via* River Sabarmathi up to Ahmedabad and thence *via* a canal would add to the prosperity of the State of Gujarat. Ahmedabad may be developed as an Inland port of intermediate size.

C. Multi-Purpose River-Valley Projects

The river valley development projects launched in India after Independence have some relevence for Inland navigation. The success of the Master Plan for Inland navigation depends upon, the extent to which the requirements of navigation are included in the design of the dams and canals. The Master Plan cannot be seen in isolation. It has to be fitted in the overall plan of water resource and transport development. The multi-purpose river valley projects implemented so far have been conceived individually and not as elements of a perspective plan for water resource development. They have been planned as irrigation-*cum*-power projects and the navigational elements have rarely found a place in them. As a consequence, the canals have been laid for irrigational purposes only. To design them for navigational purposes later would amount to investment higher than made earlier. In the context of scarce resources, how far would it be justified, has to be considered seriously. It would, therefore, be desirable to prepare a perspective plan for water resource development for the whole country keeping in view the future irrigation, power and navigational needs.

Of the several multi-purpose river-valley projects in hand or completed, the Hirakud project in Odisha; Tungabhadra of Karnataka; and Damodar valley of West Bengal have provisions for river training and navigation. Some of the other projects which have been developed on multi-purpose basis are:

1. Bhakra Nangal Project, Punjab
2. Rihand Project, U.P.
3. Chambal Valley Project, M.P. and Rajasthan
4. Rajasthan Canal Project, Rajasthan, Punjab and Haryana
5. Kakrapara Project, Maharashtra
6. Kosi Project, Bihar
7. Mahanadi Delta Irrigation Project, Odisha
8. Nagarjun Sagar Project, Andhra Pradesh
9. Mayurakshi Project, West Bengal

To have an idea of the navigational aspects of these projects we would discuss in short the Hirakud project of Odisha, Tungabhadra Project of Karnataka and Andhra Pradesh, and Damodar Valley Project of West Bengal and Bihar.

1. Hirakud

Completed in 1956, the Hirakud dam is the longest of its type in the world and the biggest in India. Included in this project of multipurpose development, is the construction of gravity and lift canals on either side of Mahanadi from the dam site which is about 9 miles north of Sambalpur town. With the construction of the dam, a content discharge of 8,800 cusecs is available in the Mahanadi river at Chiplima where the power channels join the river. To utilise this regular-flow. It is proposed to deepen the main river channel and develop navigation between Chiplima and Cuttack, a distance of about 194 miles. It is also proposed to utilise the power channel between Chiplima and Hirakud reservoir (approximately 16 miles) for Inland water transport.

2. Tungabhadra

This project lies partly in Karnataka and partly in Andhra Pradesh State. The headworks are located in Karnataka State. A navigable canal has been taken out from the headworks in Raichur district of Karnataka. This canal is 127 miles long. It passes through a very undulating relief and crosses three hill-ranges. The last range of hills is navigated by a 3557 feet long, 22 feet wide and 19 feet deep tunnel. The canal is navigable from the end of this tunnel to a distance of about 75 miles (*Also see pages 117-119*).

3. *Damodar Valley*

The Damodar valley canal connects the highly industrialized Durgapur region with the metropolitan town of Kolkata *via* river Hooghly to which it empties near Tribeni. It has a maximum head discharge of about 9400 cusecs during rains. The canal is 85 miles long, 92 feet wide and 9 feet deep. It allows 300 tonne barges of 125 x 16 feet with 6 feet draught. The maximum bed width of the canal is 172 feet and minimum 69 feet with 2:1 side slopes. The locks are of Chamber, Basin and combined types according to suitability.

D. The Gokhale Committee's Recommendations

The Gokhale committee on Inland water transport suggested for immediate investigation the following stretches of rivers during the Third Five Year Plan period, with a financial outlay of Rs. 50 crores for Inland navigation as a whole.

1. River Ganga from Allahabad to Kanpur, a distance of about 155 miles;
2. River Yamuna from Allahabad to Chambal River, a distance of about 290 miles;
3. River Tapi from Surat to Bhusawal, a distance of 232 miles;
4. River Narmada from Broach to Hoshangabad, a distance of 370 miles;
5. River Mahanadi from Cuttack to Dholpur, a distance of 107 miles;
6. River Godavari from Dowaleshwaram Anicut to Pranhita, a distance of 260 miles;
7. Rivers Sabari and Sileru (tributaries of Godavari); and
8. Krishna river.

The Committee also gave a list of schemes for further investigation and planning. The estimated cost of the schemes amounts to Rs. 167.60 crore, out of which Rs. 10 crore were earmarked for the Ganga Barrage project; Rs. 100 crore for provision of navigation facilities in river valley project, and Rs. 1 crore each for central organization and training establishments. The remaining amount of Rs. 55.60 crore was earmarked for detailed hydrographic surveys and the provision of other facilities for navigation on the existing waterways. The State-wise details of schemes with estimated cost were:

Table 10.1: State-wise Detail of Schemes with Estimated Cost

	Rs. in lakhs
1. Assam	
1. Detailed hydrographic surveys	10
2. Periodic aerial surveys of key shoals on the Brahmaputra	10
3. Terminal facilities	300
4. Approach roads to river Ghats	50
5. Ship repair facilities	30
6. Dredgers	100
7. Ferries (four)	80
8. River training	200
9. Country boat cooperatives	50
10. Navigational aids	50
11. Radio communication	10
12. Customs and security facilities at border stations and	20
13. Pilot projects on feeder rivers.	60
Total	**970**
2. West Bengal	
1. Hydrographic surveys of Sundarbans	10
2. Dredgers	100
3. Customs and security facilities at border stations (Beharikhal)	20
4. Customs and navigational aids in the Sundarban channels	10
5. Ferry for North Bengal	20
6. Improvement of terminal facilities at Kolkata	100
7. Improvement to Ghippur lock and provision of boat basin etc.	30
8. Country boat cooperatives	50
9. Navigational aids on the river Hooghly between D.V.C. canal and Kolkata port	10
10. Investigations for possible extension of the D.V.C. canal up to Sindri	10
11. Improvements to Hijli canal	10

(Contd.)

Table 10.1 (*Contd.*)

	Rs. in lakhs
12. Development of Inland water transport on D.V.G. canal	100
13. Pilot project for Sundarbans	30
Total	**500**
3. *Bihar*	
1. Navigational aids	10
2. Development of country boat cooperatives	50
3. Dredgers	30
4. Approach roads to Ghats	10
5. Terminal facilities	20
6. Ferry services	40
7. Ship repair facilities, and	30
8. River training.	50
Total	**240**
4. *Uttar Pradesh*	
1. Approach roads to Ghats	40
2. River training (Ganga, Ghaghra and Rapti)	45
3. Terminal facilities	20
4. Hydrographic surveys	5
5. Repair facilities	50
6. Country boat cooperatives	30
Total	**190**
5. *Odisha*	
1. Improvement in Mahanadi from Cuttack	50
2. Major improvements in High Level Canal to Dholpur and in Taldana and Kendrapara canals,	200
3. Dredgers for maintaining depth in canals, estuaries, and in Mahanadi	60
4. Development of country boat cooperatives	50
5. Terminal facilities at Jenapur and Paradip	40
6. Ferries in estuaries of the Mahanadi, Dharma and Devi rivers	50
Total	**450**
6. *Tamil Nadu*	
1. Dredgers for Buckingham and Vedaranyam canals and river crossings	40
2. Terminal facilities at 'Chennai wharves on Buckingham canal	10
3. Road connections, tow paths, and fresh water supply etc.	30
4. Country boat cooperatives	30
Total	**110**

(*Contd.*)

Table 10.1 (*Contd.*)

	Rs. in lakhs
7. Andhra Pradesh	
1. Dredgers for maintaining depth in Buckingham canal at river crossing	60
2. Road connections, terminal facilities, tow paths, fresh water supply etc.	40
3. Dredgers for Delta canals	40
4. Two locks on Pulleru and Masulipatnam canals	20
5. Improvement in Krishna.Godavari and their tributaries	200
6. Boat repair facilities	20
7. Country boat cooperatives	40
8. Ferries in Krishna-Godavari Delta	60
Total	**480**
8. *Kerala*	
1. Construction of tow walls	20
2. West Coast Canal north of Cochin, including the construction of locks and high bridges	200
3. West Coast Canal, Quilon to Cochin including navigational and terminal facilities at Alleppey and Quilon wharves	100
4. Beypore, Paulba and other rivers and backwaters	40
5. Other canals	20
6. Dredgers (6)	80
7. Country boat cooperatives	50
8. Alleppey Shartalai canal	40
9. Extension of West Coast canal from Badagra to Mahe	40
10. Ferries	50
Total	**640**
9. Maharashtra and Gujarat	
1. Hydrograyhic surveys	50
2. Dredgers	100
3. Navigational aids	40
4. Country boat cooperatives	50
5. Terminal facilities at Karambhavane on Vasishti River	20
6. Approach roads to Ghats	10
7. Tugs on Narmada and Tapi	20
8. Inland waterway development in Mumbai and Salsette, Island and	900
9. Ferries	30
Total	**1,220**

(*Contd.*)

Table 10.1 (*Contd.*)

	Rs. in lakhs
10. Karnataka	
1. Coastal canal between Mangalore and Coondapur	70
2. Country boat cooperatives	20
3. Ferries	20
Total	**110**
11. Others	
1. Improvement of Ferries and country boat cooperatives in M.P.	50
2. Improvement of Ferries and country boat cooperatives in Punjab	50
3. Improvements of waterways in Kashmir	50
4. Provision of works required for future navigability and head room under bridges of the Rajasthan Canal	500
5. Ganga Barrage project	1000
6. Provision of navigational facilities in river valley projects	10,000
7. Control organisation	100
8. Training establishments	100
Total	11,850
Grand total	***16,760***

E. National Water Grid*

The concept of a national water grid with a Ganga-Cauvery link canal as its mainstay has a great significance for Inland water transport in India. The basic elements of this concept are already there in the Master Plan for Inland navigation discussed above. The Master Plan has now been made more comprehensive and multi-purpose. The proposed national water grid would be by far the largest project conceived in India and one of the largest water project attempted in the world.

The possible components of the national water-grid could be (1) the Ganga Cauvery link connecting Ganga in the north with Cauvery in the south and passing in route through the basins of Son, Narmada, Tapi, Godavari, Krishna and Pennar, (2) Brahmaputra-Ganga link *via* northern districts of West Bengal, (3) a link canal to Rajasthan from Narmada, (4) a link through river Chambal, a tributary of Yamuna to pump water to areas near Ajmer in Rajasthan, (5) a link canal to carry surplus water of the

* Partly reproduced from *The Hindu*, September 29, 1972.

Mahanadi to irrigate coastal areas, and (6) a link canal girlding the peninsula along the coast. The Ganga-Cauvery link envisages diversion of up to 60,000 cusecs of the waters of the Ganga by constructing a barrage near Patna. Of this quantity, 10,000 cusecs for 300 days of the year, would be supplied to the drought-affected areas of south Uttar Pradesh and south Bihar which are located within the Ganga basin itself. The volume of 50,000 cusecs of water, pumped for 150 days in a year would be diverted during the high flow period only and would be transferred outside the basin to meet partially the water demand of the chronically drought prone areas of Rajasthan, Gujarat, Madhya Pradesh, Maharashtra, Andhra Pradesh, Karnataka and Tamil Nadu.

At the barrage on Ganga, 60,000 cusecs of water will be lifted to a canal at an elevation of 150 feet which will carry the water to Son barrage. 50,000 cusecs of water will be lifted in stages and carried along river Son. Passing through Son and a canal cutting across the ridge separating the Son and Narmada basins, the water will reach Bargi reservoir on Narmada river which has a full reservoir level (FRL) of 1,387 feet.

A part of the transferred water will be released into Narmada river for use in the drought affected areas in the adjoining basins. The rest will go to the Wainganga river and then to Inchampalli reservoir (400 FRL) on the Godavari river. Then along with the surplus waters of Godavari and Narmada, the water will be pumped to a height of 1,000 feet from where a gravity canal will carry it into the Srisailam reservoir (FRL 885 feet) which is under construction on the Krishna river.

The water from the Srisailam reservoir would be fed into Kunderu river, a tributary of the Pennar river. From Pennar, near Cuddapah a gravity canal will carry the water to the upper anicut (FRL 238.4 feet) on the Cauvery river. The total length of the link would be about 2,600 km. out of which 1500 km. will be along the river course and 1100 km. along the canal. The width of the canal will be about 75 metres and the depth will be about five metres.

If and when completed, the Ganga-Cauvery link will offer following advantages:

1. It would bring the surplus waters of the Ganga specially during the monsoon season to the south and thus (a) help extend irrigation to millions of acres of dry farming land

in Madhya Pradesh, Andhra Pradesh, Karnataka and Tamil Nadu, and (b) lessen the damage caused by floods to UP and Bihar.

2. It would give a navigable channel from north to south facilitating the movement of coal, ores, foodgrains, building materials etc. at a relatively cheaper rate. It would give rise to a number of Inland ports not only along the grand canal, but also along the riverways and other canals

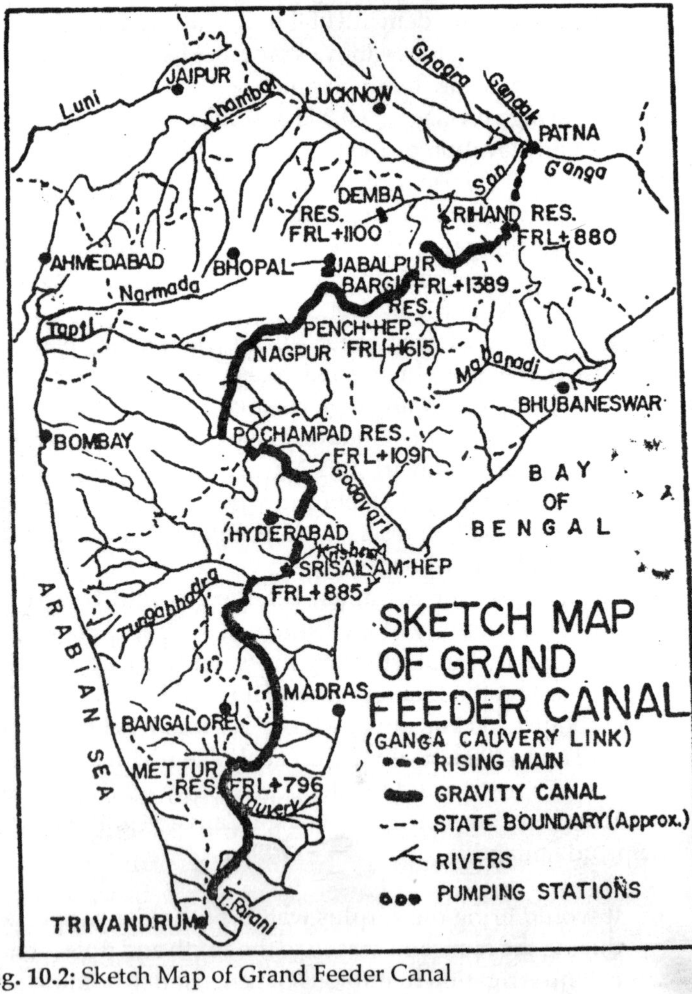

Fig. 10.2: Sketch Map of Grand Feeder Canal

linking it with the adjoining areas and other parts of the country. All these will thus provide the opportunities for the development of new urban and industrial centres.

3. The canal, if planned in an integrated way, can offer the best facilities for recreation. The reservoirs through which it would pass should help develop aquatic games, and sports, apart from a belt of forests and orchards running across the country.
4. The canal would also supply drinking water to the interior urban centres specially by 2000 A.D. when Indian economy would be confronted with increasing scarcity of water.

Several doubts have been raised about the economic viability of this project. Important among these are:

1. The cost of the project is so high and the gestation period so long that the country cannot afford to go for it at least for a few more decades.
2. There is about 300 million acre-feet of utilizable water which still remains unutilized and which will cost far less to develop. It would be better to take up these projects first.
3. The Power needed to pump the water of Ganga up to a height of 150 feet near Patna will be about 17 times of that used by Neyveli generation. This would amount to about fifty per cent of the power produced in the country at present.
4. The cost projection of about Rs. 2,500 crore for the entire project is an under-estimate. Moreover, it can be very much reduced by diverting the waters of the Ganga by means of a north Vindhya-Aravali canal with suitable modifications all along the line.

The objection on the grounds of cost does not appear to be substantive. The canal is going to be ready only by the end of the century. By that time, the country would be faced with serious problems of water supply and also of higher wages. Notwithstanding the fact that economy will be far better then, it would not be in a position to invest enough resources to complete the project in a decade or so. The project could be completed in stages, each stage becoming paying after its completion. For example, the Godavari-Krishna-Cauvery link may be completed first.

It should also be kept in view that the canal in question passes, through drought affected areas of the country. It can be considered as a part of the drought relief programme and completed much earlier than scheduled while at the same time solve the immediate employment problem of the country. It can give employment to lakhs of unemployed people residing in the rural parts of the country.

The second objection is also rather weak. By the time the Ganga-Cauvery link becomes a reality, much of the available surface water in the country would have been utilized under various other schemes. In fact, one of the reasons why this project should get priority in our perspective planning is the lack of potential water resources, to be developed after 2000 A.D. Further, the Ganga-Cauvery link could be the main channel to which water could be drawn from other sources including the west-flowing rivers of Kerala and Karnataka and from which water could be diverted to other areas. This project does not disqualify other projects which might be given priority in our periodic plans.

The third objection pertains to the requirements of power to lift the waters of Ganga to a height of 156 feet, near Patna and still higher elsewhere. It is estimated that it will consume anywhere between 40 to 50 per cent of power generated in the country to lift 60,000 cusecs of water to this height. One has, however, to keep in view that the power generating capacity of the country in 2000 A.D., for example, would not be the same as it is today. If the perspective plan for power generation is taken into account, by 2000 A.D., the power needed for this purpose may not exceed 5 per cent of the national output. The last objection pertaining to the estimates of the cost appears to be valid. But if the project is taken up as a part of the drought relief and other programmes, the cost even if higher would be justified. The point that the lifting of the water to such a great height can be avoided by building a North Vindhya-Aravali canal however, needs serious consideration. In any case, it would be desirable to have two channels diverting the waters of Ganga and its tributaries and meeting somewhere in Central India to form the grand canal. This would help divert superfluous waters of the Ganga from its upper reaches also and would provide direct navigational link between the western and the peninsular states of the country.

F. Priorities in Planning

The master plan as chalked out earlier and the national water grid proposed now are long-term programmes. It may take several decades before some of them may even be considered seriously for implementation. The available resources are so meagre and the popularity of Inland water transport is at such a low ebb that unless considered as an element of national water resource utilization and management plan, Inland water transport would not get its due priority. Even among the various modes of transportation, it is not likely to get proper priority except perhaps in the States of West Bengal, Assam and Tripura.

Given the constraints, of the resources as they are and as they are likely to be in the near future, serious attention has to be paid to setting priorities for the development of Inland navigation within the framework of a perspective plan for national water grid. There is no dispute over the need for a national water grid involving the construction of the Ganga-Cauvery Canal. When should such a project be implemented, is the question? This question can be handled fairly well if we break the whole programme of national water grid into stages.

1. Stage-I (1975-84 A.D.)

In this stage following projects should be completed:

(a) The Ganga should be made navigable by steamers from Varanasi to Kolkata;

(b) Navigability of Brahmaputra and Surma through Bangladesh should be improved and a coordinated plan for the development of Inland navigation between West Bengal, Bangladesh and Assam should be implemented in cooperation with, the Government of Bangladesh;

(c) The navigable waterways of Kerala should be further developed and missing links opened up;

(d) The Buckingham canal should be improved and made navigable;

(e) Navigational problems of Krishna, Godavari and Mahanadi Deltas and Damodar and Tungabhadra canals should be solved and commercial navigation developed.
(f) Survey of the Ganga Cauvery link should be completed and wherever the allignment and depth of the channel is determined, earth work started.

2. *Stage-II (1985-94 A.D.)*

(a) The Ganga should be made navigable up to Allahabad or if feasible up to Kanpur, and Ghaghra up to the Nepal border. Navigability of other rivers of the Ganga system can also be improved depending upon the traffic;
(b) Navigation on Brahmaputra in Assam as well as in Bangladesh should be further improved and Inland port facilities of modern types provided;
(c) The Buckingham and Vedaranyam canals should be connected by a link canal;
(d) The Odisha Coast Canal should be improved, so that, the Mahanadi Delta canals can offer direct links between Cuttack and Kolkata;
(e) Krishna should be linked with Cauvery as envisaged in the Ganga-Cauvery link scheme; and
(f) The Madhya Pradesh portion of the Ganga-Cauvery canal should be partly completed.

3. *Stage-III (1995-2004 A.D.)*

(a) The Ganga should be made navigable up to Kanpur;
(b) The Godavari and Krishna link of the Ganga-Cauvery canal should be completed and planning for the pumping of water near Patna started; and
(c) Ken and Son should be made navigable and linked with Narmada which should also be made navigable.

4. *Stage-IV (2005 to 2014 A.D.)*

(a) The Ganga-Cauvery link should be completed up to Mettur dam;

(b) Godavari and Krishna should be made navigable from their junction with the Ganga-Cauvery canal to their mouths;

(c) Attempts should be made to make Mahanadi also navigable as far as possible.

5. Stage-V (2015 to 2024 A.D.)

(a) The Ganga-Cauvery link should be extended further south to River Tambraparani and linked with the coastal waterways of Kerala and Vedaranyam canal of Tamil Nadu;

(b) The west coast waterways in Kerala should be extended northward to Mangalore;

(c) Ken-Narmada link should be further improved;

(d) Link canal connecting the delta canals of Godavari and Mahanadi should be constructed; and

(e) Narmada should be linked with the Ganga-Cauvery canal by a navigable channel. Tapi also may be canalized to link the Grand Canal with the Arabian Sea.

The total cost of all these projects may amount to Rs. 5000 crore or an annual investment of Rs. 100 crore during the next 50 years or so. When completed, the national water grid will solve the problem of water that the country will face in the early part of the next century while at the same time will offer a national grid of waterways.

ANNEXURES

Annexure-I

*Lectures on Irrigation Works in India**[1]

By Sir Arthur Cotton

LECTURE I
(DECEMBER 10, 1874)

The importance of any subject of investigation is measured by the difference between the cost of obtaining it and its value when obtained, that is, in the case of material things. The question is not what is the value of a pound or a ton of anything. If a pound gold costs more to obtain than its value, we must leave it alone; and if a pound of iron, when obtained, is worth double the cost of mining and smelting it, it is a highly profitable operation. If 1,000 cubic yards of water can be made use of at a cost of 6d., and if its value, so applied, is 10s., there is no gold mine in the world that can be compared to an irrigation work. At present, it is stated that the average result of gold mining in Victoria is that it merely affords rather high wages to the men actually employed upon it. If so, it is nothing to the results of conducting water to the land in India. If a million a year is spent in gold-mining, and it gives 6s. a day to the miners who could otherwise be only gaining 4s, there is a net profit of 330,000 pounds a year; and if a million a year is spent as the interest at 7 per cent of a capital of 14,000,000 pound's in irrigating 10,000,000 acres, yielding in increase of produce and other things 20 millions a year, it is sixty times as profitable as gold mining in Victoria. Therefore, we may like-wise engineers make sure that we have a sound foundation before we proceed to the

---

1. Lecture delivered at the School of Military Engineering, Autum Session, 1874.

superstructure; let us inquire into the value and cost of water in India and thus satisfy ourselves that we are expending our times upon a matter that is really worth it. I, therefore, propose in this first lecture to show from the actual results of works on the largest scale what is the value of water for its several uses, so far as they come within the sphere of our action as engineers.

This is especially necessary in England, because we are so generally tolerably well supplied with it that we think little about it. A gentleman, who had not been long in Australia, began a review of a book on Water with this observation: "This is a very dry subject."

Probably, he never had anything to do with water in England except to wash himself, and had always found it ready in his room for this purpose. How different would his valuation of water have been if he had to lie down to die for want of a draught of it in the plains of the interior as numbers have done; or if he had seen hundreds of thousands dying of famine around him in Africa or India from the failure of the harvest, or if he had gone into one tract and seen the population though not dying of famine yet in a State of utter despondency, ill-fed, ill-clad, ill-housed, sickly, the slaves of the money lenders, and so unfit for any of the duties of life; and then into another, where, through the blessing of water distributed through their villages and over their lands, he found the population wealthy, cheerful, active, well-fed, housed, and clad independent of all the world, and full of life and energy.

The first thing, then, we have to do in this case, as in all other, is to get our interest aroused and our judgement satisfied by a careful examination of the fundamental points. Now, the principal uses for which water is required are these:

First — For domestic purposes: drinking, washing etc.
Second — For the production of food from the land etc.
Third — For carriage by rivers etc.
Fourth — For water power.
Fifth — For sundry purposes, such as an extinguishing fire, cleaning sewers etc.

But besides the benefits arising from these uses of water, we have to consider the prevention of losses by its regulation when it would otherwise be injurious, viz.

First — In preventing or protecting from Inland floods.
Second — In draining when its excess or stagnation is injurious to health.
Third — In protecting land from the ocean wave.

With respect to the first of the uses,—that of domestic purposes, it is, of course, a matter simply of absolute necessity; and the value of pure water in abundance and at hand for drinking for man and beast, for cleanliness etc. cannot be estimated in figures. I must not attempt to go into the subject of its sanitary value in any detail, because it is not in our line. I may safely refer inquires on this point to the writings of Miss Nightingale and others I may just mention, as an instance of the value of its supply for this purpose, that, in consequence of its regular and ample supply, Calcutta has lately become one of the healthiest cities in the world. In 1871 it was more salubrious than Manchester and Liverpool. I may also mention instances of the want of it in India. I have seen a number of water holes dug in a piece of land and each watched night and day by a member of the family, to whom it belonged, to prevent the water being stolen, and sometimes it is carried for miles on the women's heads in the dry season to their homes, and often it is drawn from wells in which it is highly mineralised, or from pits in which is contained only the remains of what collected months before in the rains, and was now in such a filthy state as to be totally unfit for drinking. In Bombay, one of the charges in the municipal accounts used to be for carrying away the dead fish that were found floating on the tops of the tanks killed by the poisonous state of the water which was the sole supply of the human inhabitants.

Let us proceed to consider the second point, *viz.* the value of water for the production of food. In one respect its value in this matter also is beyond estimate—making, the difference between famine and plenty. But we may also in one way apply a measure of money value to it even in this respect; thus, about four millions of people this year in Bengal were fed by Government for an average of four months, who must have consumed about 350,000 tons of food. This would be produced on 700,000 acres, and have required for rice at 6,000 cubic yards per acre, 4200 millions cubic yards, which would give 650 cubic yards per pound. But is this case, besides this money value, who can estimate the importance of the people having been employed in their ordinary work of cultivation, etc., rather than suffering all the evil influences connected with the feeding of them by Government. One more instance may be given of the money-value of water in connection, with, famine. In Orissa, in 1866, the old Indian system of leaving the people to die was persisted in, and the official papers state that 1½ millions died. Probably, an average supply of four month's food would have preserved those lives, costing, at two-thirds of a penny a pound (the ordinary price of rice), for 1,50,000 tons, 9,00,000 pounds and 1,800 millions of cubic yards of water would have secured this produce which is 2,000 cubic yards per pound. Now, the loss of 1½ millions of people costs the Government, its loss of revenue at 2½ rupees a-head 3,75,000 pounds a year, the interest of a capital of 7,000,000 pound which would have all been saved by a supply of 1800 millions cubic yards of water giving for its value 260 cubic yards per pound. We may now consider the value of water for under ordinary circumstances.

We allow 6,000 cubic yards of water per acre of rice (allowing for great waste) to produce half-a-ton, worth at two-thirds of a penny, 3 pounds, besides straw for fodder; and allowing the average crop without irrigation to be worth 1 pound, it gives 2 pounds for the value of 6,000 cubic yards or 3,000 cubic yards per pound. If we take the case of what we call dry grains such as wheat, about 1,500 cubic yards secures an addition to the ordinary crop of about the value of 1 pound 10 shillings which is 1,000 cubic yards per pound. We have data for this now from a multitude of irrigation works all over India, from the Himalayan mountains to Cape Comorin—some of them on a very large scale—calculated to irrigate from ½ to 2,000,000 acres. To compare this with the value of the water raised from rivers and from millions of wells scattered over India, the cost of raising it on an average from wells of 15 feet deep is about 3,000 cubic yards per pound, and it is evident that the value must be greater than this for such filtered well water, which is greatly inferior to river water, otherwise it would not be raised; perhaps 2,000 cubic yards per pound for well water against from 1,000 to 3,000 cubic yards per pound for river water as above given. These are quite sufficient to enable us to form a substantially correct judgement of the value of water for production.

The third point is the value of water for carriage.

This will necessarily vary very much especially according to the extent of traffic, but to give a probable case, in order to show the mode in which this may be calculated the consumption of water in a canal is—first, by evaporation, and second by leakage. There might be in some countries a third, by what is called 'Absorption,' but there is no such thing in Indian canal filled by rivers and having a moderate current, as the fine silt in the river water perfectly puddels the canal in a short time, so that, not a drop escapes by the bottom or sides. I have cut a trench 6 feet deep in the loose sands close by the side of water, flowing in a canal and found it perfectly dry—not a drop of water passing through the lining of the fine silt like butter with which sandy bed of the canal was covered. Evaporation in India is, on the hottest days, with a strong land wind of the temperature of 110° blowing, half an inch in shallow water, and the total evaporation in the year is about two yards, though I am not aware that this has been accurately ascertained. But allowing a canal 30 yards broad, suited to a first class traffic of several million tons per annum, the loss by evaporation will be about 100,000 cubic yards per mile; and if 3/4 of a million tons moved in one direction and the same boat with ¼ of a million ton returning carrying 100 tons, there will be 15,000 passages of the locks per hour; and allowing that half the boats find the locks full or empty according as it is going up or down, so that, it consumes no water in passing, the number of locks full of water per annum, will be 11,000, which, with the locks 150 feet by 20 with a lift of 9 feet or 1,000 cubic yards per lock full, will be 11,000,000 cubic yards per annum. Now, if such a canal is 300 miles long, the consumption of water will be 37,000 cubic yards per mile, making the total for evaporation and leakage in such a case 1,37,000 cubic yards per mile, or allowing for waste 2,00,000. If such a canal is worked at 1/10 of a penny per mile, and a river by the side of it at half a penny, and allowing for winding 3 farthings to compare it with a nearly straight canal, the saving will be two-thirds of a penney per ton per mile, or nearly 3,000 pounds per mile for a consumption of water of 2,00,000 cubic yards which is 70 cubic yards per pound against 2,000 cubic yards for production—so great is the value of water for carriage. If we compare the canal with land carriage, either by railway or road at 3d per ton, the saving will be four times as great, of the value of water 18 cubic yards per pound; and if, as will be the case on almost all the great lines in

India, the canals are used for both irrigation and transit, the value will be still rather greater.

This calculation is quite sufficient to show that the value of water for transit is enormous, and the cost of water (as will be shown hereafter) utterly insignificant in comparison of the value.

I may mention here that the traffic on such canals in India carrying at that cost, one-tenth of a penny per ton per mile, will be several million tons, up the valley of the Ganges when the canal is completed for 1,200 miles and fitted for steamers of 250 tons. The traffic will probably be at 2,000,000 tons almost at first, and will probably increase to 4 or 5 millions.

To give some idea of the value of water for irrigation in comparison of that for production, let us suppose that the various irrigation projects between Calcutta and Loodeena, on the Sutlej, a distance of 1,200 miles, namely, the Sirhind, Ganges, Sone, and Rajmahal projects, form a complete communication. Their cost will be about 12 millions, watering five million acres, yielding an increased produce of grain of 8 millions a year.

The saving in the one main line, carrying 2 million tons a year, and saving a half-penny a ton a mile compared with the river, would be five millions a year and that on the innumerable branches could not be less than 3 millions—or together equal to the profit in produce; i.e. to say, that on that great line, through this immense population the saving on the transit alone, would be equal to the whole profit of irrigation. In other words, where the water is used both for irrigation and navigation, the profit on such an important line would be doubled, and this supposed that there is effective water carriage on the same line by river. If there were only land carriage, either by road or rail, the whole of the traffic would in fact, be produced by water carriage. On one main line, the Peninsular Railway, where there is no water carriage by the side of it, the whole of the transit is only 140 thousand tons a year. The traffic on that line, (if there were really cheap transit) would probably be from one to two million sterling, and rapidly increase on that, i.e. where there is only land carriage, there is no traffic worth mentioning.

In the United States, they estimate for a traffic of 10 million tons a year in the present state of things, between the central States and the Atlantic. On the three canals terminating in the Mersey there are more than 3 million tons carriage, besides that on a river navigation, and four lines of railway, and the common road.

It is important to state these things here, because so few are aware of the vast extent to which traffic will reach when it is extremely cheap, so that, the coarsest thing may be conveyed hundreds of miles at an almost nominal cost.

In the above calculations goods only have been supposed, but there will be a great addition to the value of water in passenger traffic. One of the peculiar features of India is the extraordinary locomotive propensities of its population.

Even without any facilities for travelling, when they can only move by days marches of 20 or 25 miles on foot, they travel in multitude. Many years ago, at a point 11 miles from Madras, on one of the four main roads that enter that city, the number of travellers was 3,300 per day almost all on foot. On the canals in Godavari, by boats at 3 miles per hour, the charge being 7 or 8 miles for a penny, multitudes travel, by calculation from the number of boats about 5,000 a day over 20 miles each. The expense of travelling on foot may be taken at 25 miles per day for the value of a day's labour, or 3d or 4d—one-seventh of a penny per mile.

With steamers moving at 10 or 12 miles an hour, for the great mass of travellers, they could be carried about 8 miles for a penny, but moving night and day so as to accomplish about 300 miles a day. At this charge and speed, the travellers on the main line, up the plain of the Ganges, would perhaps be 5,000 a day. On the Railway, at a charge 1/3 of a penny, the number on that line averages, about 1,000 a day, besides multitudes on the road and river.

When I was in India some years ago, the main road from Calcutta to Allahabad was crowded with travellers, just like a street in London, and that, too by the side of a railway. I enquired recently about this phenomenon, of a gentleman who was living on the high road, and he said, that the same state of things still existed.

If such steamers were placed on the Godavari canals, no doubt the number of passengers would be increased three or four fold. On the railways, 96 per cent travel in 3rd class, and 3 per cent in 2nd class, leaving only 1 per cent in first class.

For the mails and a few first class passengers, boats could be built to run at the same speed, as the railways are now worked at, *viz.* from 15 to 25 miles. A boat built for the Governor of Bengal lately ran at nearly 24 miles an hour on the trial and would keep up about 22. She was 90 feet long and similar boat 150 feet the length of the locks, would run 30 miles, so that, any speed may be used.

If 5,000 passengers a day use the canal on an average over its whole length, and the charge is one-eight of a penny against one-third of a penny on the rail, the saving would be one-fifth of a penny, or 4 pound per day per mile, 1,200 pounds per annum, for a consumption of water of 2,00,000 cubic yards per annum, which would give for the value of water for passenger traffic 170 cubic yard per pound, in addition to 70 cubic yards per pound for goods traffic at a 1 million tons, or together 50 cubic yards per pound. This is sufficient to show the enormous value of water for transit, both for goods and passengers, so far as money can measure it, but there is no way of estimating the full value of such means of cheap transit. The value of a means that sets every district at liberty to grow whatever is most suited to its soil and climate, and places at its disposal everything else that it requires whatever it may be most cheaply produced cannot be estimated. If the Isle of France, instead of being surrounded by water, and so enable fully to turn to account its wonderful powers of soil for the production of sugar, while it lays all the world under contribution for everything else, were surrounded by hundreds of miles breadth of land, and was thereby compelled to grow all its own food, clothing etc., instead of its sugar, it would be a miserably poor country compared with what it is. And the transit of goods is only a part of the effects of cheap carriage, the free intercourse of the inhabitants is a matter also that cannot be estimated.

If all India could be traversed at a cost of 8 miles for a penny, and at 10 to 20 miles an hour, the effect of it upon the whole population would be beyond all calculation. I may here remark that the great mass of people cannot afford the railway prices, and either go by the common roads or remain isolated, and even with respect to those who do afford it, the number is quite in significant on account of the trifling length of railway that is or can be executed.

We next come to the value of water for power. On all the great irrigation work, there is of necessity, an enormous power of water available. Everywhere there is a greater fall of the country than can be allowed in the canals.

The current must be kept so low as not to cut the bed and banks, and also not to spoil the transit. For either of these a current of 3,000 yards at the utmost cannot be exceeded, which is due to a depth of 9 feet, with a fall of 5 inches, and if the fall of the country is more than this, there must be locks and weirs in the line of the canals.

If on the line of the canal there is 50 feet fall in the country, above 4 or 5 inches a mile, most of the water must pass round the locks before it is used in the field, and there would be 1,700 lbs. by 50 ft., 85,000 lbs. falling 1 feet for every cubic yard of water, or about 28 cubic yards per horse power per hour, against one penny for steam horse power 7,000 cubic yards per pound for the value of the water falling 50 feet per power; and if compared with the cost of human labour, 3,000 cubic yard for horse power. Of course, there will be a great difference in the height which the irrigation water falls in the different localities. In Godavari, for instance, the average is probably 20 feet, while in the Ganges canal it may be 200 feet.

But to this we may add the consideration of the great advantage of water power over steam, in its safety, convenience etc.

The advantages which India thus enjoys in the vast waterpower distributed over all the tracts irrigated, situated in the midst of population, on the lines of cheap transit, and so with every facility for both collecting the raw material to the mills and distributing the manufactured good without land carriage, these advantages are enormous.

In the Godavari works 8,000 million cubic yards of water are conveyed by the canal, falling on an average 20 feet at the locks, which would be about 27,000 horse power for the whole year, at 10 hours a day. And on the Ganges canal about 6,000 millions fall 200 ft., giving about 20,00,000 horse power throughout the year.

It is only necessary to give these calculations roughly to show the immense of water power that is thus available in India in connection with irrigation.

India will thus have the advantage over every country in the world, in having the power so distributed in the most convenient localities. The charge for it may be quite nominal, as the interest of the money expended on the irrigation works will be paid over. and over by the irrigation and transit.

But the total value of it for power in the Ganges canal, allowing one penny per hour, the cost of steam power would be 800 pounds per hour and 25,00,000 pounds per annum. And of the Godavari water, the value would be 110 pounds per hour, or 3,50,000 pounds per annum. So, that on the 10 great irrigation works now under execution there must be water power of the value of many millions a year.

Of the value of water under the fifth head, namely for the extinguishing of fire, and all the various other minor purposes, of course, no estimate can be given in money, though they give a vast additional value to it, besides the great one estimated. But thus taking the combined value of water for domestic purposes, and health, for securing an increasing food by irrigation, for providing extremely cheap, convenient and speedy transit for goods and passengers, as shown in a measure by the calculations above given, we can come to no other conclusion than that it is incomparably the greatest treasure India possesses.

If we allow 1 pound for 2,000 cubic yards for the value, that of the Ganges canal water 6,000 million cubic yards would be, if all were used, 3 millions per annum, and of the Godavari water 4 millions, but a large portion of what enters the canal is not used. The actual value of the former taking a million acres at 15 rupees, is one and a half million a year for produce only.

And of the latter 600,000 acres, at 2 pounds, one and a quarter millions. And the actual total money receipt from them is much above this; certainly above 3 millions a year for the two.

When the present great works are completed, they will water at least 10 million acres, and the money value will be at least 25 millions, much more than half the amount of taxes paid by India at present. Besides the work now in hand, several great projects have been fully planned and estimated, but not yet begun. If these were executed, the total increased income received by India from water would be fully equal to the whole of the taxes, 40 millions.

And if the same system were carried out through all the remaining districts, so that, there was an average of only a quarter of a million acres irrigated in each of 200 districts, there would be 50 million acres, and the money value in produce, navigation, power etc., would be at least 120 millions or three times the present taxation, so that, if instead of this, all taxes are abolished, India would be 80 millions a year poorer than under a general systems of irrigation and navigation, while all the present taxes were continued. And this 50 millions of acres could be completed for about 120 millions, including what was already been expended.

Now, what should we think of gold mines in India that yielded 120 millions a year, without all the inestimable benefit from water not included in that estimated money return; and is not 120 millions the same whether it is the value of gold or water ? Is not 1,000 pound worth of Iron, or wood, or water, or anything else just as valuable as 1,000 pound worth of gold ?

How strange it seems that men cannot understand this. The income of Godavari is increased by about 1,250,000 pounds a year from water, and you will scarcely find an official paper even that takes the least notice of it.

How every newspaper would have been filled with the accounts if the district yielded 1¼ millions a year in gold.

I have given above the cost of water for irrigation and for canals of navigation separately, but in the great majority of cases in India, in the great works, the two would be combined, and nothings would be required to make the irrigation canals navigable, but locks. There would, of course, be roads on both banks of every such canal, which would answer for tow-paths. The cost of locks would depend on the fall of the country. Over a large extent of the most important lines this is very small, under a foot a mile, besides the slope of the canal, which might cost 200 pounds for locks fitted for steamers of 250 tons, quite an insignificant addition to the cost of irrigation.

Thus wherever, there is extensive irrigation from rivers, we have not only main lines of navigation, but innumerable branches pervading the whole, built for nothing while the railways cost from 6,000 to 28,000 pounds a mile.

I must now show the data we have for the whole cost of a canal for navigation, independent of irrigation. The actual cost of large canals has varied from 1,000 pounds per mile for one of 25 yards broad in the instance of the Krishna and Godavari canal, 93 miles long, with only one lock, and in a very flat country, but across the lay of it, so that, all the drainage was crossed and had to be provided for, up to that of the main Tungbudra canal, 190 miles long, 60 yards broad at the head, and, I suppose, 15 yards at the end, or averaging 35 yards with a considerable fall of 500 feets, 2½ feets per mile, which cost about 6,000 pounds a mile. This is in the upper country where there are considerable undulations, much rock cutting, and very heavy drainage to cross. It is about an extreme case for the populous part of the country.

The Ganges canal has about 700 miles of main lines, from 10 to 60 yards broad, averaging perhaps 35 yards, with a total fall of about 500 feet in 350 miles, or 1½ feet per mile. The whole cost of the works including many thousand miles of distributaries and etc., has been 2½ millions, but of this 1 million was the cost of bringing it out of the hills in a kind of country where no canal would have to be made. Of the remaining 1 million, if we take half of the distribution, it leaves about 1,000 pound per mile for the cost of such a canal in the plains. But this canal follows the water shed of the country, and crosses no drainage.

If we take an average of 3,000 pounds a mile for main lines of navigation, 30 yards broad, it would include probably all such lines for a complete system of Inland water transit, or one-sixth of what the railway lines have hitherto cost without interest. And a less sum would be sufficient for river improvement. The Godavari navigation work, when completed, will have cost 2,000 pounds a mile, without any additional supply of water, and with it about 2,500 pounds.

Some of the rivers of India can never be made very good for navigation. Such is the case with the Indus and the Ganges, the latter especially on account of its winding; but both on account of changes in their beds, and of their great width making them so dangerous in storms. Hunderds of boats are lost every year in the Ganges, and it is stated that the loss between Calcutta and Goalundo, the junction of the Ganges and Burhampootra, is 4 per cent, every voyage. Some of the rivers are, on the country, very capable of improvement, as the Godavari, part of the Krishna, and the Beema, and probably many others.

On the lines of the Godavari, there is no alternative, but to improve the river, as it is impossible to make a canal anywhere near it, owing to a great rise of the river, in one place 80 feet, so that, every little stream that enters it at every two or three miles, has a channel for 40 to 80 feet deep. But with the weirs and, locks at the three barriers, an additional water, the river will from a very fair navigation capable of being worked at ½d. a ton a mile or less. I am not acquainted with the Burhampootra myself, but I am informed that it is a good navigation in its unimproved stage, and

I conclude, it could be much improved by stored water in the dry season. For 800,000 pounds or 1000 pounds a mile, perhaps 4,000 million cubic yards could be stored, which would supply an average of 1 million cubic yards per hour for 160 days, or 2 millions at the end of the dry season, providing for a stream 1,000 yards broad, and 1 yard deep, with a velocity of 2,000 yards, which could not, but be an important addition to the river when it is at its lowest. The terrible mistake has been neglecting those natural lines where money would have effected so much, and spending such enormous sum on land carriage, which has entirely failed in the two essential points, to carry large quantity, and to carry cheaply. In this case, for instance, which will be most valuable, 40 miles of railway carrying a small quantity at l½d., and not paying its interest, or 800 miles of river carrying one or two million tons at ¼ d., and leaving no burden on its treasury.

We thus come to these conclusion:

First – Cost of water drawn from the rivers and distributed to the land, from 20,000 to 70,000 cubic yards, per pound.

Second – Ditto of stored water, from 40,000 to 60,000.

Third – Ditto raised 20 feet by steam, 20,000. Ditto raised 15 feet by animal power, 3,000.

This data are quite sufficient to afford a perfectly correct notion of the cost of water generally, and it will be easy to make such a calculation in each particular case. The vast amount of water already distributed in such a great variety of situation, from Cape Comorin to the Himalayas, affords unquestionable means of calculation.

As I have said so much about the cost of water for irrigation, I may here try to investigate the subject of water carriage in comparison with land transit. This is now by far the most important question for modern engineers. The difficulty always is to get men fairly to compare things. The tendency always is to run away with some idea, and to refuse even to look at any other. In nothing has this been more disastrous in its consequences than in the case of Inland transit. The public everywhere till very lately have been thus so completely carried away by the success of the railways, that no comparison has been made between them and canals.

Happily, in most civilized countries, men have not been so completely blinded by them as to neglect roads, and the latter have been most deligently attended to all the time of the railway mania, so that, in England, and still more in France, they have been greatly improved, indeed to such a degree that I have no doubt we are on the eve of a revolution, by the extended use of them. It has now been proved by the bicycles that human labour can accomplish a speed, and that at a low cost, that no horse power could possibly attend to. A speed of 17 miles has been reached by the present very imperfect machines worked by the feet, and consequently, only about two-thirds of the powers of the arms, and with several other sources of waste of power, from which it is certain that a speed of 20 miles on the road can easily be reached by human power, and that at much less cost than by horse at 10.

But the examination of the subject of water transit has not yet been fairly begun in England. In France they are now reforming their waterways, though strange to say, leaving out of sight the main point, the use of steam power. And even in England there has been a sort of enquiry into the subject by a Parliamentary Commission, but they also, incredible as it may appear, left out the point upon which all turned, the use of steam.

Imagine, in our day, men not observing that in such things the omission of the item of steam power falsifies every calculation. I have a standard book, which in the most plausible manner possible compares railways and canals, and pursues the investigations through whole chapters, and never observes that all the time he is comparing a horse and a steam engine. Suppose he had reversed the case, and compared a horse tramway with a steam boat canal, would his conclusion have been the same. In America they are now at last really looking into this matter and the last Massage of the President pressed it upon the attention of the different States, promising them that if they would each reform their canals for large steamers, he would have the rivers improved to suit them. One calculation will show how this now pressing upon them there. They estimate that they have to provide for the carriage of 10 million tons a year from the western States to the cost, 1,200 miles and whether this is brought by land at even so low a cost as a penny a ton or by steam boat canal at one-tenth of a penny a ton, or much less, will make a difference of 45 millions sterling a year. They have at last relised the fact that railways cannot carry cheaply.

But let us try now really to campare the two means applying steam to both.

The advantages of railway are that, first, they can carry at almost any speed. Second, that they can be carried over very great changes of level without any essential defects. Third, they can carry considerable quantities of goods, perhaps as much as a million tons a year in a double railway with 1,000 passengers a day. Fourth, they are not in this country often stopped by frost and snow.

And what are their disadvantages ? First, they cannot carry cheaply, certainly not under 3 farthings a mile per ton in this country, and passengers under a penny, while carrying also many passengers. Second, they cannot carry any great quantities, certainly not several million tons a year. Third, they cost enormous sums; the average in this country is 35,000 found a mile. Fourth, they can only receive or deliver goods, or passengers at stations several miles apart, an immense evil. Fifth, the trains cannot pass each other going in the same direction, causing inconveniences, dangers, and losses in various ways. Sixth, if an accident happens the whole traffic is stopped. Seventh, the vibration so injurious to many passengers. Eighth, even in wealthy England they only return on an average 4½ per cent and in a poor country like India they are absolutely ruinous. The annual loss there on them, including interest of debt being 4 millions a year. Ninth, the highest speed on them is in a great measure deceptive. Between getting to and from station, and waiting for trains, the average speed of all travellers, from house to house, is certainly not above 8 miles an hour in England. Tenth, no private carriage can be used; all who use the railways are at the mercy of the railway company. Eleventh, the time is almost all lost; one cannot read in comfort, write, walk, eat etc.

The advantages of steam boat canals are:—First, the cheapness; in this country, about one tenth of a penny per ten for considerable distance, and perhaps a half-penny for passengers. Second, the power of conveying any amount of goods and number of passengers. Third, the ability to receive and deliver at any point on both sides. Fourth, the lower cost, perhaps, 15,000 found a mile in this country, and not more than 3,000 on an average in India. Fifth, ample speed. A small boat of only 90 ft. long lately ran the measured half mile at the rate of nearly 25 miles and a similar boat 150 ft. long would run more than 30 miles and there is no limit really to this. Sixth, with the help of inclined planes, as in the Monkland canal, they can be carried over very great changes of level. Seventh, everything can be carried at its own most suitable speed, independent of anything else, because the boats can pass each other in the same direction. Eighth, every boat can be worked by the most suitable power, whether by steam, animal or human power. Ninth, every man may have his own independent of the Canal Company. Tenth, an accident to a boat would not stop the traffic. Eleventh, the absence of vibrations; Twelfth, the power to walk sit, lie down, eat, drink, read, write etc. A gentleman in his private boat would not lose a minute of time. Thirteenth, freedom from the terrible accidents on the railways, in a great measure. These are main fest and vast advantages, especially, the two essential ones, the conveying large quantities, and the carrying cheaply both for goods and passengers.

The imaginary disadvantages are:--First, the locks. By proper arrangements these could be pressed in one or two minutes. Second, the wave from the passports. This can be provided for by the width of the canal, the form of the boat and the lining of the banks. Third, the want of the speed. This is shown to be fancy, by the actual speed of the boats at present. Fourth, the windings of the canals, that is of the present horse canals; of course, a steam boat canal would be nearly straight. The only real advantage is the stopping of the canal by frost in this country; but this would not be very frequent, and it is now stated in America that they can afford to keep them open, even there by steam blown into the water, and which I think can be done in this country. This objection does not exist in India.

When these things are fairly considered there is not a shadow of a question, as to which is the best mode of transit in India. The railways have cost 140 millions including debt for 5,600 miles, carry 1,30,000 tons at three-half pence, and 700 passengers a day at three-eighths of a penny and require 4 millions a year from the treasury. The same sum would have made 60,000 miles of canal, capable of conveying millions of tons per annum at one-tenth or one-twentieth of a penny, thousands of passengers a day at one-eighth of a penny and have required no payment from the treasury, even if they had all to be paid for solely as navigations, whereas, most of them would have been paid for by irrigation. Further, they would be far more defensible in times of rebellions, and would be great objects for defence by the population as their property would depend upon them.

Even in England what would be the effect of a steam boat canal from London to Liverpool, carrying at all speeds from 5 to 30 miles at a cost of farthing to a half penny for passengers, and of one-tenth of a penny per ton for goods, conveying probably 5 or 6 million tons a year, the boats loading and discharging at every point on either side, men of property having their own private boats to start whenever they please, carrying on their business on the way etc. At present nobody can conceive what the effect of such a highway would be. It would save the city of London alone several millions a year in cost of carriage.

I must give the actual state of the case in respect of speed, about which we have so deluded by the high speed that a few passengers travel at a long distances. The average price of a ticket for all England is only a shilling, showing the average distance travelled is only 8 miles, i.e. the great mass of travellers only go two or three stations and out of the towns. They take, perhaps, 10 or 20 minutes to walk to the station, and the same from it, and wait 10 minutes on an average, making an hour for 8 miles, so that the real average of all travellers by the railway from house to house is certainly is about eight miles an hour, while a bicycle could go 20, and as the cost of the two men to work it would not be about a shilling an hour, the cost would be only a little more than a half-penny a mile, from a half to fifth of that by the railway.

To go from my house in Dorking to an office in London takes me about two hours, and costs there and back, 6s. This distance is 25 miles, 12½ miles an hour, 2d. per mile, first class for the railway. I feel sure that a tricycle would take me the distance in 1¼ hour, and cost about 3s 6d for two men for half a day, there and back, or, under a penny a mile, less time, and leaving me quite independent to start and return at anytime, without waiting for trains, or the chance of losing one. And four young men could join in a tricycle and work it themselves 20 miles and back without any cost at all.

It is impossible to over-rate the importance of these considerations, to young engineers, now, that the actual results of the railways and waterways have been fully ascertained, and we know perfectly what they can do, and what they cannot do.

We do not, indeed, yet know so fully what roads can do, but most certainly what the cycles are doing demand a complete revision of all our notions on the subject.

If a man can do on a bicycle by himself—what no horse could enable him to do—go 8 miles in 28 minutes, 17 miles in an hour, 100 miles in 8 hours, and 168 miles in a day, with a very, imperfect machine, constructed in defiance of several of the fundamental principles of mechanics, certainly a young engineer requires to take a new look into the subject of transit. And so with the waterways. The boat that has been sent out to Bengal is calculated to run at 20 miles per hour, and to carry 150 passengers if full, at a total cost of a shilling a mile, including interest and everything, or if only half full, costing Id per six miles per head.

Surely the time has come for revising the whole subject. If it is said that what has this about railways and rivers to do with water? I answer, the question of course is not confined to what waterways can do and what they cannot do, but what is their case in comparison of other means; what in any particular case will meet the demands of that case most effectively. In respect of railways, especially in India, this has been the fundamental mistake, the authorities absolutely refuse to have any comparison made of railways and waterways, and roads. So in general, railways have been made where waterways would have been in every way preferable, but above all, the railways have essentially failed in the two main point-cheapness and quantity, in which canals would have answered perfectly.

And they are now making railways where even common roads would have been preferable, as for instance, from Oomruwatte in Berar to the Peninsular railway 5½ miles which has cost 8,000 pound a mile, and does not pay its working expenses, charging 2½d a ton a mile, and the whole interest has to be paid out of taxes, making the actual cost of transit of goods 3,360 pound for 1,60,000 tons carried 1 mile, or 5¼d a ton a mile, while a good road would have conveyed at 2d or 3d., the amount paid by the senders being 1,600, pound and the interest at 4 per cent 1760 pound and the traffic is so insignificant for part of the year that the railways is actually closed for some months. If such a work is not a mistake, what is? If we refuse to compare the effects of the different ways of accomplishing our object, whatever it is, we are certain of one result, that is, mistakes. Instead of this 5½ miles of railway, carrying at 5½d. a ton a mile, and closed for part of the year, we might have had 20 miles of road and carrying at probably at 2d. and open for the year. In this very district probably, 1,000 miles of road are required to be made, while they have spent about 1,00,000 pound on 13 miles of railway, and saddled its treasury with a charge of 4,000 pound a year.

In a very poor country like India where there is not perhaps a hundredth part of the wealth per head that there is in England, and where everything in the way of material improvement has to be done, it is especially important to consider well what are the best means of accomplishing the object of improving the conditions of the people. How can we be justified in imposing in a tremendous berthen on the country when the people have no-whatever voice in the matter, without first honestly and thoroughly investigating the case.

Who can dare to think of 140 millions having been laid out in railways there, and a permanent berthen of 4 millions a year levied upon the people, when certainly 50 times as much benefit could have conferred upon it for the same money by waterways and roads and in some places, probably, very light railways, of 1 to 2 ft. gauge, like the Dolgelly railway in North Wales.

Suppose for instance 600,000 pounds had been spent on 30 miles of railways on Godavari, instead of irrigating 600,000 acres, giving them 500 miles of waterway, sending fresh water through every village, securing the land from floods, draining it etc., increasing the income by 1 million and a half a year (3 times the whole amount of taxation) for the same expenditure. Such is the prodigious difference and money judiciously expended according to the peculiar circumstances wants, and advantages of a country, and that expended without the least consideration, and when refusing to hear both sides of the question. Propose now to the inhabitants of Godavari or even to the authorities, to abolish the irrigation and navigation and substitute for it, 30 miles of railway, what would they say to the proposition?

LECTURE II
(DECEMBER 14, 1874)

There are three methods of obtaining water for its various uses:

1st — Leading it from rivers as they flow;
2nd — Storing it in reservoirs and tanks; and

3rd — Raising it from rivers, lakes, or wells.

All these methods have been used by the natives of India from time immemorial, and we have learnt from them; only from our superior means we have done it upon a larger scale.

There are multitudes of old native works in various parts of India, but principally in the southern parts of the peninsula, where there are numerous river channels, some of considerable extent, and innumerable tanks, containing from 100 million cubic yards. downwards. These are noble works, and show both boldness and engineering talent. They have stood for hundreds of years. Many of the weirs are built in the sandy beds of rivers, without any rock or sound stratum to found them on, and it was from them we learnt how to secure a foundation in loose sand of unmeasured depth. In fact, what we learnt from them made the difference between financial success and failure, for the Chennai river irrigations executed by our engineers have been from the first the greatest financial successes of any engineering works in the world, solely because we learnt from them how to make secure and cheap foundations in loose sand, and the Ganges canal was a financial failure for 25 years solely from a fear to attempt to build a weir in such a situation, which drove the engineers to go up into the hills to lead off the water, where the river bed consisted of pebbles, and it cost them a million to lead the water from there into the plains, the whole of which would have been saved if the water had been taken off at a point clear of the hills, and the loss of this million made the whole difference between financial failure and great success. Having got over this fancy, the engineers are now building weirs in the rivers in the N.W., in the plains, where, as in Chennai, there is nothing, but sand in their beds.

And so with the tanks, the natives have constructed tens of thousands of tanks, in almost every kind of soil, with earthen bunds without the puddle banks which English engineers have fancied necessary, and which only increase the risk of failure.

With this lesson about foundations, we have built bridges, weirs aqueducts and every kind of hydraulic work, without a foundation more then 8 feet deep in loose sand, and these works have stood perfectly. We are thus deeply in debited to the native engineers.

With respect to the cost of water led from the rivers by means of weirs and canals, without storing, we have now ample experience in this, so that, we can calculate from works on a very large scale, and that have been in operation many years. There are such large works in actual operation in the deltas of the Cauvery, Kistna, Godavari, Toombudra, Mahanuddee and in the Pallaur, Sone, Ganges, Jumna and Ravee, 12, besides many smaller ones in the Madras Presidency, where almost every river has several weirs or anicuts across them built by us.

As specimens of the cost of water from these works, I will here give the Godavery, the Ganges, and the Toombudra works. The first distributes about 1 million cubic yards per hour for 200 days, and about half a million for the remainder of the year, or in all 7,000 million cubic yards. The cost of these works up to the time has been 6,00,000 pound the interest and repairs at 7 per cent being 42,000 pound a year, which gives 1,70,000 cubic yards per pound. At present a large portion of this runs to waste on account of the distribution works not being completed, and even when they are there will always be much water that is not used, especially at the time between the main and second crop. The actual consumption of water is about 6,00,000 acres at 5,000 cubic yards, or 3000 millions cubic yards—not half the total quantity that the canals can receive; but more will be eventually used. At this rate the cost of the water used is 70,000 cubic yards per pound.

In the Toombudra work the cost has been 1½ millions, or at 7 per cent, 1,05,000 pound per annum, and the quantity is 400,000 cubic yards per hour for 200 days, besides some during the remainder of the year, about 2,400 millions in all, which gives 23,000 cubic yards per pound. In this, most probably, almost all the water will be used eventually, making about 20,000 cubic yards per pound for used water. This work is in the upper country, where the work is more expensive, but, on the other hand, the water is more valuable.

In the Ganges Canal the cost has been 2½ millions, besides 1 million of debt no due upon it, giving at 7 per cent, on both 2,40,000 pounds per annum. The quantity is about 7,50,000 cubic per hour throughout the year, or 6500 millions per annum, 26,000 cubic yards per pound. Of this not above one-third is used, I believe, at present. The area of irrigation varies considerably, and the larger part of it is for wheat or other dry crops, requiring only 1,500 cubic yards per hour. The area irrigated varies from about 80,000 to a million acres. No doubt a much larger proportion of the water will be used ultimately. But the cost of the used water is at present about 8,000 cubic yards per pound. But as I have before stated, this great cost was entirely owing to the needless expense of bringing the water from high up in the hills. Had it been brought from below the hills, where they are now leading off a canal, it would have cost a million less, have been in operation several years sooner, and have paid its interest abundantly, so that, there would have been no debt, and the capital sunk would then have been at the utmost 1½ millions, instead of 3½ millions, so that, the cost of used water would have been only 23,000 cubic yards per pound.

Of course, in future works such mistakes won't be repeated, and many new works have the benefit of all the mistakes made in the early ones. Thus, the actual cost of water so obtained has been from 23,000 cubic yards to 70,000 and average is perhaps, 40,000 cubic yards per pound.

And it must be observed that this is the cost of the rich river water, full of the materials of fertilization, so that, lands so watered continue to bear grain crops for hundreds of years without manure, though of course manure might be added with benefit. But without it the soil is not exhausted Tanjore is in a high state of fertility, after a long period of cropping although owing to the land ignorant system of using dung for fuel, very little is ever returned to the land.

In calculating the cost of water from these works, it must be kept in view that there may be a great change in the value of money hereafter. The enormous influx of bullion from cotton during the American War (more than 100 million sterlings in 4 years above the previous receipts from this source), produced a violent change in the value of money at that time; but it has since gone back to nearly its former value, and probably will recede still more with the present low price of that product; but the general effect of the change in the circumstances of India, and its increasing trade with England, will necessarily be to assimilate the value there to that of England. At present the difference is, I believe, about 3 to 1, comparing the average value of human labour and food in the two countries.

But, if we take 20,000 cubic yards per pound in the upland district, and 40,000 in the plains for future works, I think it will give us substantially correct grounds for calculation for such works for some time to come. I will only say here, by the way, there are millions of private patches of irrigation all over India, by raising water 12 or 15 feet from wells, rivers, or lagoons, by means of bullocks at a cost of about 3000 cubic yards per pound, and if poor filtered water is thus raised from wells profitably (and if it were not profitable it would not be continued), what must be the profit on rich river water supplied at from 1/6 to 1/12 of that cost. This alone is quite conclusive as to the enormous profit from these works on a large scale.

We next come to the cost of water stored in tanks. We have not such complete data for this as for the river water. It seems very strange that with the noble example of the innumerable native tanks before our eyes, and their incalculable benefits, we should have been so backward as not to initiate them with our immensely superior means and science. Till within the last 30 years, very little was done even to keep the old works in repair. When I was called upon to report on irrigation works in 1836, there were many thousand tanks in every state of disrepair or ruin, and scarcely any in good repair; and not one of our construction. By degrees the most important tanks were put into good order, and improved, and a very large number have now been put into some sort of repair. In Mysore, indeed, under the charge of commissioners who have more power, I believe the whole of these works have been reformed. But there are numbers in Madras either in ruin or in a disgraceful state of disrepair still. But it was impossible to get anything done in the way of new tanks, till lately two noble works have been at last constructed by our Government in Bombay and one large one by the municipality for the city of Bombay.

The initiation of this work of storing water constitute an era in our management of India. There were very few countries that have such facilities for this improvement as India. There are multitudes of sites for such reservoirs where short bunds of 100 feet height would retain the water for a length of 10 or 20 miles, and continued applications have been made for the sanction of such works, but as yet nothing has been done, excepting in these three instances. Many fine sites have been examined, and the works fully projected and estimated, but when it comes to the execution there is always some reasons found for more investigation. When I first arrived in India, the contempt with which the natives justly spoke of us on account of this neglect of material improvements was very striking; they used to say we were a kind of civilized savages, wonderfully expert about fighting, but so inferior to their great men, that we would not even keep in repair the works that they had constructed, much less even imitate them in extending the system. All this was perfectly true, till lately.

The new Government works in Bombay have been both formed by shutting up capacious valleys, one by a masonry bund, and the other by one of earth. They will each contain about 140 million cubic yards when the waste-weir is closed. But it must be remembered, that a tank supplied much more water than it contains, because it is continually supplying during the four months of the monsoon, while it is filling, so that, these tanks might supply, perhaps, 60 million cubic yards during the monsoon, and be full at the end of it, making a total of 200 millions.

But there is a loss by evaporation, which by the best information I have, amounts to about 6 feet in the year there. During the cold months, when the area of the surface of the tank is greatest, this evaporation is very moderate, increasing up to a ½ inch per day in the extreme hot weather, when the surface will be very small. If the full tank is in the above cases 5 square miles, or 15 million square yards, and the average during the dry season half that, or 7½ million, and the evaporation of that part of the year 5 feet, the loss will be 12½ million cubic yards, or 6 per cent of the whole supply that the tank affords.

I have not the separate cost of the tank near Poona with the masonry bund, but that hear Sholapur cost 90,000 pounds including distribution, perhaps 70,000 pounds for the tank only, for 200 million cubic yards per annum, which, at 7 per cent gives 5,000 pounds for that quantity, or about 40,000 cubic yards per pound, and including distribution 30,000 cubic yards per pound. This was a good site, but there are many where from two to four times this could be obtained with the same bund, and consequently, from 80,000 to 1,60,000 cubic yards per found could be stored. And the capital required was in the above case 370 pound per million cubic yards of water supplied, or 500 pounds per million of the mere contents of the tanks.

I have no doubt that immense quantities of water may be stored at a cost of 200 pound per million cubic yards of content, or 140 pound per million supplied, and at a cost in interest and repairs at

6 per cent of 850,000 cubic yards per pound, besides the cost of distribution. Some vast sites have been examined, and estimated, one to contain 2,000 million cubic yards, 500 times the capacity of the Sheffield reservcir, that burst some years ago.

But in judging of the cost of water so stored, it is essential that two things be kept in view. One is, that if the irrigation is situated a long distance from the tank, the navigation of a length of river may be so improved by the water discharged, that the whole interest may be covered by the value of the navigation. Thus, if the dry season supply of the Krishna or Godavari deltas were improved by storing water in the upper part of the basins of those rivers, several hundred miles of river navigation would be improved. If the above mentioned site for 2,000 millions near Nagpoor were filled with water, it would provide an average stream of 4,00,000 cubic yards per hour for 200 days, or 8,00,000 at the end of the dry season, when there is about 2,00,000 cubic yards in the river at present, thus, increasing the stream five-fold, greatly improving 400 or 500 miles of navigation, so that, if the tank cost 200 pound per million cubic yards, or 4,00,000 pound it would cost 1,000 pound a mile charging it all to the river, to be compared with 20,000 pounds per mile, the cost of the railways.

Thus, it may be abundantly worthwhile to store water solely for the improvement of the river navigation. Perhaps, for instance the important line of the Burhampootra navigation of 800 miles might be thus improved at a nominal cost, for an annual charge of 10 pound a mile would be nothing in a line connecting the important province of Assam with Calcutta; it would be only a charge of 1. 60d—per mile per ton on a million tons.

The other point to be kept in view in storing water is that, it is of vast importance in regulating the rivers and diminishing floods. In France, they have been planning great works solely with this view.

In proportion as the country increases in wealth and population, this point will become everyday of greater importance. I go into more detail on this point hereafter. But it would be quite right in such a case as that of the. Godavari to charge one-third of the cost of the tank to the navigation, which would be a charge of 330 pound a mile, one-third to the irrigation, which would then be say 1 pound for 2,40,000 cubic yards, and one-third to the protection of the delta and intermediate country from floods, which would be only 8,000 found a year, 2d. per acre on the Delta area alone.

So, in the Kistna, many hundred miles of fine navigation by the Beema and Kistna might be obtained by storing water for the irrigation of the delta in the dry months, and for keeping its canals navigable, which are now nearly empty for three months.

This storing of water is thus one of the very first question in the management of India, and the returns from it alone would be far beyond those from any gold mine. Dry season irrigation water could be supplied to the delta of the Godavari at 1/80 of the cost at which water is now raised from wells with profit by private enterprise, and every million cubic yards so stored will help to regulate the rivers and diminish floods.

This stored water, though not equal to river water, in consequence of its not holding fertilizing materials in suspension, will yet be much more valuable than well water, because it is not filtered, and contains much manure in a state of solution.

We come now to the third point, of obtaining water by raising it by steam or other power. Immense quantities are raised by bullock and human labour in India, but, as I have stated, at a comparatively great cost, about 3,000 cubic yards per pound. This, however, gives us an unquestionable standard for the value of water and in this respect it is of the greatest importance. If filtered water can be used profitably at a cost of 3,000 cubic yards per pound, how can there be any possible question about Government works, which supply rich water at from 20,000 to 40,000 Cubic yards per pound. There is also an immense quantity of water raised from rivers and lagoons a few feet by human labour, by the Picottah.

I do not know of any use of wind power for this or any other purpose in India. Now, the country is peculiarly fitted for it, because calms are so very rare there in most parts, and I observed that they are resorting very much to this power in some countries of late. I have no doubt, that it might be used to an immense extent in India.

But there is no room for expecting any means that could ever raise water to the land so cheaply as it can be distributed by the present irrigation works of canals and tanks.

I am not aware, also, of steam power having been used for irrigation or navigation purposes, though it may have been in a few instances.

With respect to the cost of these means of raising water, I do not think there is any great difference between the cost of human and bullock power for this purpose in India. I have often calculated the cost of bullock power, and make it about 3,000 cubic yards of water, raised 15 feet for 1 pound, or 75,000,000 lbs. raised 1 foot for 1 pound, and I think human labour is not dearer.

Steam power, of course, will vary greatly with the price of fuel, but taking the cost of Indian coal at 1 pound a ton, and allowing a 4 lbs. per indicator house power per hour, it gives 2/3d. an hour for fuel for 2,000,000 lbs. raised 1 foot gross or Id. net, and allowing the cost of management, interest, etc., to be equal to the cost of fuel, which, I think, with moderate engines would be not far from the truth, it gives 2d. for 2,000,000 lbs. raised 1 foot, or 2,40,000,000 per 1 pound, besides wear and tear of raising machinery, perhaps 2,00,000,000 in all, against 75,000,000 for bullock or human power. This is where fuel is cheap. But I know that in some places, for certain purposes, steam has been found more expensive than human labour in India upon actual trails.

There can, however, be no doubt that on a large scale steam power could be never compare with great hydraulic works, such as, for instance, 20,000 cubic yards brought from 20 feet below the bank of a river for a pound, which would be 700 million pounds raised 1 foot per 5, and this includes distribution.

But there is a case in navigation where, I have no doubt, steam power for raising water might be used with wonderful advantage. This is in making a line of canal above the level of the country.

Suppose a canal made 20 feet above the level at which the water stands on an average in a river, that the canal is 40 yards broad, and the evaporation 6 feet per annum. This would require 1,40,000 cubic yards, raised 20 feet per mile per annum or 5,000 million pounds raised one foot, which, at the rate given above, 200 million pounds. One foot per pound, would be pound 25, a year, the interest of a capital of 350 pound a mile of canal.

It is evident that this would be a small item compared with the difference between cutting a canal of the least depth compatible with providing earth for its embankments, and cutting it deep enough to admit the river water. In an alluvial country, a navigation canal so formed would be the simplest thing possible. A cutting 40 yards broad and 1½ deep would provide banks for a canal of 9 feet of water, requiring only 1,08,000 cubic yards of dry excavation per mile, which at 3d. a cubic yard, would be only 1,200 pound a mile; and no deep foundations would be required for bridges etc., whereas to cut it down to the level of the river would make a most expensive work of it, both from the amount of excavation and from the cutting it below level of water. It is evident that the addition of 350 pound a mile, the capital represented by the cost of raising water would be a very small sum in comparison. This, however, provides only for evaporation.

Supposing the canal to be 200 miles long, that the locks are 150 feet by 20 feet by 12, and that these will admit boats of 250 tons, there would be required 1,400 cubic yards of water, raised 20 feet or 50 ft. one foot for 250 tons, there would be required 1,400 cubic yards of water raised 20 feet, or 50 million pounds one foot for 250 tons of traffic for 200 miles, 250,000 pounds one foot per boat mile, and if 200 million tons pass per annum 2,000 million pounds per mile per hour for lockage or 10 pounds per mile per hour, representing a capital of 70 pounds per mile for a traffic of 2 million tons.

In this case, therefore, the difference between cutting a canal only 1½ yard deep, and, perhaps, 6 yards, would be met by a capital for raising water of 420 pound a mile, probably not-tenth of the additional expense or cutting the canal to a depth to admit water from the river, besides the saving of time in executing the work. If it would take five years to cut the deep canal, the shallow one might be cut in one year. This is just the case of a line of canal from Calcutta to the main Ganges. Probably the shallow one could be cut for 3,000, pounds including the capital for raising the water, while the deep one would cost, perhaps 10,000 pound a mile.

To show in a simple way the case of this raising the water by steam power for canal navigation; if there were such a steamboat canal from London to Birmingham, and each ton of goods required 3 cubic yards of water to pass it through the 110 miles for lockage, it would be 5,000 pounds raising 400 feet, or 2 million pounds 1 foot which would cost in this country, I believe, about 1d, that is, if the lockage water were returned from the Thames to the apex of the country at Birmingham by steam power, it would cost only 1d per ton for 110 miles, and I estimate that the water for evaporation for a canal 30 yards wide, with a traffic of 4 million tons, would be about the same, together representing a capital of 4,200 pound a mile, for the supply of water.

For the purpose of irrigation generally, the cost of steam power to raise water from the rivers a height of suppose 20 feet, would be, at the before-stated cost of 200 million pounds, 1 foot per 6,000 pound cubic yards per pound, and as in this case there would be no waste as in the canal system, we may allow 4,000 cubic yards per acre of raise, which would be 13s. 4d. per acre, and 1,500 cubic yards per acre of wheat, which would cost 5s. per acre, or one-third the value of the increase of produce in rise, and one-sixth of that in wheat etc. There seems no reason whatever why this system should not be extensively resorted to by individuals who have land on the banks of the great rivers, with the advantages of being able to commence irrigation at once, and of being independent of Government in their improvements, though the water would certainly cost more than canal water for rice. But, according to this calculation, the cost would be the same for wheat as the present Government charge in the North-West. The land-owner would not, however, in this case, have the benefit of the navigation by the Government canals, which would make a great difference. When I was examining the country for the Sone project and others, I was greatly surprised that the European Zamindars holding great fertile estates on the banks of the permanent rivers had not adopted this plan, especially as in one estate the owner showed us a well he had dug, and told us what enormous returns of interest it had made in the increased rent that the tenants had gladly paid.

I have no data for the cost of wind power in India, but I have no doubt it might be used very economically, and with a much smaller first outlay than for steam power. Even in England wind power still extensively used, and the wind is by no means so constant here as in most parts of India. And of late years great improvements have been made in wind-mills, so as to make them more manageable and cheaper. If a small raised tank were formed by a circular embankment, to hold a few days' water, there would be a constant supply, and the windmill might work at any time of the day or night, as it could be made quite independent of attendance.

But besides these uses of water, as I have said, we have the amount of loss caused by water in the natural state of things, which we may prevent.

First of Floods: This is a very extensive subject. We have read of the terrible devastation caused by these in most countries especially almost all the delta countries of the great rivers, usually filled with a dense population, are subject to such calamities.

The Yellow River in China has been called China's Sorrow from this cause. It not only overflows over immense tracts, but it has of late years taken an entirely new course, forcing for its vast volume of water a new channel through hundreds of miles of populous country.

In 1858 I was ordered from Madras to inspect the Mahanudee River, at Cuttack, and report upon works constructed to protect that city, which stands in the delta, and was in imminent danger of being entirely submerged, being 10 or 15 below the level of the water in floods.

It is impossible to estimate in money the amount of these losses, which may be prevented by the restraint and regulation of the rivers.

But just in proportion as these fertile tracts are improved by irrigation etc. in the extent of population and property that will prevent it.

In Godavery, for instance, the present irrigation is 6,00,000 acres, and the value of crop is about 2 millions, so that, an uncontrolled flood there would destroy a vast amount of property and many lives.

The destruction this year on the plains of the Mississippi has been most extensive, but I have no estimate of the amount.

The prevention to these things is, therefore, one of the first points for the engineer's consideration in the question of regulation of water. And besides these great river floods there is the other points I have mentioned, viz., drainage—that is the carrying off the superfluous water of the local rains, and this both in the agricultural district and in cities. All the most fertile plains of the world are exposed to terrible evils from these accumulations of water, chiefly in the way of diseases caused by them. There has been of late years a most fatal fever desolating the country round. Calcutta greatly owing to this cause, and the want of effective drainage in cities, especially those situated in alluvial plains, is the source of innumerable deaths and attacks of sickness. No money value can be assigned to the prevention of these things, but an idea may be formed of it by the consideration, that in a city of half-a-million inhabitants, if an assessment of one rupee a head per annum were levied to construct such works it would represent at 7 per cent. A capital of ¾ of a million. The mere loss of money from deaths and sickness would, in a city, no doubt far exceed one rupee per head, or 10s. per family annum.

Third—We have on the sea-board the danger from the ocean wave. We have dreadful examples of this in India. In Orissa, in Godavery, and other places there have been tens of thousands of the population swept away in a few hours by the inroads of the seas in hurricanes. A few years ago, the city of Musulipatam, though situated three miles Inland, was almost destroyed and some 20,000 or 30,000 lives lost in it and the adjoining country. In Orissa, a vast work has been constructed by the government in the way of an embankment of, I believe, more than 100 miles in length (but I have not the particulars) for the protection of the country from such an inroad. The last news from India states that it did protect that tract from a hurricane wave, but it is said that it was only effective in consequence of the strength of the gale occurring when the tide was out, and that had the storm happened at the time of high water and at spring tides it would probably have given way. Hurricanes always cross the Bay of Bengal from the east to the west at rather different angles, and strike the coast from 10°N up to Calcutta, and those that strike high up drive in a tremendous wave (indicating it on the map), and consequently this district is specially exposed to injury. These calamities require the more to be pressed upon the attention, because of their irregularity. There are long intervals between them as they are due to a concurrence, of circumstances which tends to their generally or entirely being lost sight of. A hurricane only strikes any particular point of a coast at long intervals, and them if the times for high water and of the strength of the gale do not concur there may be little damage done. Thus, it is now 40 years since the destruction of the population of Cocanada, in Godavery, and it may be many years before there is another hurricane at that precise point at the time of high water, but if one did occur now, the loss of life would be far greater that it was in 1832, as the population is rapidly increasing. No provision whatever has been made against such a calamity in that part. This is thus a very serious and difficult question to deal with on account of the almost impossibility of getting men to provide against a calamity which does not immediately threaten, however certain in may be that it will one day occur. It is undoubtedly one of the great points in water engineering, but what may be done in this way does not belong to this lecture.

These remarks will give some idea of the value of water, and of the importance of using and regulating it, especially in a country like India with periodical rains.

But let us now further consider the amount of this material available in India. What quantity of water have we in India that is at present totally lost, or worse than lost, and from want of controlling and direction works is allowed to destroy instead of refresh and fertilize? When the Godavery is full for instance, it contains about 180 millions of cubic yards per hour, or more than 4,000 millions per day. This, at 2,000 cubic yards per pound, is worth 2,000,000 pound a day. It is, however, seldon full-perhaps only once in four or five years, and then from one to ten days; but the total volume flowing into the sea in the year from this one river is enormous. The average fall of rain in its basin is about 40 inches, so far as I can judge, and of this, perhaps. One half flows by the river which would be 2,00,000 million cubic yards, worth, if it could be all used, 1,00,000,000 pound sterling a year. This river drains about one-tenth of the area of India.

Leaving out the rainless tract, if an average of one yard of rain falls throughout India it would supply 7,500 cubic yards, sufficient for one crop of rice, and one other grain on an acre for two-thirds of the whole area, perhaps, nearly all that is fit for cultivation. Land so irrigated would produce not much under a ton of food-grains per acres, or sufficient for a population of 1,500 per square mile, or six times the present population, and allowing one-third of the area for other things there would be food for four times the present population. This is sufficient to show the main point, that we have an unlimited supply of this material as far as any present prospects are concerned. We have, therefore, not only a mine of incalculably more value than any gold mine to work upon, but one of unlimited extent. We have in the case of the Godavery added to the income of the people by this means 1 pound per head, or 5 pound per family, and when the works are completed there will be half as much more, making 7 pounds 10s. The average income of a family throughout India is, I believe, about 5 pound a year, at which rate the income in Godavery has been already doubled, and will be eventually increased still more. There are in India fifty million families, so that, if the same blessing were extended to the whole of the country it would add 3,75,000,000 pound a year to its income, or nine times the amount of the taxes now paid besides all the incalculable benefits of health, comfort, security, freedom from famine, satisfaction of the people under our rule, free intercourse of goods, passengers etc., and this would be only with the present population which is rapidly increasing. Before long, the population will probably be 60,000,000 of families, and the increase of income, if all were supplied with water, would then be 3,50,000,000 pounds a year. And so with respect to transit. The great feature of India next to its ample supply of this inestimable gift of water is its extraordinary facilities for water transit. Throughout India, in all parts capable of bearing a considerable population, the most perfect communications possible may be made by means of water at an expense quite trifling, compared with its importance. About 7,000 miles of canal in connection with some fair river navigation would from a network of main lines connecting all India, and branch lines in all directions would be connected with them. There is thus an unlimited field in India in this respect also, that is, for giving it cheap transit. To give some idea of the extent of the benefits of such a system of transit, if an average of 2,000,000 tons were carried over these 7000 miles, it would cost 1,80,000,000 pound a—year to carry it by road at 3d. per ton a mile, and 90,000,000 pound by rail at the present charge, while by the steamboat canal at one-twentieth of a penny it would cost 3,000,000 pounds—a saving of 1,77,000,000 pound and if as much more were carried over the minor lines, the total saving would be 3,50,000,000 pound or equal to the increased value of produce from irrigation. I speak of the railway charge, but besides this there is a sum equal to the whole charge for goods paid out of the treasury to cover the interest, so that, the actual cost by rail is the same as by road. Of course, I do not mean to say that this 1,80,000,000 pound is now paid for transit on the main lines. The cost is so great as entirely to prohibit 19/20ths of the traffic, there ought to be on all the lines where there is not natural water carriage by the rivers, but what the amount of traffic would be if such thoroughly effective transit were extended from one end of India to the other is clearly shown by that on the main Godavari canal—a short isolated line, hundreds of miles from a great city, where it is about 2,00,000 tons a year, though it only affects about 2,000,000 of people. There is no great city nearer than Madras 400 miles distant, Calcutta 760 miles, and Bombay 700 miles. It is thus quite out of way. What would it be, for instance, on a main line up the valley of the Ganges affecting 1,00,000,000 of people, and terminating at a capital city, besides passing through many others of several hundred thousand inhabitants? Even with the present very imperfect river transit between Calcutta and the Burhampootra though the direct distance is 130 miles, and the circuit by river is 420 miles, the traffic is nearly 2,000,000 tons per annum. This is for the eastern traffic alone-from and to Calcutta.

These statements and calculations are quite sufficient to show the enormous value of water in India, and the unbounded field for increasing its comfort and wealth by making use of this water instead of letting it flow into the sea. That its wealth can be increased by several hundred millions a year by means of it is indisputable. Of course, the remaining question is, can this be done at a practicable cost. Can a hundred million sterling a year be added to its income at a less cost than 1400,000,000 pounds of outlay, which would allow 4 per cent, interest and 3 per cent for repairs and management? Whatever it would cost, less than that would be clear gain. I propose this subject of the cost of water for various purposes for consideration in another lecture. I may mention here that we have three districts in Madras that have been to a considerable extent improved by this means of regulating the water. In Tanjore, containing now nearly 2,000,000 of inhabitants, and the adjoining districts which also include part of Delta of the Cauvery about 1,200,000 acres are irrigated; a considerable portion of it for two crops a year. The value of produce on this is at least 5,000,000 pound a year. But this tract has not been provided with navigable canals, so that, it is only half improved. Still it is such a picture of fertility and industry as could hardly be equaled in the world, and the mass of the people are for India, well to do. There, as everywhere also the poor are too much at the mercy of the rich, and the horrible system of caste is a dreadful plight, but still, the people are in the main tolerably well fed and clad and famine is never thought of. Its progress is also shown by the increase of the Revenue and the improvement of irrigation which was seriously taken in hand in 1830. The Revenue was then 4,20,000 pound a year, it is now 7,20,000 pound an increase of tax of 3,00,000 pound whilst the increase of produce on a million acres has probably been 20,00,000 pound leaving a profit the people of 1¾ millions sterling. In the same way Godavari and Krishna have been improved, with this difference, that they have also a complete system of canal transit, though as yet in the case of the latter only for nine, months in the year, the supply of water from the river being very small, in the other three for want of storage works high up the river which have not been constructed.

The Godavery Works were began in 1846, and they have been carried on in the usual pattering way till now with long intervals—when they were not even kept in effective repair, 6,00,000 acres are now irrigated, and the completion of the works is now carried on with some vigour, and the result has been far beyond expectation. The district is now the most thriving in India from having been one of the poorest. The exports have increased from 60,000 pound to 8,00,000, pounds and the revenue from 2,30,000 pound to 5,30,000 pound. The canals are swarming with both cargo and passenger boats, and people passing through take district are struck with the well-to-do look of the people. The Kistna district is progressing in the same way though the works are not so far advanced. About 2,00,000 acres are now irrigated. These three districts yield a revenue of 6,00,000 pound a year each on an average and if the 200 districts of India had been improved in the same way of the total revenue would be 1,20,000,000 pounds a year instead of 40,000,000 pounds as it is now—if so much had been required.

I must not detain you any further to-night, but I hope on Monday evening to continue the second lecture on the Cost of Water.

LECTURE III
(DECEMBER 17, 1874)

We now come to the great question of comparative cost and value, upon which, as I have tried show, the whole matter depends.

Whether the material we have to deal with is gold, iron, water etc., is of no significance; the sole point, is which has the greatest difference between cost and value, supposing of course that the quantities obtainable are sufficient.

I have shown by our actual results that the value of river water for production; as shown by careful investigation by different persons in various localities, is:

For rice	3,000 cubic yards per pound
For dry grains	1,000 cubic yards per pound

in increase of produce in grain only; of course it is much more valuable for sugar, plantains, cotton etc., but the quantities used for such products will be small compared with grains. And this value is fully corroborated by the fact that in innumerable cases inferior water is raised from wells throughout India by private individuals, at a cost of 3,000 cubic yards per pound, which necessarily implies a good profit to the landowner.

And the cost has been shown to be from 23,000 to 70,000 cubic yards per pound, averaging perhaps 40,000. And the value above stated is also, besides the use of the same water, for navigation and all other purposes.

If we take the average value, including navigation at 1,500 cubic yards per pound, and the average cost at 40,000 cubic yards per pound, it gives the latter 27 times the former.

If we take the Godavery district alone, the annual expense of the works is 42,000 pound and the value of increased produce, and navigation at least 1,500,000 pound or 35 times as great. Incredible as this might appear, the data are unquestionable. What mining or any other undertaking has ever equalled this ?

And this money return is, besides all the other benefits of health, comfort and convenience arising from a plentiful supply of pure water in the dry season, and the carrying off that which is superfluous in the monsoon, which cannot be stated in money.

If a gold mine could be found in which it would cost 2 pound to obtain a pound of gold, what would be thought of it? or a silver mine that would cost 1¼ d to produce an ounce of silver worth 4s? How every newspaper would be full of it; but because these very results are obtained by water, they are not thought worthy of moment's notice. That the Godavery works are at this moment costing 42,000 pound a year, producing a million and a half from 600,000 acres of irrigation, and about 500 miles of navigation, is as simple and palpable a fact as could possibly be brought before us. And so with the fact of the Sone works this year, that before any part of them is finished they have watered 160,000 acres producing 500,000 pound worth of grain, in the midst of a famine, about the whole cost of the works up to that time.

Is it possible that any question could lie in a smaller compass?

I have spoken throughout these papers of the actual total cost and total benefits of these works, because that is of course the essential point for Government works. There is certainly a secondary question which must also be attended to, *viz.* Can the treasury be re-paid for the outlay? Out of this enormous result, can a small portion be obtained from the cultivators and carriers to cover the interests and current expenses? The first answer to this is, what must be the mismanagement, if out of a total return of 100 or 200 per cent, seven per cent, cannot be levied for this purpose ? But has been the actual results in this respect? The increase of revenue in, Godaveri has been 3,00,000 pound a year, 50 per cent on the outlay by far the greater part due to the irrigation; and the water rate alone is 1,80,000 pound 30 per cent. In the Ganges Canal the net return is about 4 per cent, in the Ravee about 3 per cent, in Tanjore it is by the Government returns more than a 100 per cent the average of all the great works now extensively in operation is not under 15 per cent net.

But the difference in the water rate levied in different districts is unaccountable. The average rate under the Tambrapoorny, in Tinnivelly including land tax, is Rs. 14 an acre or about Rs. 12 for water; probably most of this is for two crops, leaving about Rs. 9 for the main crop. In the Toombudra the rate paid is Rs. 6, in the Godavery Rs. 4, in Orissa 1½ to be increased to, 2½ rupees for rice, in the, Ganges and Ravee 2½ for wheat. In Tanjore the whole land tax is 5½ rupees; leaving 4 for the water for rice.

As for the lowest rate of 1½ rupees for rice, in Orissa, where the increased crop is worth 15 rupees it is simply coming to monstrous mis-management under the Zamindari system. And this brings to the point which is now the grand weapon if the opponents of irrigation, that the people will not use the water. Let us look into this point. First—Is this the usual thing or exceptional ? It is the case of two irrigation out of innumerable ones. One is that of the irrigation company's works in Madras, where it is simply owing to the Government not permitting the company to manage their own affairs.

When the inhabitants are asked why they do not use the water, they reply that the native Government officials are so opposed to them that they cannot encounter the persecution that it bring upon them. But the Government have now modified their proceedings in a measure, and about 35,000 acres are now irrigated, with every prospect that it will rapidly extend. But what must the mismanagement be when an energetic race like the Teloogoos, with the keenest possible apprehension of the value of water, will not take it at 6 rupees an acre, when it is worth to them 20 rupees.

Without going the least into particulars, we are quite certain that in such a case there is some gross mismanagement. Every other district in Madras has irrigation works, both new and old, where nobody dreams of the water being refused. But one thing is certain, that so absurd an anomaly cannot go on long, and the water will certainly be all used within a few years.

The other case is of Orissa, where however, there is a very inferior race, who have been reduced to the lowest state by the dreadful Zemindary system. Their answer about using the water is—What is the use of our taking it, when half the profit will go to the Zemindary, and half to the money lender ? But there also in the northern part, in the Midnapoor district, the difficulty is being got over, and I believe about 100,000 acres will be irrigated this year altogether, and, as under the Toombudra, such an anomaly cannot long continue. In general, in Bengal and the north-west, we may take the cost of the works at 3 pound per acre, and the water rate of 2½ rupees will be 8½ per cent, besides navigation tolls, so that, there is no question about all these works making ample returns to the treasury eventually.

But of course whether they return 3 or 10 per cent, to the treasury is a very small matter compared with their returning 1 or 200 per cent in all.

Up to this time, including all that has been spent, including the works only just beginning to irrigate, the net returns are about 15 per cent, and in a few years they will certainly be 20 per cent and this includes in the calculation all the mistakes made in the initiatory works which will not be repeated, such as the waste of a million in the Ganges canal, and the consequent incurring of another million of debt there.

The danger always is of official men forgetting that they are not private investors to whom the direct money returns to those who construct the works is a sole question and losing sight altogether of the real point, the total returns to community.

We then come to the unquestionable conclusion, that water is incomparable India's great treasure, and that were this generally turned to account she would be in the highest state of temporal prosperity. If only half a million were spent in each of two hundred districts, yielding cent, per cent, her income would be increased two and a half times her whole taxation.

What would be thought of the rule of our nation over India if we abolished all taxes? Yet it would certainly be a small matter compared with such a general regulation of the water.

Having then considered the fundamental points I would proceed to enter upon various details.

First: With respect Engineering details. Let us see what is the mode of leading the water from the great rivers out upon the land. We will take the case of the Godavery contains a million acres. The river at its head is four miles broad including low islands, which are covered with water from three to ten feet deep into the freshes. By these the stream is divided into four channels. When the river is not full measuring together 4,000 yards in breadth. In the end of the dry season the water is only a foot deep at the fords, but it rises thirty one feet in extreme floods. It then contains about 180 million cubic yards per hour, but at the end of the dry season there is only 3,00,000 cubic yards in it. The fall of the river at this point, is 11/8 feet per mile, and the level of the land adjoining about three feet under the flood level, 28 feet about the low water level, but the land rapidly slopes away from the edge of the river, so that, with the weir or anicut, as we call it in Madras, 14 feet high, capable of being raised 2 feet in the dry season, by planks, we have not to cut a canal for before the water is brought to the surface of the land. It is raised 15 feet by the anicut out of the 28, and it reaches the surface of the land within five or six miles of the head of the delta, so that, only and insignificant narrow strip of land is left above the level of the canal water.

The anicut consists of masonary 48 feet thick 18 feet being level, and the remaining 30 feet forming a curved slope; this whole breadth is covered with well fitted out stone of a hard sand stone in large blocks 2 feet thick. Below the slope is a loose stone arron of 25 yards broad in large blocks carefully packed with a very slight slope. From each end of the anicut and from the middle three main canals are led. Each of them now, I believe, about 60 yards broad, and carrying 8 feet of water when full. They have a fall of about 4 inches a mile, giving a current of 2500 yards per hour, and conveying in all one million cubic yards of water per hour. They have a head sluice, with a lock 150 feet by for passing the boats from the river.

There is also in the anicut adjoining each head sluice, what we call a under-sluice, that is having a floor 4 feet below that of the canal and capable of discharging about a million cubic yards per hour each. This is for the purpose of keeping the sandy beds of the river low near the heads of the canals, and preventing the sand being carried into them.

Along the crest of the anicut are iron posts with grooves, 8 feet apart and 2½ feet high to receive planks, and this to raise the water in the dry season. These planks are removed before the monsoon though they have occasionally been left in position through part of the freshes, in consequence of the sudden rise of the river, but no evil consequences ensued.

This cannot now happen, because the rise of the river is known many days before it reaches the anicut.

We have thus to begin with a very heavy work, which required 8,00,000 tons of stone, besides many millions of bricks, before we could lead the water out of the river. This work has failed once, a breach was made in one of the anicuts, but, providentially, it occurred at such a time of the year that the crop was not extensively hurt and the cost of repairs was very small—I think 6,000 pound. Excepting this, the work has now stood for 25 years and, of course, its weak points have been well ascertained and strengthed. We had on the spot a hill containing sand-stone sufficiently hard to answer our purposes temporarily, but the whole work has since been raised two feet, and covered with an excellent stone admirably laid.

We had also, near the spot, within a few miles, one of the very best hydraulic lines, which set extremely hard in a short time.

The water is carried on a level two or three feet above the land so as to water direct by sluices in the canal banks; and between every two irrigating canals and drains are cut to carry off the local rains. Some of these are of large dimensions, 20 or 30 yards broad, as the falls of rain are exceedingly heavy.

But it must be remembered that numerous mistakes in the original works have been gradually corrected, and especially in this last two or three years a through improvement of the whole works has been carried out by a very able officer. Unaccountable as it may appear in spite of the astonishing results of these works it has been impossible to persuade the authorities to complete them to this day though they are now setting about it in earnest. Only 6,00,000 acres have yet been irrigated out of a million. Twenty-eight years after the commencement.

The cost has been 600,000 pound and probably 4,00,000 pound will be expended in completing and improving them, making 1 pound an acre. The charge for water is 4 rupees for the main crop and the increase of produce 20 rupees per acre. There are about 500 miles of canal and river navigation, besides thousands of miles of branch lines. The locks are 150 by 15 feet, sufficient for boats of 180 tons. But the canals cannot be kept full in the dry season for want of stored water. This has been continuously urged, but no work has yet been ordered. I have before spoken of the great effects of this work of storage in three ways: improving the river and canal navigation, providing for dry season, irrigation and diminishing the danger of floods; and the returns would be so great in these three ways that the cost would be quite insignificant. About the foundations in these sandy beds of rivers it must be remembered that complete foundations require three things, that the status should be lst incompressible; 2nd indestructible; 3rd immovable. Sand is perfect in respect of the first of these, but is easily moved, though work resting on it, never settles a hair's breadth, and it cannot decay; and we have only therefore to keep the current away from it, so that, it may not be moved and the foundation is then quite safe. The native way of making foundations, for all sorts of works in this material, is by building up wells of brick in clay on the sand with a rough ring of wood under them, and then swathing them round completely with straw ropes just to prevent them from falling to pieces from sinking. A man then gets into them and digs out the sand working under water when the well has sunk a few feet and continues this till the top of the well is levelled with the bed. When the well is filled with stone and clay. We have never sunk them above 8 feet in Madras where the sand was liable to be washed away by the stream as in bridges, etc. loose stone is thrown up round the masonry. Thousands of works of every sort thus founded are now standing in Madras. In the north-west they have greatly improved upon this by sinking solid blocks of masonry with holes left in them by which the sand is drawn up by a beautiful apparatus worked from above, invented by Mr. Fouracres, of the Soane

Works, formally in Godavery. By this means the, blocks are sunk at expense little more than nominal. Thus, by this simple means, taught us by the natives instead of loose sand proving a difficult and expensive foundation it is about the soundest and cheapest of any.

Upon the whole nothing can be more satisfactory than results of these Godavery works. The canals swarm with boats, both for passengers and goods, about 2,00,000 tons including rafts of timber and bamboos, being conveyed along the main canal from the head of the delta to the port of Cocanada. And this, although steam has not yet been used on them, excepting in a Government boat, and although it is only a small isolated patch of navigation, unconnected with any extensive tract of country, or any capital city. The longest line is from Cocanada to Nizampatam in Kistna, 160 miles, along the coast and to the second barrier 220 miles up to the Godavery. but through a very poor forest country. If it were continued up the Godaveri into the populous interior above the second barrier and connected with the north coast canal from Madras (and interval of 40 miles), the traffic would be increased manifold; and if it were continued, 280 miles to the north to connect it with the Orissa Works and so with the Ganges and Burhampootra, and continued from Madras to Cape Comorin or to Ponany on the west coast, it would form a link of immense system of internal' navigation, on which there would be a traffic of millions of tons per hour, and thousands of passengers per day.

This account of the Godavery works will give a general idea of the nature of these great river irrigations. The Sone works which are the last projected, and have the benefit of all the experience gained in eight others, will be the most complete of all hitherto. They will cost four millions and irrigate two million acres, and the main line of the canal will form a portion, 300 miles in length, of the Ganges valley canal, between Calcutta and the Punjab. The anicut across the Sone is 2½ miles in length in one unbroken line, and one of the main canals has been cut already to the breadth of 75 yards. To convey the whole of the water for this 2 millions acres, the two main canals must be each 150, yards broad and ten feet deep, with a slope of five inches and a current of 3,000 yards. Such is the scale on which we have to work in India. About three-fourths of a million have been spent on these works, and the present expenditure is about one fourths of a million employing thirty or

40,000 people. This is a very slow process for such a work but at present all these important and wonderfully renumerative works are sacrificed to railways which do not pay even working expenses like that above mentioned at Oomerawattee. Orders have been lately issued to stop the main north canal of this work. Three new great projects of this kind have been fully planned and estimated, but they are also stopped; they are the Sooja River Project for the irrigation of Oude; the Gunduck river for north Bihar of the Ganges; and the Rajmahaul project from the Ganges two hundred miles from Calcutta to be led from an anicut from across the river where it is two and a half miles broad, to irrigate all the country down to Calcutta and from the first part of the Ganges valley navigation.

To show in a striking light the state of the case of Inland navigation, I must give some of the particulars of the transit between Calcutta and the Ganges. At present, the great traffic goes either by the river Bhagerratti and others, very winding and imperfect navigators, closed or nearly so for four months in the year, or by what is called the Soonderband route, a circuitous line of 400 miles through the tidal creeks to the south-east of Calcutta. The traffic to the East alone for the Burhampootra, was lately taken at Goalundo, at the confluence of the Ganges and that river, and found to be by native boats, 1,700,000 tons, through a distance of 420 miles, the direct distance being 130 miles.

On this line there is a railway by a route of 160 miles, which carries 1,70,000 tons, and by steamers 30,000 tons are conveyed. Probably, the western traffic for the Ganges is equal to this making a total of four million tons. The cost of this traffic is one farthing a ton, making a total of one-and-a-half millions a year paid on a single line of 130 miles, besides cost of insurance.

Now, a steamboat canal on a high level, on the plan before mentioned in these lectures, would cost at 3,000 pound a mile 4,00,000, pound one-fourth of the cost of the traffic in a single year.

The cost of transit by such a canal would be quite nominal, about one twentieth of a penny per ton per mile, or six pence for the whole distance, so that, the saving in three months traffic would pay for the whole cost. And this would enable the steamers navigating the Burhampootra to the important province of Assam, rapidly filling up with Europeans, to come direct to Calcutta in a night, instead of seven days steaming by the Soonderbunds. On this, line a railway has been laid costing with its debt three millions, which carries one-twelfth of the Burhampootra traffic, and what it does carry has to be transferred to boats. Since, I was ordered to report upon this line of communication in 1858, about twenty millions have been paid for transit, besides three millions for the railway, while 400,000 pound would have saved almost the whole of it. Could anything put in a more striking light the difference between land water transit in India.

I now return to the subject of storing water. The old native tanks of Madras are simple, but most noble works. There are tens of thousands of them. They are formed by earthen bunds lined with stone to resist the waves; either closing valleys, or in horse shoe form in the plains. They are furnished with excellent granite sluices, and what we call Calingulahs; waste weirs to carry off the water when the tank is full.

One of these, the Veranum tank in South Arcot has a bund 12 miles long and about 20 feet high; the water is 2½ miles broad in widest part. It contains about 100 million cubic yards of water, but of course supplies much more. It is filled both by small streams, and by a canal of 12 miles from the Colleroon the main stream of the Cauvery, which supplies water for about 6 months.

The history of this work will give an idea of the state of things under the Company's Government. In 1927 was sent to inspect it, as the people were stated to be nearly in a state of rebellion, from its neglect. I found the works in uttar disrepair; the Colleroon Canal had 6 feet of silt in its bed, so that, when it ought to have had 8 feet of water flowing down it, it had 2. Thus, this work which had a population of perhaps 1,00,000 and a revenue of 40,000 pound dependent upon it, had not been allowed 500 pound a year to keep it in repair. The Government could not afford it. Is it surprising the natives thought us savages ? I made, a small estimate of 3,500 pound for some immediate repairs, but knowing what its fate would be, I proceeded to Madras and arrived just in time to hear, as I expected that the Government could not squander such sums as this, upon the wild demands of an engineer. We had however a Governor at that time who was accessible, and I asked the Chief Engineer to go to him and speak to him about it. He said the papers had never been laid before him, and ordered the expenditure. In my ignorance at that time I thought the point was gained, as orders were sent to the Collector of the District who had first called for my report on the case, and whose business it was according to the absurd arrangement of that time, to execute this work. Soon after, I left the district, and did not return till, 1933, when to my astonishment I found that the Collector had not taken the trouble to spend the money or the Government to enforce it; a small sum only had been spent and the people were in such a state of rebellion, that it had been feared troops would have to be sent into the district. Such was the inconceivable state of things under that admirable middle class government.

We now set to work to put those works in a real state of repair, and to build the lower Colleroon anicut at the head of the channel, and in a few years the revenue which had fallen to 10,000 pounds rose to 40 or 50,000 pound paying to the Treasury some 100 per cent. What a comment on the India House not being able to afford to repair those vital works. And what will be said 20 or 30 years hence about the communication between Calcutta and the Ganges? Matters have indeed greatly altered since those days; some money is now spent in material improvements, and a portion of it really on the most suitable works; but the lesson has yet to be learnt, not to spend 3 millions in a way that leaves 11/12 of the traffic to go on just as it did before, and entails a permanent burden on the finances, when an effective work could have been constructed for pound which would have provided for the whole traffic, have entailed to loss on the Treasury, but (if it was thought advisable) an immense profit, have sent on that traffic without a transfer, and enable the great steamers to go direct from Calcutta to Assam.

When this further lesson has been learnt, and the money is expended according to the actual circumstances and wants of the country, India will make the most astonishing advance in wealth and prosperity; when all India will undergo the same change that has passed over the Godavery.

There are many other very large tanks, though none equal to the Veranum in capacity; the highest bund I have seen was 54 feet high, but I believe there is a tank with 60 feet of water in it.

Most of these very large ones have now been put into good order and some enlarged and improved; many of them supplied by channels from the large rivers. I have said that these bunds are simply mounds of earth thrown up without any order whatever. The ideas the English Engineers have that they must be made in layers with a puddle trench etc., are all pure fancies. I thought of such contrivances myself 50 years ago, but when I had seen 10,000 safe and sound works without any of these clever things, I began to think they might not be necessary. It must be remembered that these works extend over an immense range of country and are consequently made of almost every possible kind of earth, so that, it is not likely that any kind can now be found that can need any particular contrivance, but it is possible that with some kind of material it might be advisable to make the inner slope with some selected earth that would certainly be water tight. But a paddle trench is actually a mischievous thing, because to have the bund made of two different materials, one that will settle differently from the other, may lead to cracks through the mass. I once had to close up the mouth of a feeder to a river with such an earthen bund and the moment it was high enough, with out giving it a day to settle, I let the water against it, 17 feet deep, without any leaks, though I had to keep people at work on it to raise it for some weeks as it settled down. The one point is to have the mount homogeneous that it may all settle equally.

About the lining with stone to bear the wash of the waves; this is very necessary, in tanks several miles long and ten or 20 yards deep, and requires to be carefully done. The natives make the lining of large blocks with a slope of about 45 degrees, but in this I think the English method, the best, to give a long slope of 2 or 3 to one and let the lining stones rest chiefly on the earth. There should be a thin layer of smaller stones under the large ones to prevent the earth from being washed out between the large stones by the receding wave.

The most important point of all in these tanks is the waste weir. In this the old native works are very generally defeated. Most of them had insufficient escapes. The burst of rains in the Garnatic are tremendous often five inches; and I have known 12. Thus, a very large portion of these tanks, have burst, at one time or another from having their bunds overflowed. They are now generally in a much better state, most of them having had their weirs enlarged of late years. At times indeed the floods are so overwhelming, that they defy all calculations. On one occasion the water in the Viranum is said to have overflowed its banks of 12 miles throughout, and it was breached in 13 places. There seems no possibility of providing against such catastrophes. But they are happily extremely rare, and certainly these tanks can be secured against all, but such, and in fact are generally at this time. The essential point is that these escapes should not be placed in the high part of the bund, but near the ends, and, of course, if possible, on rocky ground. They are made with granite floors and wing walls with a line of granite posts along, the crest, from 3 to 6 feet high. By the natives they were closed with sods after every burst of the monsoon, which could be cut away in a short time whenever the weather appeared to require it. It was a clumsy way of doing things and was often the cause of the tank bursting because the persons in charge would not take the trouble to go out in a storm to open them, so that, a great number of breached tanks were always found with their Callingulahs closed. As I have not been in these districts for many years, I do not know whether a better system has been, substituted, but it would be easy to close them with wooden shutters that could be quickly opened or shut.

In a tank with a very high bund it is most essential that the sluices for supplying the irrigation should not be in the bund itself, but in the solid ground at each end, in the side of the valley. How strange it seems that an engineer should ever put the sluice in the very last place it ought to be, *viz.*, in the highest part of the bund, where if it fails, it will most effectively destroy the tank. This was the cause in the Sheffield reservoire. In a very long bund, in the planes, of course, there must be many sluices under it, but still they may be let into the solid ground, and in such shallow tanks there is no great pressure of water. In one of the new tanks in Bombay, near Poona, the bund is made of masonary, what the object of this is I have no idea; it must be much more expensive than earth, and it has this terrible objection that if it bursts it gives at once, and the whole tank will be empty in a few minutes, whereas in an earthen one it will take sometime to form a large breach. At Sheffield it took an hour or two, and 250 people were drowned; had it emptied in a quarter or half an hour probably thousands would have been drowned. The construction of these great tanks, holding several hundred million cubic yards of water, is perhaps the most serious work an engineer could be employed upon as the effects of a failure may be so terrible. It should always be kept in view, that it should be made many miles above any great population, that the water may be disbursed in some measure before it reaches them, in case of a failure. But none but a very experienced engineer should be intrusted with such a work, who has had the opportunity of making himself well acquainted with numerous tanks in a variety of situations, and especially with such as have failed. But to place a tank at all, like the Sheffield one, just above an immense town, at the bottom of the valley, seems to me insufferable, as running a risk that nothing can justify.

I would now add some remarks on the details of navigation works.

First about the locks. They are objected to, as helping to make water carriage intolerably slow. But this is simple because the old locks are so absurdly defective. When a thousandth part of the thought and outlay have been spent upon locks for steam-boat canals that have been expended upon railways, locks will cause very little detention. What are required for them are these things: First—that ample water passages should be provided, so that, the lock can be filled or emptied in a minute or less. Second—that the sluices should be made to open instaneously, by a quarter revolution of a winch. Third—that the gates should also be made to open and shut nearly instantaneously, by springs, or by weights suspended from a post. Such a weight ought to be sufficient to open the gate before the water is level by some inches. Fourth—besides water passages in the masonary, a considerable portion of the surface of the gates might be made in vertical Venetians, so that, a quarter revolution of a handle would open them, and admit of a great volume of water passing through.

By these and other expedients which will soon be thought of the detention by locks will soon be reduced to a very trifling time.

But further, in many main lines in India the number of locks will be very small. In the Ellore canal, in Madras, there is one lock in 90 miles. In the great line, up the valley of the Ganges, there will not probably be more than 40 locks in 1,200 miles. The total fall is not 1,000 feet, and a great portion of this will be provided for by the slope of the canal.

About the wave caused by fast boats. It must be allowed that in boats of the present form, this is very considerable at 25 miles an hour, as was seen in the Thames in trying the Orissa boat. This must be provided for Ist—By making wide canals such as all the great irrigation canals must necessarily be in India. 2nd—By keeping the water 2 or 3 feet below the top of the banks. 3rd—By allowing an easy slope of 2 or 3 to 1 to the upper part of the bank. 4th—If needful, by covering that part with stone, as has been done in the Gloster ship canal. 5th—By the form of the boat.

On the upper Godavery navigation the steamers are made with a vertical entrance like a punt, but with a very easy slope of 5 to 1, and it ought to be less than this. The deck of these boats is a complete oblong; thus they, throw off no wave from the bow, as in a boat with a horizontal entrance. Such a boat, I suppose, would produce a very moderate wave in a broad canal, but I have not seen none tried. These steamers on the Godavery have been a complete success, working very cheaply at about 10 miles an hour.

All these supposed objections of water transit will be got over when great lines of traffic are thus worked. But it must be always kept in mind that this matter of high speed is a very small one compared with that of cheapness, especially in India. The first class passengers there are only 1 per cent, and on some lines much less, so that, it is certain on a perfect steam boat canal, there would be only 1 or 2 very small fast boats a day on main lines, just to carry the mails and half a dozen passengers. The great mass of the traffic, both in goods and passengers, would be moved at from 5 to 10 miles, or under the former. I have stated that eleven-twelfths of the goods traffic from Calcutta to the Burhampootra goes by the river, 130 miles only in direct distance to Goalundo, though it takes 6 weeks by native boats, and 8 days by steamers, 400 miles by the river.

This chapter does not propose to deal with details further than seems absolutely necessary for the support of general principles. My main object is to prove that incomparably the most important subject for the engineer in the civil part of his duties is water, especially in India. The data shows that nothing can at all compare with it in cheapness, either for production or transit, and that its regulation is an absolute necessity for health and comfort.

And the unbounded field that is before us in India must inevitably be more completely occupied, in spite of all intentions of any set of men.

Let us consider the progress that has been made of late. If any of the authorities had been told 20 years ago that they would be sanctioning single irrigation works to cost 4 million sterling, and ordering canal steamers to run at 20 miles an hour, they would have considered it a most impossible folly for them to be guilty of.

But thus it is, the pressure of facts is too great for men's intentions, and they constantly find themselves doing the very last things they intended.

It is now much easier to get a million sterling for irrigation or navigation than it was after I had been in the service 20 years to get a lac of rupees (10,000 pounds), that is the ideas of men in authority have expanded more than one hundred fold in 30 or 40 years.

Now, that they have spent 6½ millions in meeting the wants of a single famine, and keeping alive 4 millions of people, men cannot conceal from themselves that it would be much wiser to spend this same in saving for ever from famine twelve districts, containing 12 or 15 millions of people, by irrigation works, than in making 7 or 800 miles of railways that would not pay its working expenses, but leave the whole a permanent charge upon the taxes, as is certainly the case with all the new railways. Men may shut their eyes to facts, but they cannot get rid of them. And thus we may confidently conclude that what has happened will continue to happen, and that such improvements will advance at increasing speed, inspite of intentions, and will be often carried on by the very men who will tell you that they are entirely opposed to them.

The difficulty is to realise what it is to reduce an immense unimproved country to anything like tolerable order in respect of P. Works. I believe about 800 millions have been spent in this way in England, not one-tenth the size of India which, allowing for the difference in the equal to 2700 millions spent in India. What we are doing at present is the nearest trifling with a matter, but if we increase our scale of operation in the next 30 years, one hundred fold, as we have done in the last, you will see some really ineffective inroad made upon this vast field before you have been half the time in the public service that I have.

The progress of ideas in the management of India is shown in the strongest manner by the achievement of the late famine. No such attempt, was ever made before, and nobody imagined it possible, (Myself among the number). Actually, to prevent deaths, at all in so awful a calamity affecting 20 millions of people. Previously, even to within only 4 or 5 years the idea was of course, the people must die by hundreds of thousands in a famine, but now this has been completely prevented.

This indicates an entirely new era in the Government of India and opens the way for the brightest hopes in respect of all other matters and especially in the expansion of the P. Works system which will provide against famines before hand and make it in a manner impossible for famines to take place at all, that is while God pleased to continue to India the same seasons, as we have hitherto had including the irregular distribution of rains.

Nobody ever thinks of famine now in the irrigated districts of Chennai or those around them.

I look upon it therefore as much as certainty as anything can be, that the demand for engineers in India will rapidly increase and the means at their disposal and certainly no finer field could be found for young men to be, in God's hands, the instruments of immense good to this vast multitude, now stated to be about 300 millions.

I must add one remark on the main network of proposed water communications for India. 1st—The first line would be a very complete one around India, viz., from Chennai by Ahmedabad up the valley of the Indus, across by the Sirhind Canal to the Ganges canal, down the valley of the Ganges to Calcutta, along the east coast to Cape Comonrin and up the west coast to the new port of Karwar, near Goa. The only impracticable piece of country is that from Goa to Bombay. 2nd—Across the Peninsula by the valleys of the Godaveri, Wurdah and Tapi, to meet the former line at Baroda. 3rd—A second line across peninsula from Nellore, hundred miles north of Madras, by the valleys of the Pennair Toombudra and Kala Nuddee to Karwar in the West Coast. 4th—From Madras across the Carnatic, and by the valleys of the Ambravatti and Paulghant River to Ponany, on the west coast.

The Wurda line of navigation may also be connected with the valley of the Mahanuddy, down to the east coast line at Cuttack.

Further, I believe the Wurda may be connected by the valley of the Wainganga with the Nerbudda and that with the valley of the Chumbul, down to the Ganges Valley lying, near Allahabad.

The Burhampootra is a very fair line of navigation at present, though no doubt it could be greatly improved.

And from it a land line of 300 to 500 miles would connect the whole system of Indian navigation with Yangtse and the internal navigation of China, thus giving it us a private entrance into China of the utmost political importance, and uniting the immense population of India and China, each now supposed to be three hundred millions, together with half the population of the globe.

Annexure-II

Coastal Navigation in India

D.C. Jayasankar

India has a coastline of more 6000 km., but it has only eight major ports, twenty intermediate ports and 150 minor ports.[1] The major ports are Kolkata, Mumbai, Chennai, Visakhapatnam, Cochin, Kandla, Marmugao and Paradip. Two more ports Mangalore and Tuticorin are being elevated to the category of Major ports. Of twenty intermediate and 150 minor ports, only 125 are active ports. Majority of the intermediate and minor ports are situated on the west coast and only a small number on the east coast (115: 10). Some of the minor ports and two major ports namely Kolkata and Paradip are river ports. It has been estimated that about 4 million tons of goods are handled on the coastal trade out of a total trade of about 50 million tons of goods handled by all ports. The major ports except Kolkata and Cochin have minor role to play so far as coastal trade is concerned. The quantum of coastal trade handled by these ports is less than 25 per cent of the trade volume of these ports. In 1965-66 these ports handled the following amount of coastal trade:

		(In million tons)
1.	Mumbai	24.5
2.	Kolkata	30.6
3.	Marmugao	2.2
4.	Chennai	24.2
5.	Visakhapatnam	15.5
6.	Cochin	43.3
7.	Kandla	22.7
8.	Paradeep	not available

Even today the pattern has not changed much appreciably and therefore, it is patent that the intermediate and minor ports have a greater role to play in coastal trade.

Minor ports have been in existence from a long time. Some of the mincr ports in the east coast and the west coast like Poompahar, Cranganore, Cochin, Calicut, Broach, Surat etc., had trade relations

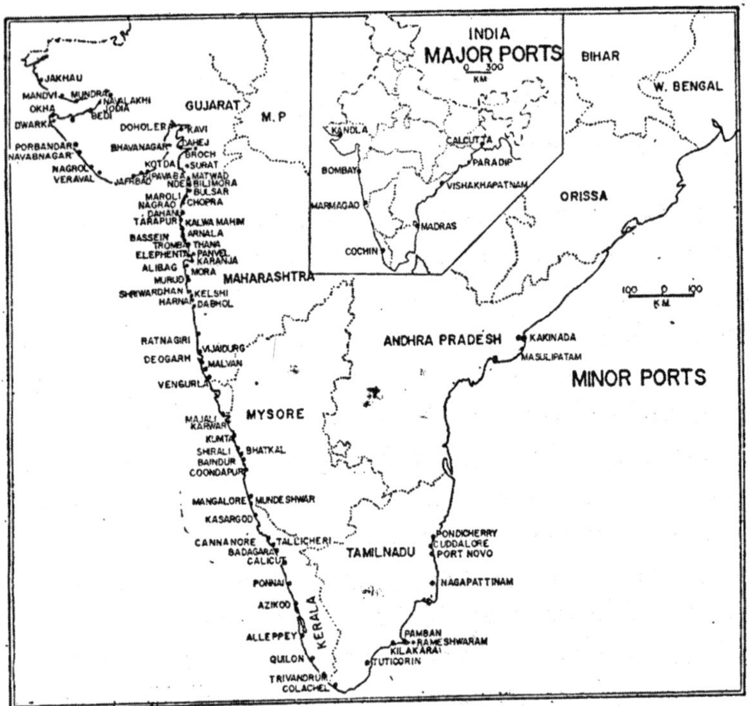

Fig. A-II.1: Location of Major Ports and Minor Ports of India

even with foreign countries. With the emergence of major ports and their special position as garrisoned ports under the East India Company and direct British rule, the minor ports languished. The East India Company's system of collection of raw-materials through the garrisoned ports reduced the importance of minor ports even as coastal traders. They are re-emerging as trading partners of major ports after the Independence. Let us now take close look at these intermediate and minor ports and the role they play in the coastal trade of India.

Minor Ports

As stated earlier there are about 18 intermediate and 150 minor ports in India. But only 125 of them are situated on the west and only 10 of them on the east coast. These minor ports must have performed a great service in the days gone by. Navigable rivers and minor ports situated at their mouths must have played very significant roles in the days when roads and railways were not in existence. With the advent of roads and railways the Inland navigation slowed down. Along with them the ports situated at their mouths which had a crucial role to play had also dwindled. The roads and railways saw phenomenal development during the British regime. In some cases as described earlier in the book the road and railway development hit hard the navigation by rivers. Since, the British were primarily interested in trade and protection of territories (defence needs) the navigational aspect was given scant attention. Roads and railways developed in many cases as competitors to water transport. This left the ports which were serving as focal point for coastal trade high and dry.

The Independence of the country, the surging population, the need for redistribution of goods to consuming centres within the country, the inability of the railways and roads to cope with the added traffic particularly in times of famine and cheapness of water transport has brought the coastal trade and Inland water transport into prominence. In 1950, Government of India accepted the policy of reservation of coastal shipping for Indian tonnage and by 1952 coastal trade was being catered for entirely by Indian Companies. In 1965 the total tonnage operations on the coast was 4.2 lakh G.R.T. and consisted of 112 coastal ships including three tankers. Today the coastal tonanage has decreased of 2.5 lakh G.R.T.[2] on account of dilicensing of overaged ships.

The coastal traffic is divided broadly into two categories: (a) the west coast trade and (b) wider coast trade. The main commodities which are carried by ships around the coast are coal, salt, cement and general cargo comprising foodgrains, fertilizers, jute, tea, iron and steel products, refinery products, cotton and piece goods etc.

West Coast Trade

In the west coast of India apart from the four major ports (present)—Kandla, Mumbai, Marmugao and Cochin, there are 12 intermediate ports. The intermediate ports are Mandvi, Bhavnagar, Veraval, Porbandar, Bedi, Navlakhi, Okha, Broach, Ratnagiri, Karwar, Calicut and Alleppy. Mangalore is being raised to major port and will start functioning as such from 1974.

Majority of the minor ports are situated in the state of Gujarat and Maharashtra. They alone have 60 minor ports apart from 60 sub-ports. Many explanations are possible for the large number of minor and sub-ports found in the two states alone.

1. The Western Coast had the early impact of Europeans and even earlier of the Arabs.
2. The Western Coastal regions from Saurashtra to Ratnagiri produce cotton which was required by the Europeans particularly British.
3. Except during the monsoon months, the coast is comparatively free from cyclones and winds of high velocity.
4. The coast is more indented compared to the southern half.
5. The coast has a variety of marine wealth which finds a ready market in the Metropolitan centres of Mumbai, Baroda, Surat, Ahmedabad etc.
6. The lower density of roads and comparative inaccessibility of several centres along the coast have promoted the development of many ports.

In spite of all these, these ports do not handle a large volume of coastal trade. A paradox indeed ! The reasons are not far to seek. The main items that feature in the coastal trade of India are coal, cement, salt and general cargo comprising foodgrains, fertilizers, jute, tea, iron and steel products, refinery products, cotton and piece goods etc.

The west coast hinterland does not have materials like coal, salt, and many items of the general cargo which need redistribution. They are the receivers of these materials. But from the Bengal-Bihar-Odisha mining area all-rail route is much cheaper as ships have to round Sri Lanka to reach these ports. As a consequence, these ports deal mainly with cotton piece goods, cement, fertilizers, foodgrains refinery products and fish.

On the other hand intermediate ports found in Karnataka and Kerala have a better trade. The hinterland is rich in forest products, plantation crops like coffee and the spices, ropes, cashew nuts iron ore, manganese and fish. Therefore, there is a large bilateral trade from port to port and with the major ports in the area. Some of the intermediate ports like Mangalore have a definite quantum of foreign trade also, particularly in iron ore and manganese. The establishment of refinery at Cochin had accelerated the movement of refinery products to most of these ports as landed cost by tanker is less than rail transport. As stated earlier, Cochin port handles a large volume of coastal trade among the western ports. This is primarily due to its situation hemmed in by Western Ghats on the east and a rich hinterland of forest, sea and spice products. The recent establishment of refinery coupled with the fact that the back-water transport (canal navigation) is well developed in this State, is another important reason.

In spite of all these advantages, it is found that wider coastal trade particularly the trade between the west coast and the east is not as much as normally can be expected. This is primarily due to the bottleneck experienced by ships going round the island of Sri Lanka. This long journey and time add to the landed cost of materials.

Wider Coast Trade

Under this term is included the East coast trade and the trade between East Coast and West Coast. Of the two, the pure East Coast trade is more than the bicoastal trade. In the East coast trade, the port of Kolkata assumes a very great significance. Kolkata and now Haldia are so situated that all Ganga and Brahmaputra navigation channels converge on it. The hinderland of Kolkata is rich in coal, jute, tea, iron and steel products, textiles and cement. Southern part of India particularly Odisha, Andhra Pradesh and Tamil Nadu find it convenient to receive these products through coastal ships. The ships that are employed in the Eastern coastal trade have another advantage also. The ships going to Tuticorin with coal for example can expect a return cargo of salt. Therefore, the empty haulage is not that much a problem in the east coast as compared to the West Coast.

The ports that serve the East Coast trade are Kolkata, Haldia, Paradip, Masulipatnam, Kakinada, Cuddalore, Nagapattinam, Chennai, Puducherry, Tuticorin and 6 minor ports. Of these ports, Kakinada, Cuddalore, Nagapattinam and Tuticorin serve a larger area and cater to a larger volume than other ports. Tuticorin will be upgraded as a major port by 1974. Tuticorin has a richer hinterland constituting of petro-chemical complex, salt extraction, cement production and textile production. The, nearness to Neyveli Lignite Complex has enhanced the value of Cuddalore as a port. The machinery and other requirements of the Lignite Complex are unloaded at Cuddalore and briquattes, urea etc., loaded at this port. Kakinada is the only port in Andhra Pradesh which has considerable coastal trade. Its hinterland is rich in sugar and tobacco. It requires a lot of fertilizers and salt. Therefore, it still retains its position as a port. On the other hand Masulipatnam has dwindled in importance.

The bicoastal trade is confined to only a few items and that too only from the southern coast of Tamil Nadu to Kerala and Karnataka. The inherent difficulties faced in this trade can be summarised as follows:

1. The need for circulating the island of Ceylon in the absence of a passage through the Strait of Talimannar.
2. The cheapness of all-rail route compared to rail-ship-rail route.
3. The necessity for transhipment at two points—one at loading point and second at unloading point.
4. Absence of coordination between railways and shipping companies.
5. Irregular schedules of coastal ships.

The Planning Commission is aware of these problems and has remarked about the future of Coastal shipping as follows:[3]

> "The future role of coastal shipping has to be considered in relation to its overall national and strategic importance. Coastal shipping has a certain basic importance for a country like India with its geographical position and its long costline. In times of emergency coastal shipping may have a special role in national defence and economic strategy. While these aspects deserve to be given weightage in considering the future development of coastal shipping, an essential determinant of the pace of coastal shipping as part of an integrated transport network in the country is its comparative economics in relation to other modes of transport. From the foregoing analysis, it is clear that the future expansion of coastal shipping has to be planned with reference to a few selected commodities which

> constitute important components of coastal cargo, namely coal, salt, and cement. These together account for the bulk of the traffic of the traffic along the coast."

The Planning Commission has also recommended the Sethu-Samudram Project in order to obviate the circum navigation of the island of Sri Lanka. Further such a canal will not only shorten the distance and time, but will also make the rail-ship-rail route competitive with all-rail route.

They have also recommended certain policy steps for the Railway and the Transport Ministry to follow:

> "The advantage of coastal shipping for the movement of general cargo will increase if steps are taken to arrange for through booking facilities with railways and the necessary facilities are developed at a number of ports in the country. It would also be desirable to provide for specially designed vessels suited for carrying general cargo from port to port."[4]

Regarding the organizational aspect of the coastal shipping industry, the Planning Commission is of the opinion that:

> "For an adequate coastal fleet to be maintained and employed efficiently in national interest, it will not be sufficient merely to assume the requisite cargo in commodities like coal, salt and cement. It is essential also to consider whether important economies in capital cost and operational expenses will not be secured if, in place of as many as 27 companies of varying size many of them operating their small fleets in an indifferent manner round the coast, a scheme for unified control and operation cannot be evolved with the cooperation of the industry. This would take the form of a corporation promoted by the Central Government to which the Central Government and the existing shipping companies might subscribe... A single corporation operating the coastal fleet will be in a position to secure a fuller utilisation of the existing ships, provide regular services, improve operational efficiency both directly and through improvement of facilities at the

> ports arid take steps to replace overaged ships. It is certain that this will help improve the comparative costs of coastal shipping and facilitate coordination in rates and traffic with the railways....In the last analysis, it will be by creating conditions in which the coastal sea transport can be operated more efficiently and at lower cost that it can become a viable national industry."[5]

The reorganization of coastal shipping and reopening of coastal trade will reinvigorate and rejuvenate the Inland navigation which is the central theme of this book by linking the navigable rivers with each other along the Coast.

References

1. Government of India, Planning Commission, *Committee on Transport Policy and Coordination*, New Delhi, 1965, p. 134.
2. Government of India, Ministry of Finance, *Economic Information*, New Delhi, 1971, p. 103.
3. Government of India, Planning Commission, "Committee on Transport Policy and Coordination", *Final Report*, New Delhi, 1966, p. 131.
4. *Ibid.*, p. 132.
5. *Ibid.*, p. 133.

Annexure-III

The National Waterways Bill, 2015

Introduced by Shri Nitin Gadkari, Minister of Road Transport & Highways and Shipping in Lok Sabha in 2015

A BILL to make provisions for existing national waterways and to provide for the declaration of certain Inland waterways to be national waterways and also to provide for the regulation and development of the said waterways for the purposes of shipping and navigation and for matters connected therewith or incidental thereto.

BE it enacted by Parliament in the Sixty-sixth Year of the Republic of India as follows:

1. This Act may be called the National Waterways Act, 2015.
2. It shall come into force on such date as the Central Government may, by notification in the Official Gazette, appoint.

Short title and commencement as Introduced in Lok Sabha Bill No. 122 of 2015.

1. The existing national waterways specified at serial numbers 1 to 5 in the Schedule along with their limits given in column (3) thereof, which have been declared as such under the Acts referred to in sub-section (1) of section 5, shall continue to be national waterways for the purposes of shipping and navigation under this Act.

2. The regulation and development of the waterways referred to in sub-section (1) which have been under the control of the Central Government shall continue, as if the said waterways are declared as national waterways under the provisions of this Act. (3) The Inland waterways specified at serial numbers 6 to 106 in the Schedule along with their limits given in column (3) thereof are hereby declared to be national waterways for the purposes of shipping and navigation.

3. Save as provided in sub-sections (1) and (2) of section 2, it is

hereby declared that it is expedient in the public interest that the Union should take under its control the regulation and development of the waterways specified in the Schedule for the purposes of shipping and navigation to the extent provided in the Inland Waterways Authority of India Act 1985.

4. In the Inland Waterways Authority of India Act, 1985, in section 2, for clause (h), the following clause shall be substituted, namely: – "(h) "national waterway" means the Inland waterway declared by section 2 of the National Waterways Act, 2015, to be a national waterway.

Explanation.—If Parliament declares by law any other waterway to be a national waterway, then, from the date on which such declaration takes effect, such other waterway— (i) shall also be deemed to be a national waterway within the meaning of this clause; and (ii) the provisions of this Act shall, with necessary modifications (including modification for construing any reference to the commencement of this Act as a reference to the date aforesaid), apply to such national waterway".

5. (1) The following Acts, namely:—(a) the National Waterway (Allahabad-Haldia Stretch of the Ganga Bhagirathi-Hugli River) Act 1982; (b) the National Waterway (Sadiya-Dhubri Stretch of Brahmaputra River) Act, 1988; (c) the National Waterway (Kollam-Kottapuram Stretch of West Coast Canal and Champakara and Udyogmandal Canals) Act, 1992; (d) the National Waterway (Talcher-Dhamra Stretch of Rivers, Geonkhali-Charbatia Stretch of East Coast Canal, Charbatia-Dhamra Stretch of Matai River and Mahanadi Delta Rivers) Act, 2008; and (e) the National Waterway (Kakinada-Puducherry Stretch of Canals and the Kaluvelly Tank, Bhadrachalam-Rajahmundry Stretch of River Godavari and Wazirabad-Vijayawada Stretch of River Krishna) Act, 2008, are hereby repealed.

(2) Notwithstanding such repeal, anything done or any action taken under the Acts referred to in sub-section (1), in so far as they are in conformity with the provisions of this Act, shall be deemed to have been done or omitted to be done or taken or not taken under the provisions of this Act.

National Waterway 1: Allahabad-Haldia Stretch of the Ganga-Bhagirathi-Hugli River with the following limits, namely:— From road bridge at Allahabad across the river Ganga, about 2 km. upstream of the confluence of the rivers Ganga and Yamuna at

Triveni to the Inland waterway limit on the tidal waters of the river Hugli from a line drawn between No. 1 Refuge house at the entrance to Baratola river commonly called channel creek, to a position 2.5 km. due south of Saugor lighthouse, and then connected to the right or south bank at the entrance to the Hijili or Russulpore river, through river Ganga, lock canal and feeder canal at Farakka, river Bhagirathi and river Hugli.

National Waterway 2: Sadiya-Dhubri Stretch of Brahmaputra River with the following limits, namely:– From a line drawn across the Brahmaputra river from the point on the north bank of the Kundil river at its confluence with the Brahmaputra river near Sadiya to the beginning of the river island Majuli and therefrom through all the channels of the Brahmaputra river on either side of the river island Majuli up to the end of the river island Majuli and then up to the international border downstream of Dhubri.

National Waterway 3: Kollam-Kottapuram Stretch of West Coast Canal and Champakara and Udyogmandal Canals with the following limits, namely:— The northern limit of the West Coast Canal shall be a line drawn across the river Periyar parallel to Kottapuram road bridge (NH-17) connecting Maliankara and Valiapanikan Thuruthu at a distance of 1.0 km. upstream, and the southern limit shall be a line drawn across the Ashtamudi Kayal at a distance of 100 metres south of Kollam jetty. The Champakara Canal starting from the confluence with the West Coast Canal and ending at the railway bridge (railway siding for Cochin Oil Refinery) near Fertilisers and Chemicals Travancore Limited, boat basin. The Udyogmandal Canal starts from the confluence with West Coast Canal and ends at the Padalarn road bridge (Eloor-Edayar).

National Waterway 4: Kakinada-Puducherry Stretch of Canals and the Kaluvelly Tank, Bhadrachalam-Rajahmundry Stretch of River Godavari and Wazirabad-Vijayawada Stretch of River Krishna with the following limits, namely: Kakinada-Puducherry canal (Canal system consisting of Kakinada canal, Eluru canal, Commamur canal and North Buckingham canal, portion of the Coovum river linking North and South Buckingham canals, South Buckingham canal and Kaluvelly tank) Northern limit: A line drawn across the Kakinada canal parallel to the Jagannadhapuram road bridge, Kakinada at a distance of 500 metres down stream at Lat. 16° 56′ 24″ N, Long. 82° 14′ 20″; Southern limit: Junction of

East Coast Highway and Chinnakalawari-Kanakachettikulam road at Kanakachettikulam which is the end point of the artificial canal link to Kaluvelly tank at Lat. 12° 02′ 36″ N, Long. 79° 52′ 12″ E. River Godavari Western limit: Road bridge at Bhadrachalam across river Godavari at Lat. 17° 40′ 39″ N, Long. 80° 52′ 52″ E; Eastern limit: Sir Arthur Cotton barrage across river Godavari at Dowlaiswaram, Rajahmundry at Lat. 16° 56′ 05″ N, Long. 81° 45′ 32″ E. River Krishna Western limit: Road bridge at Wazirabad across river Krishna at Lat. 16° 40′ 50″ N, Long. 79° 39′ 29″ E. Eastern limit: Prakasam barrage across river Krishna at Vijayawada at Lat. 16° 30′ 18″ N, Long. 80° 36′ 23″ E.

National Waterway 5: Talcher-Dhamra Stretch of Brahmani-Kharsua-Dhamra Rivers, Geonkhali-Charbatia Stretch of East Coast Canal, Charbatia-Dhamra Stretch of Matai River and Mahanadi Delta Rivers with the following limits, namely:— East Coast Canal and Matai river (Consisting of old Hijli tidal canal, Orissa coast canal and Matai river) Northern limit: Confluence point of Hugli river and Hijli tidal canal at Geonkhali at Lat. 22° 12′ 20″ N, Long. 88° 03′ 07″ E; Southern limit: Confluence of Matai river and Dhamra river near Dhamra Fishing harbour at Lat. 20° 47′ 42″ N, Long. 86° 53′ 03″ E. Brahmani-Kharsua-Dhamra river system (Consisting of Brahmani-Kharsua-Dhamra rivers).

North-Western limit: Samal barrage across river Brahmani, Talcher at Lat. 21° 04′ 26″ N, Long. 86° 08′ 05″ E; South-Eastern limit: An imaginary line drawn across Dhamra river at East Point of Kalibhanj Dian Reserved Forest near Chandnipal at Lat. 20° 46′ 26″ N, Long. 86° 57′ 15″ E. Mahanadi delta rivers (Consisting of Hansua river, Nuna nala, Gobri nala, Kharnasi river and Mahanadi river) (Alternate route-Hansua river enters into Bay of Bengal through northern point of False point bay, then enters river Kharnasi at southern end of False point bay, river Atharabanko, a northernly distributory of river Mahanadi) Northern limit: Confluence of Kharsua river with Brahmani river at Ramchandrapur at Lat. 20° 36′ 55″ N, Long. 86° 45′ 05″ E; Southern limit: An imaginary line in continuation to the Northern break-water structure across the entrance channel at Paradip Port at Lat. 20° 15′ 38″ N, Long. 86°′ 40′ 55″ E.

National Waterway 6: Aai River: 71 km. length of the river from Upstream of Bridge at Adalguri No. 3 at Lat. 26°33′32.17″ N, Long. 90°34′0.86″ E to confluence with Brahmaputra river at Lat.

26°12′49.90″ N, Long. 90°36′ 24.40″ E (4.7 km. upstream of Naranarayan Setu at Jogighopa).

National Waterway 7: Ajoy River: 96 km. from Bridge on Morgram-Panagarh State Highway No. 14 at Illambazar Lat. 23°36′56.10″ N, Long. 87°31′58.07″ E to confluence of river Ajoy with river Bhagirathi at Lat. 23°39′23.33″ N, Long. 88° 7′56.72″ E at Katwa.

National Waterway 8: Amba River: 45 km. length of the river from Arabian Sea, Dharamtaar creek near village Revas at Lat. 18°50′15.14″ N, Long. 72°56′31.22″ E to a Bridge near Nagothane ST Stand at Lat. 18°32′19.82″ N, Long. 73° 8′0.29″ E.

National Waterway 9: Arunawati/Aran River: 98 km. length of the river from a Bridge on State Highway No. 211 at Lat. 20°13′32.91″ N, Long. 77°33′23.32″ E to confluence of Arunawati and Aran rivers near Ratnapur village at Lat. 19°59′30.70″ N, Long. 78° 9′37.51″ E to confluence of Aran and Penganga rivers near Chimata village at Lat. 19°54′8.32″ N, Long. 78°12′36.43″ E.

National Waterway 10: Asi River: 5.5 km. length of the river from Ganga river confluence at Assi Ghat, Varanasi at Lat. 25°17′18.64″ N, Long. 83° (1) (2) (3) 5 10 15 20 25 30 35 40 45 50 6 0′25.46″ E to near Newada, Varanasi at Lat. 25°16′37.28″ N, Long. 82°58′17.60″ E.

National Waterway 11: AVM Canal: 11 km. length of the canal from Poovar Beach at Lat. 8°18′29.73″ N, Long. 77° 4′45.20″ E to Erayumanthurai Bus Stop at Lat. 8°14′54.16″ N, Long. 77°9′33.50″ E.

National Waterway 12: Baitarni River: 49 km. length of the river from Dattapur village at Lat. 20°51′44.61″ N, Long. 86°33′30.45″ E to confluence with Dhamra river near Laxmiprasad Dia at Lat. 20°45′13.32″ N, Long. 86°49′15.36″ E.

National Waterway 13: Bakreswar/Mayurakshi River: 110 km. length of the Bakreswar river from Nil Nirjan Dam at Lat. 23°49′30.77″ N, Long. 87°24′59.04″ E to confluence of Bakreswar and Mayūrakshi rivers near Talgram village at Lat. 23°51′58.01″ N, Long. 88° 2′21.04″ E and 27 km. Mayurakshi river from Talgram village to confluence with Dwarka river near Dakshin Hijal village at Lat. 23°58′22.24″ N, Long. 88° 9′2.

National Waterway 14: Barak River: 121 km. length of the river from Lakhipur Ferry Ghat Lat. 24°47′17.73″ N, Long. 93° 1′16.33″ E to Tuker Gram Lat. 24°52′33.96″ N, Long. 92°29′20.60″ E.

National Waterway 15: Beas River: 191 km. length of the river from Talwara Barrage at Lat. 31°57′21.93″ N, Long. 75°53′37.44″ E to confluence of Beas and Sutlej rivers near Harike at Lat. 31° 9′9.17″ N, Long. 74°58′7.93″E.

National Waterway 16: Beki River: 73 km. length of the river from Elenagamari Lat. 26°38′37.19″ N, Long. 90°59′2.15″ E to Brahmaputra confluence at Lat. 26°14′23.80″ N, Long. 90°47′20.86″.

National Waterway 17: Betwa River: 68 km. length of the river from Rirwa Buzurg Dariya at Lat. 25°54′16.78″ N, Long. 79°45′6.46″ E to confluence of Betwa and Yamuna rivers near Merapur Daria village at Lat. 25°55′11.48″ N, Long. 80°13′7.65″ E.

National Waterway 18: Bharathappuzha River: 61 km. length of the river from 80 m upstream of Shornur Railway bridge at Lat. 10°45′6.38″ N, Long. 76°16′52.94″ E to Lakshadweep Sea, location Koottayi Padinijarekkara Azhimugam, Ponnani at Lat. 10°47′12.03″ N, Long. 75°54′40.04″ E. (1) (2) (3) 5 10 15 20 25 30 35 40 7.

National Waterway 19: Bhavani River: 94 km. length of the river from Bhavani Sagar Dam, Sathyamangalam at Lat. 11°28′16.21″ N, Long. 77° 6′49.11″ E to confluence of Bhavani and Kaveri rivers at Kaveri river bridge on Salem-Coimbatore Highway: NH-47 Lat. 11°25′54.41″ N, Long. 77°41′1.92″ E.

National Waterway 20: Bheema River: 139 km. length of the river from Barrage (approx 1 km. from Hippargi village) at Lat. 17° 9′4.50″ N, Long. 76°46′34.14″ E to confluence of Bheema and Krishna rivers at Gundloor Lat. 16°24′27.96″ N, Long. 77°17′12.60″ E.

National Waterway 21: Birupa/Badi Genguti/Brahmani River System: 102 km. length of the river from Birupa Barrage at Choudwar at Lat. 20°30′49.00″ N, Long. 85°55′20.17″ E to confluence of Birupa and Brahmani rivers near Upperkai Pada village at Lat. 20°37′36.25″ N, Long. 86°24′19.13″ E including alternative route of 25 km. from Samaspur village Lat. 20°35′40.59″ N, Long. 86° 6′31.50″ E to near Kharagpur village Lat. 20°38′27.77″ N, Long. 86°17′31.81″ E and additional 54 km. length of Brahmani river from confluence of Birupa and Brahmani rivers near Upperkai Pada village at Lat. 20°37′36.25″ N, Long. 86°24′19.13″ E to Brahmani river at Katana Lat. 20°39′26.28″ N, Long. 86°44′52.86″ E.

National Waterway 22: Budha Balanga: 56 km. length of the river from Barrage (approx 300m from Patalipura village) at Lat. 21°38′12.96″ N, Long. 86°50′53.17″ E to confluence of Budha Balanga river with Bay of Bengal at Chandipur Fishing Port Lat. 21°28′12.14″ N, Long. 87° 4′11.60″ E.

National Waterway 23: Chaliyar River: 88 km. length of the river from Bridge on Panamkayam road at Lat. 11°23′50.87″ N, Long. 76°14′45.90″ E to confluence of Chaliyar river with Lakshadweep Sea at Beypore Port at Lat. 11° 9′42.21″ N, Long. 75°48′10.61″ E (part of the river also under West Coast Canal).

National Waterway 24: Chambal River: 402 km. length of the river from Sawai Madhopur-Sheopur road bridge on State Highway No. 30 near Jailalpura village Lat. 25°51′48.77″ N, Long. 76°34′34.27″ E to confluence of Chambal and Yamuna rivers at Charakpura village Lat. 26°29′29.89″ N Long. 79°15′0.89″ E. (1) (2) (3) 5 10 15 20 25 30 35 40 8.

National Waterway 25: Chapora River: 33 km. length of the river from Bridge at State Highway No.124 (1km from Maneri village) Lat. 15°42′47.31″ N, Long. 73°57′23.38″ E to confluence of Chapora river with Arabian Sea at Morjim Lat. 15°36′ 33.27″ N, Long. 73°44′0.93″ E.

National Waterway 26: Chenab River: 53 km. length of the river from Chenab road bridge at Lat. 33° 5′7.34″ N, Long. 74°48′6.16″ E to Bridge near Bhardakalan at Lat. 32°48′12.42″ N, Long. 74°34′53.24″ E.

National Waterway 27: Cumberjua River: 17 km. length of the river at confluence of Cumberjua and Zuvari rivers near Cortalim ferry terminal Lat. 15°24′39.76″ N, Long. 73°54′47.94″ E to confluence of Cumberjua and Mandovi rivers near Sao Martias Vidhan Parishad Lat. 15°31′26.44″ N, Long. 73°55′34.30″ E.

National Waterway 28: Damodar River: 135 km. length of the river from Krishak Setu, Bardhman on State Highway No. 8 at Lat. 23°12′39.83″ N, Long. 87°50′53.85″ E to confluence with Hugli river near Purbba Basudebpur at Lat. 22°21′0.58″ N, Long. 88° 5′19.31″ E.

National Waterway 29: Dehing River: 114 km. length of the river from rail Bridge at Merbil Majuli No.1 Lat. 27°19′24.58″ N, Long. 95°18′44.60″ E to confluence of Dehing and Brahmaputra rivers near village Lachan at Lat. 27°15′10.21″ N, Long. 94°40′1.33″ E.

National Waterway 30: Dhansiri/Chathe: 110 km. length of the river from Bridge near Morongi T.E. village Lat. 26°24′40.65″ N, Long. 93°53′46.75″ E to Numaligarh Lat. 26°42′1.20″ N, Long. 93°35′15.42″ E.

National Waterway 31: Dikhu River: 63 km. length of the river from Bridge at Nazira on State Highway No.1 Lat. 26°55′18.43″ N, Long. 94°44′27.03″ E to confluence of Dikhu and Brahmaputra rivers at Lat. 26°59′58.33″ N, Long. 94°27′41.73″ E.

National Waterway 32: Doyans River: 61 km. length of the river from Bridge near Sialmari Lat. 26°10′47.45″ N, Long. 93°59′10.26″ E to confluence of Doyans and Subansiri rivers at Lat. 26°26′53.34″ N, Long. 93°57′11.61″ E. (1) (2) (3) 5 10 15 20 25 30 35 40 9.

National Waterway 33: DVC Canal: 130 km. length of the canal from Durgapur Barrage Lat. 23°28′47.36″ N, Long. 87°18′19.04″ E to confluence point of DVC canal with Hugli river near Tribeni Lat. 23° 0′30.95″ N, Long. 88°24′54.72″ E.

National Waterway 34: Dwarekeswar River: 113 km. length of the river from Bridge near Abantika Lat. 23° 6′54.76″ N, Long. 87°18′46.99″ E to confluence of Dwarakeswar and Silai rivers at Pratappur Lat. 22°40′16.94″ N, Long. 87°46′42.57″ E.

National Waterway 35: Dwarka River: 121 km. length of the river from Bridge at Tarapith at Lat. 24°6′57.70″ N, Long. 87°47′51.48″ E to confluence with Bhagirathi river near Maugram village at Lat. 23°43′52.56″ N, Long. 88°10′51.44″ E.

National Waterway 36: Gandak River: 300 km. length of the river from Bhaisaslotan Barrage near Triveni Ghat at Lat. 27°26′21.75″ N, Long. 83°54′23.90″ E to Gandak and Ganga Rivers confluence at Hajipur Lat. 25°39′17.59″ N, Long. 85°10′27.85″ E.

National Waterway 37: Gangadhar River: 62 km. length of the river from Pakriguri Bridge on NH 31C at Lat. 26°27′29.98″ N, Long. 89°51′24.97″ E to Bangladesh Border at Binnachara Point III Lat. 26° 0′31.81″ N, Long. 89°49′57.18″ E.

National Waterway 38: Ghaghra River: 340 km. length of the river from Faizabad Lat. 26°47′51.38″ N, Long. 82° 6′46.10″ E to Ghaghra and Ganga Rivers confluence at Manjhi Ghat Lat. 25°44′12.56″ N, Long. 84°42′2.89″ E.

National Waterway 39: Ghataprabha River: 112 km. length of the river from Barrage near Malali Lat. 16°20′1.13″ N, Long. 75°11′23.14″ E to confluence with River Krishna at Chicksangam Lat. 16°20′13.37″ N, Long. 75°47′53.52″ E.

National Waterway 40: Gomati River: 518 km. length of the river from Bara Imambara, Lucknow Lat. 26°52′21.23″ N, Long.

80°54′58.08″ E to confluence of Gomati with River Ganga Lat. 25°30′31.41″ N, Long. 83°10′16.86″ E.

National Waterway 41: Ichamati River: 64 km. length of the river from Bridge on Border Main Road at Gobra near Bangladesh Border at Lat. 22°53′49.64″ N, Long. 88°53′48.87″ E to near (1) (2) (3) 5 10 15 20 25 30 35 40 45 10 Bangladesh Border at Bansjhari Mallikpur Lat. 22°39′6.71″ N, Long. 88°55′35.35″ E.

National Waterway 42: Indira Gandhi Canal: 277 km. length of the canal from Harike Barrage at Lat. 31° 8′33.11″ N, Long. 74°56′56.72″ E to Bridge on NH 15 near village Piperan Lat. 29°12′18.49″ N, Long. 73°53′58.09″ E.

National Waterway 43: Indus River: 35 km. length of the river from Bridge on highway at Upshi village Lat. 33°49′42.69″ N, Long. 77°48′56.23″ E to Bridge on Shey-Chuchol road near Shey village Lat. 34° 3′35.41″ N, Long. 77°38′33.14″ E.

National Waterway 44: Jalangi River: 131 km. length of the river from Bridge on State Highway No. 14 near Plashipara at Lat. 23°47′47.15″ N, Long 88°27′8.97″ E to confluence of Jalangi with Hugli/Bhagirathi rivers at Nabadwip Lat. 23°24′38.73″ N, Long. 88°22′48.38″ E.

National Waterway 45: Jhelum River: 110 km. length of the river from Bridge on highway at Lat. 33°49′25.78″ N, Long. 75° 3′50.14″ E to Wuler lake, Srinagar at Lat. 34°21′37.16″ N, Long. 74°36′36.35″ E.

National Waterway 46: Kadalundy River: 53 km. length of the river from old bridge near Parappuram village at Lat. 11° 3′15.98″ N, Long. 76° 1′42.58″ E to confluence of Kadalundy river with Arabian Sea at Kadalundy bridge Lat. 11° 7′26.15″ N, Long. 75°49′32.37″ E (part of the river also under West Coast Canal).

National Waterway 47: Kali River: 54 km. length of the river from Kodasalli Dam Lat. 14°55′8.24″ N, Long. 74°32′6.90″ E to confluence of Kali River with Arabian Sea near Sadashivgad bridge at Lat. 14°50′30.95″ N, Long. 74° 7′21.32″ E.

National Waterway 48: Kallada River: 69 km. length of the river from PPM Dam at Lat. 9° 2′7.30″ N, Long. 76°54′46.03″ E to Lakshadweep Sea, Neendakara Lat. 8°56′1.94″ N, Long. 76°32′16.52″ E *via* Ashtamudi Lake.

National Waterway 49: Kalyan-Thane-Mumbai Waterway: 57 km. length of the river from Bridge on Kalyan-Badlapur road near Kalyan railway yard at Kalyan Lat. 19°14′6.39″ N, Long. 73° 8′49.13″

E to Navi Mumbai Lat. 19° 0′7.65″ N, Long. 72°58′55.10″ E *via* Ulhas river. (1) (2) (3) 5 10 15 20 25 30 35 40 45 11.

National Waterway 50: Karamnasa River: 86 km. length of the river from Bridge at Kakarait Lat. 25°18′11.21″ N, Long. 83°31′38.43″ E to confluence of Karamanasa and Ganga rivers at Kutubpur Lat. 25°31′6.21″ N, Long. 83°52′47.32″ E.

National Waterway 51: Kaveri/Kollidam River: 364 km. length of the river from Uratchikottai Barrage at Lat. 11°29′3.09″ N, Long. 77°42′13.68″ E to confluence of river Kollidam with Bay of Bengal at Pazhaiyar Lat. 11°21′37.97″ N, Long. 79°49′53.23″ E.

National Waterway 52: Kherkai River: 23 km. length of the river from Dam near Gangia village at Lat. 22°45′11.99″ N, Long. 86° 5′9.19″ E to confluence with Subarnrekha River at Jamshedpur Lat. 22°50′13.26″ N, Long. 86° 9′37.11″ E.

National Waterway 53: Kopili River: 46 km. length of the river from Bridge at Banthai Gaon Tinali Bus Stop at Lat. 26°10′41.02″ N, Long. 92°13′5.31″ E to confluence with Brahmaputra River at Chandrapur No. 2 Lat. 26°15′7.22″ N, Long. 91°56′48.71″ E.

National Waterway 54: Korapuzha River: 23 km. length of the river from Bridge near Theruvathukadavu on State Highway No. 38 at Lat. 11°27′59.35″ N, Long. 75°46′20.40″ E to confluence of Korapuzha River with Lakshadweep Sea at Elathur Lat. 11°20′46.69″ N, Long. 75°44′8.46″ E.

National Waterway 55: Kosi River: 236 km. length of the river from Kosi Barrage at Hanuman Nagar Lat. 26°31′39.85″ N, Long. 86°55′28.95″ E to confluence of Kosi with Ganga River at Kursela Lat. 25°24′40.44″ N, Long. 87°15′13.61″ E.

National Waterway 56: Krishna River: (1) 628 km. length of the river from Bridge near village Galagali Lat. 16°25′27.87″ N, Long. 75°26′18.70″ E to Wazirabad Barrage (NW-4 limit) at Lat. 16°40′55.99″ N, Long. 79°39′26.82″ E; (2) 99 km. length of the river from Vijayawada Barrage (NW-4 limit) at Lat. 16°30′23.46″ N, Long. 80°36′19.62″ E to confluence with Bay of Bengal at Hamasaladeevi (near Koduru) Lat. 15°42′47.09″ N, Long. 80°49′55.74″ E.

National Waterway 57: Kumari River: 77 km. length of the river from Dam near Amruhasa village at Lat. 23° 6′36.54″ N, Long. 86°15′50.92″ E to Mukutmanipur Dam at Chiada Lat. 22°57′18.24″ N, Long. 86°44′42.87″ E. (1) (2) (3) 5 10 15 20 25 30 35 40 45 12.

National Waterway 58: Lohit River: 100 km. length of the river from Parasuram Kund Lat. 27°52′40.06″ N, Long. 96°21′39.70″ E to Saikhowa Ghat, Sadiya Lat. 27°47'49.14" N, Long. 95°38'13.84" E.

National Waterway 59: Luni River: 327 km. length of the river from Dam at Jaswantpura Lat. 26°13'34.99" N, Long. 73°41'20.07" E to Barrage near Malipura Lat. 24°57'4.42" N, Long. 71°38'1.51" E.

National Waterway 60: Mahanadi River: 425 km. length of the river from Sambalpur Barrage at Lat. 21°27'34.33" N, Long. 83°57'49.80" E to Paradip at Lat. 20°19'38.12" N, Long. 86°40'16.96" E.

National Waterway 61: Mahananda River: 81 km. length of the river from Bridge near Gosaipur at Lat. 25°26'41.22" N, Long. 88° 5'26.36" E to Bangladesh Border near Adampur at Lat. 24°57'16.56" N, Long. 88°10'59.38" E.

National Waterway 62: Mahi River: 248 km. length of the river from Kadana Dam Lat. 23°18'22.35" N, Long. 73°49'37.45" E to confluence with Gulf of Khambhat near Kavi railway station Lat. 22°10'34.71" N, Long. 72°30'36.31" E.

National Waterway 63: Malaprabha River: 94 km. length of the river from Jakanuru Lat. 15°49'50.87" N, Long. 75°38'53.93" E to confluence with river Krishna at Kudalasangama Lat. 16°12'30.22" N, Long. 76° 4'15.60" E.

National Waterway 64: Mandovi River: 41 km. length of the river from a Bridge at Usgaon at Lat. 15°26'41.55" N, Long. 74° 3'12.23" E to confluence of Mandovi River with Arabian Sea at Reis Magos Lat. 15°28'32.46" N, Long. 73°46'45.56" E.

National Waterway 65: Manimala River: 67 km. length of the river from a bridge on Murani-Anikadu road at Murani Lat. 9°27'18.26" N, Long. 76°40'30.66" E to Vembanad Lake at Kainakary Lat. 9°31'15.55" N, Long. 76°22'51.64" E.

National Waterway 66: Manimutharu River: 5 km. length of the river from Manimutharu Dam Lat. 8°39'13.71" N, Long. 77°24'47.44" E to confluence with Tamraparni River near Aladiur Lat. 8°41'2.68" N, Long. 77°26'7.23" E. (1) (2) (3) 5 10 15 20 25 30 35 40 13.

National Waterway 67: Manjara River: 242 km. length of the river from Singur Dam at Lat. 17°44'58.35" N, Long. 77°55'40.79" E to confluence with River Godavari at Kandakurthi at Lat. 18°49'6.80" N, Long. 77°52'20.48" E.

National Waterway 68: Mapusa River: 27 km. length of the river (including Moide River) from bridge on NH 17 at Mapusa Lat. 15°35'20.79" N, Long. 73°49'17.20" E to confluence point of

Mapua and Mandovi Rivers at Porvorim Lat. 15°30′20.01″ N, Long. 73°50′42.09″ E.

National Waterway 69: Meenachil River: 44 km. length of the river from check Dam at Kidangoor Lat. 9°40′27.39″ N, Long. 76°36′8.72″ E to Kumarakom, Vembanad lake Lat. 9°35′52.58″ N, Long. 76°25′29.10″ E and from Illickal at Lat. 9°34′56.65″ N, Long. 76°29′15.00″ E to Vembanad Kayal at Lat. 9°33′51.04″ N, Long. 76°24′53.76″ E.

National Waterway 70: Muvattupuzha River: 56 km. length of the river from Bridge on State Highway No.41 at Muvattupuzha at Lat. 9°59′16.59″ N, Long. 76°34′40.84″ E to Vembanad Lake at downstream of Murinjapuzha bridge Lat. 9°49′45.69″ N, Long. 76°22′48.36″ E.

National Waterway 71: Nag River: 60 km. length of the river from Bridge near NIT Colony, Nagpur Lat. 21° 6′17.25″ N, Long. 79° 6′2.62″ E to confluence with river Kanhan near Sawangi village at Lat. 21° 5′38.27″ N, Long. 79°27′53.84″ E.

National Waterway 72: Narmada River: 637 km. length of the river from Hoshangabad at Lat. 22°45′29.28″ N, Long. 77°44′5.41″ E to confluence of Narmada with Arabian Sea at Gulf of Khambhat Lat. 21°38′26.81″ N, Long. 72°33′28.24″ E.

National Waterway 73: Netravathi River: 78 km. length of the river from Netravathi Dam, Dharmsthala Lat. 12°57′55.23″ N, Long. 75°22′10.19″ E to confluence with Arabian Sea at Bengre Lat. 12°50′42.73″ N, Long. 74°49′28.86″ E.

National Waterway 74: Palar River: 141 km. length of the river from rail bridge at Virudampattu, Vellore at Lat. 12°56′14.07″ N, Long. 79° 7′29.70″ E to confluence with Bay of Bengal at Sadurangapattinam Lat. 12°27′52.16″ N, Long. 80° 9′13.47″ E. (1) (2) (3) 5 10 15 20 25 30 35 40 45 14.

National Waterway 75: Pamba River: 100 km. length of the river from Cherukolpuzha Lat. 9°21′3.13″ N, Long. 76°44′17.55″ E to confluence of Pamba River with NW 3 (West Coast Canal) at Lat. 9°21′1.18″ N, Long. 76°25′47.63″ E and from Manimala River at Nedumpuram Lat. 9°22′5.67″ N, Long. 76°31′26.07″ E to Vembanad Lake, Kainakary at Lat. 9°32′29.36″ N, Long. 76°21′47.36″ E.

National Waterway 76: Pazhyar River: 20 km. length of the river from Bridge near Veeranarayana Mangalam village at Lat. 8°13′48.97″ N, Long. 77°26′27.34″ E to confluence with Arabian Sea at Manakudi at Lat. 8° 5′15.01″ N, Long. 77°29′7.61″ E.

National Waterway 77: Pengang/Wardha River: 265 km. length of the river from confluence of Aran and Penganga rivers near Chimata village at Lat. 19°54′8.32″ N, Long. 78°12′36.43″ E to confluence with Wardha river to confluence of Wardha and Pranahita rivers near Ravalli village at Lat. 19°33′59.30″ N, Long. 79°49′0.39″ E.

National Waterway 78: Pennar River: 29 km. length of the river from Penna Barrage, Pothireddypalem at Lat. 14°28′8.38″ N, Long. 79°59′9.31″ E to confluence with Bay of Bengal near Kudithipalem at Lat. 14°35′36.75″ N, Long. 80°11′30.61″ E.

National Waterway 79: Punpun River: 35 km. length of the river from Bridge on NH 83 Dudhaila near Pakri village Lat. 25°29′49.79″ N, Long. 85° 6′19.44″ E to confluence with river Ganga at Fatuha Lat. 25°30′50.37″ N, Long. 85°18′16.72″ E.

National Waterway 80: Puthimari River: 72 kms length of the river from Bridge on NH 31 near village Ghopla at Lat. 26°22′1.10″ N, Long. 91°39′10.92″ E to confluence with Brahmaputra river near Bamunbori at Lat. 26°15′27.52″ N, Long. 91°20′34.84″ E.

National Waterway 81: Ravi River: 42 km. length of the river from Dam at Gandhiar Lat. 32°35′51.27″ N, Long. 75°59′4.96″ E to Ranjeet Sagar Dam at Basoli Lat. 32°26′35.86″ N, Long. 75°43′45.19″ E.

National Waterway 82: Rupnarayan River: 72 km. length of the river from confluence of Dwarakeswar and Silai rivers at Pratappur Lat. 22°40′16.94″ N, Long. 87°46′42.57″ E to confluence with Hugli river at Geonkhali Lat. 22°12′41.58″ N, Long. 88° 3′13.99″ E. (1) (2) (3) 5 10 15 20 25 30 35 40 45 15.

National Waterway 83: Sabarmati River: 212 km. length of the river from Barrage near Sadoliya Lat. 23°26′49.66″ N, Long. 72°48′34.85″ E to confluence with Gulf of Khambhat near Khambhat Lat. 22° 9′17.99″ N, Long. 72°27′27.81″ E.

National Waterway 84: Sal River: 14 km. length of the river from Orlim Deusa Bridge Lat. 15°13′11.41″ N, Long. 73°57′29.77″ E to confluence with Arabian Sea at Mobor Lat. 15° 8′31.93″ N, Long. 73°56′59.89″ E.

National Waterway 85: Savitri River: 44 km. length of the river from Bridge near Sape at Lat. 18° 5′54.11″ N, Long. 73°20′8.81″ E to Arabian Sea at Harihareswar Lat. 17°58′47.10″ N, Long. 73° 2′15.01″ E.

National Waterway 86: Shastri River/Jaigad: 52 km. length of the river from to Sangmeshwar at Lat. 17°11′15.83″ N, Long. 73°33′2.57″ E to confluence with Arabian Sea at Jaigad Lat. 17°19′11.92″ N, Long. 73°12′39.30″ E.

National Waterway 87: Silabati River: 26 km. length of the river from Barrage near Shimulia village at Lat. 22°34′53.20″ N, Long. 87°38′30.54″ E to confluence of Dwarakeswar and Silai rivers at Pratappur Lat. 22°40′16.94″ N, Long. 87°46′42.57″ E.

National Waterway 88: Sone River: 160 km. length of the river from Sone Barrage near Dehri at Lat. 24°50′14.39″ N, Long. 84° 8′2.79″ E to confluence of Sone and Ganga rivers at Lat. 25°42′15.20″ N, Long. 84°52′2.07″ E.

National Waterway 89: Subansiri River: 111 km. length of the river from Gerukamukh Lat. 27°27′3.14″ N, Long. 94°15′16.12″ E to Brahmaputra confluence at Lat. 26°52′24.93″ N, Long. 93°54′31.26″ E.

National Waterway 90: Subarnrekha River: 314 km. length of the river from Chandil Dam at Lat. 22°58′29.39″ N, Long. 86° 1′14.03″ E to confluence with Bay of Bengal at Lat. 21°33′28.75″ N, Long. 87°22′58.60″ E.

National Waterway 91: Sunderbans Waterway: 201 km. length of the river from Namkhana Lat. 21°45′45.60″ N, Long. 88°13′5.84″ E to Athra Banki Khal Lat. 21°56′56.95″ N, Long. 89° 5′32.44″ E. (1) (2) (3) 5 10 15 20 25 30 35 40 16.

National Waterway 92: Sutlej River: 240 km. length of the river from Nangal Dam at Lat. 31°22′47.84″ N, Long. 76°21′59.38″ E to Harike Dam at Lat. 31° 8′41.21″ N, Long. 74°56′47.99″ E.

National Waterway 93: Tamraparni River: 64 km. length of the river from Sulochana Mudalir bridge, Tirunelveli Lat. 8°43′43.17″ N, Long. 77°42′53.94″ E to confluence with Bay of Bengal near Punnaikayal at Lat. 8°38′24.90″ N, Long. 78° 7′37.85″ E.

National Waterway 94: Tapi River: 436 km. length of the river from Hatnur Dam near Mangalwadi Lat. 21° 4′21.99″ N, Long 75°56′44.88″ E to Gulf of Khambhat (Arabian Sea) at Lat. 21° 2′15.51″ N, Long. 72°39′29.63″ E.

National Waterway 95: Tizu and Zungki Rivers: 42 km. length of the river from Longmatra at Lat. 25°46′11.98″ N, Long. 94°44′35.04″ E to Avanghku at Myanmar border Lat. 25°35′2.94″ N, Long. 94°53′6.12″ E and in Zungki river from bridge at Lat.

25°48′26.10″ N, Long. 94°46′35.96″ E to confluence of Zungki and Tizu rivers at Lat. 25°46′58.03″ N, Long. 94°45′20.51″ E.

National Waterway 96: Tlwang (Dhaleswari River): 86 km. length of the river from Khamrang near NH 54 Lat. 23°55′21.50″ N, Long. 92°39′8.15″ E to Bridge on NH 154 at Gharmura Lat. 24°17′18.92″ N, Long. 92°30′59.51″ E.

National Waterway 97: Tons River: 123 km. length of the river from Bridge on State Highway No. 9 on MDR road at Lat. 24°55′32.51″ N, Long. 81°24′2.07″ E to Ganga confluence at Sirsa Lat. 25°16′31.82″ N, Long. 82° 4′59.82″ E.

National Waterway 98: Tungabhadra River: 230 km. length of the river from Bridge on State Highway No. 29 near Chikka Jantakal village at Lat. 15°24′33.39″ N, Long. 76°35′12.62″ E to confluence with river Krishna near village Murva Konda at Lat. 15°57′20.28″ N, Long. 78°14′29.60″ E.

National Waterway 99: Ulhas River: 45 km. length of the river from Bridge on State Highway No. 76 near Malegaon T. Waredi Lat. 19° 2′38.20″ N, Long. 73°19′53.79″ E to Kalyan Lat. 19°15′35.03″ N, Long. 73° 9′27.77″ E linking to Kalyan-Thane-Mumbai waterways. (1) (2) (3) 5 10 15 20 25 30 35 40 17.

National Waterway 100: Vaigai River: 45 km. length of the river from Barrage near Anai Patti at Lat. 10° 5′19.23″ N, Long. 77°51′10.19″ E to Viragnoor Dam at Lat. 9°53′51.66″ N, Long. 78°10′34.06″ E.

National Waterway 101: Valpattnam River: 39 km. length of the river from Bridge on Thalassery Irikkur road at Irikkur Lat. 11°59′26.65″ N, Long. 75°32′48.94″ E to confluence with Arabian Sea at Azheekkal Lat. 11°56′36.26″ N, Long. 75°17′46.01″ E.

National Waterway 102: Varuna River: 53 km. length of the river from Road bridge near Kuru at Lat. 25°23′14.86″ N, Long. 82°44′6.64″ E to Ganga confluence at Saray Mohana, Varanasi Lat. 25°19′45.45″ N, Long. 83° 2′40.76″ E.

National Waterway 103: Wainganga/Pranahita River: 164 km. length of the river from Bridge near Chandapur village at Lat. 20° 0′30.16″ N, Long. 79°47′7.96″ E to confluence of river Godavari at Kaleshwaram Lat. 18°49′33.45″ N, Long. 79°54′32.82″ E.

National Waterway 104: West Coast Canal: 160 km. length of the canal as extension of NW-3 towards north of Kottapuram from Kottapuram Lat. 10°11′38.32″ N, Long. 76°12′4.39″ E to Kozhikode Lat. 11°13′38.83″ N, Long. 75°46′43.90″ E and 78 kms. towards

South of Kollam from Kollam Lat. 8°53′44.75″ N, Long. 76°35′0.30″ E to Kovalam Lat. 8°24′11.20″ N, Long. 76°58′19.41″ E.

National Waterway 105: Yamuna River: (1) 345 km. length of the river from Jagatpur (6 kms. upstream of Wazirabad Barrage) Delhi Lat. 28°45′27.63″ N, Long. 77°13′49.79″ E to road bridge upstream of Tajmahal, Agra near Samogar Mustkil at Lat. 27°10′49.47″ N, Long. 78° 7′50.90″ E; (2) 459 kms length of the river from confluence of Chambal and Yamuna rivers at Charakpura village Lat. 26°29′29.89″ N Long. 79°15′0.89″ E to confluence of Yamuna and Ganga rivers at Sangam, Allahabad at Lat. 25°25′24.45″ N, Long. 81°53′20.16″ E.

National Waterway 106: Zuari River: 55 km. length of the river from Sanvardan Lat. 15°13′57.87″ N, Long. 74° 8′57.89″ E to Marmugao Lat. 15°25′54.89″ N, Long. 73°48′13.20″ E. (1) (2) (3) 5 10 15 20 25 30 35 40.

Statement of Objects and Reasons

1. In many countries, the Inland water transport is recognised as fuel efficient, cost effective and environment friendly mode of transport, especially for bulk goods, hazardous goods and over dimensional cargos. It also reduces time, cost of transportation of goods and cargos, as well as congestion and accidents on highways. Yet, when compared to road and rail sectors, required investment has not been made by the Government so far on the preservation and development of Inland waterways mode of transportation in the country. The Inland waterways mode of transportation has immense potential for domestic cargo transportation as well as for cruise, tourism and passenger traffic. Its systematic development will open up progressive economic and transport opportunities in the country.

2. Five Inland waterways, namely, the—

(a) Allahabad-Haldia Stretch of the Ganga Bhagirathi-Hugli River;
(b) Sadiya-Dhubri Stretch of Brahmaputra River;
(c) Kollam-Kottapuram Stretch of West Coast Canal and Champakara and Udyogmandal Canals;
(d) Kakinada-Puducherry Stretch of Canals and the Kaluvelly Tank, Bhadrachalam-Rajahmundry Stretch of River

Godavari and Wazirabad-Vijayawada Stretch of River Krishna; and

(e) Talcher-Dhamra Stretch of Rivers, Geonkhali-Charbatia Stretch of East Coast Canal, Charbatia-Dhamra Stretch of Matai River and Mahanadi Delta Rivers; have been so far declared to be national waterways by Acts of Parliament.

3. The regulation and development of Inland waterways for the purposes of shipping and navigation and matters related thereto are undertaken by the Inland Waterways Authority of India constituted under the provisions of the Inland Waterways Authority of India Act, 1985.

4. Since the Inland waterways is lagging behind road and rail sectors in the country, the Central Government has evolved a policy for integrated development of Inland waterways throughout the country and has accordingly identified 101 new Inland waterways in addition to five existing national waterways to be declared as national waterways for the purposes of shipping and navigation by a standalone legislation in terms of Entry 24 of the Union List of the Seventh Schedule to the Constitution. The enactments by which the existing national waterways have been declared as national waterways are also proposed to be covered under the proposed legislation, namely the National Waterways Bill, 2015, by repealing them with a suitable saving clause.

5. The extent of development, the prioritisation of Inland waterways for development and related matters shall be finalised after carrying out necessary techno-economic feasibility studies through Inland Waterways Authority of India consequent upon enactment of the National Waterways Bill, 2015. Thereafter, these waterways will be developed by providing adequate infrastructure for safe, convenient and sustained shipping operations. The systematic development for navigation of these Inland waterways shall open up the progressive economic and cost effective, fuel efficient and eco-freindly transport potential in the country.

6. The enactment of the proposed legislation will in no way impinge on the rights of the State Governments for usage of water, ownership of appurtenant land, minerals, metal, sand etc., rather usher in development of transportation and tourism in States.

7. The Bill seeks to achieve the above objects.

Annexure Extract from the Inland Waterways Authority of India Act, 1985 (82 of 1985)

In this Act, unless the context otherwise requires,—* * * * * (h) "national waterway" means the Inland waterway declared by section 2 of the National Waterway (Allahabad-Haldia Stretch of the Ganga-Bhagirathi-Hugli River) Act, 1982, to be a national waterway.

Explanation.—If Parliament declares by law any other waterway to be a national waterway, then from the date on which such declaration takes effect, such other waterway—(i) shall be deemed also to be a national waterway within the meaning of this clause; and (ii) the provisions of this Act shall, with necessary modifications (including modification for construing any reference to the commencement of this Act as a reference to the date aforesaid), apply to such national waterway;

The Bill has made provisions for existing national waterways and to provide for the declaration of certain Inland waterways to be national waterways and also to provide for the regulation and development of the said waterways for the purposes of shipping and navigation and for matters connected therewith or incidental thereto.

Index